Work and Livelihoods

This volume presents a global range of ethnographic case studies to explore the ways in which—in the context of the restructuring of industrial work, the ongoing financial crisis, and the surge in unemployment and precarious employment—local and global actors engage with complex social processes and devise ideological, political, and economic responses to them. It shows how the reorganization and re-signification of work, notably shifts in the perception and valorization of work, affect domestic and community arrangements and shape the conditions of life of workers and their families.

Victoria Goddard is Professor and National Teaching Fellow at the Anthropology Department at Goldsmiths.

Susana Narotzky is Professor of Social Anthropology at the Universitat de Barcelona, Spain.

Routledge Studies in Anthropology

27 **The Anthropology of Postindustrialism**
Ethnographies of Disconnection
Edited by Ismael Vaccaro, Krista Harper and Seth Murray

28 **Islam, Standards, and Technoscience**
In Global Halal Zones
Johan Fischer

29 **After the Crisis**
Anthropological thought, neoliberalism and the aftermath
James G. Carrier

30 **Hope and Uncertainty in Contemporary African Migration**
Edited by Nauja Kleist and Dorte Thorsen

31 **Industry and Work in Contemporary Capitalism: Global Models, Local Lives?**
Edited by Victoria Goddard and Susana Narotzky

32 **Anthropology and Alterity**
Edited by Bernhard Leistle

33 **Mixed Race Identities in Australia, New Zealand and the Pacific Islands**
Edited by Farida Fozdar and Kirsten McGavin

34 **Freedom in Practice**
Edited by Moises Lino e Silva and Huon Ward

35 **Work and Livelihoods**
History, Ethnography and Models in Times of Crisis
Edited By Susana Narotzky and Victoria Goddard

Work and Livelihoods
History, Ethnography and Models in Times of Crisis

Edited by
Susana Narotzky and
Victoria Goddard

LONDON AND NEW YORK

First published 2017 by Routledge

2 Park Square, Milton Park, Abingdon, Oxfordshire OX14 4RN
711 Third Avenue, New York, NY 10017

Routledge is an imprint of the Taylor & Francis Group, an informa business

First issued in paperback 2018

Copyright © 2017 Susana Narotzky and Victoria Goddard

The right of the editors to be identified as the authors of the editorial material, and of the authors for their individual chapters, has been asserted in accordance with sections 77 and 78 of the Copyright, Designs and Patents Act 1988.

All rights reserved. No part of this book may be reprinted or reproduced or utilised in any form or by any electronic, mechanical, or other means, now known or hereafter invented, including photocopying and recording, or in any information storage or retrieval system, without permission in writing from the publishers.

Notice:
Product or corporate names may be trademarks or registered trademarks, and are used only for identification and explanation without intent to infringe.

British Library Cataloguing in Publication Data
A catalogue record for this book is available from the British Library

Library of Congress Cataloging in Publication Data
A catalog record for this book has been requested.

ISBN: 978-1-138-81398-4 (hbk)
ISBN: 978-1-138-61286-0 (pbk)

Typeset in Sabon
by Apex CoVantage, LLC

Contents

List of Figures viii
Acknowledgments ix
List of Contributors x

1 Work and Livelihoods: An Introduction 1
  VICTORIA GODDARD

SECTION I
Past, Present and Future: Generations in Times of Crisis 29

2 Lost Generations? Unemployment, Migration
  and New Knowledge Regimes in Post EU Poland 31
  FRANCES PINE

3 Credentialism and Recommendations: The Bases of the
  Reproduction of the Metallurgical Working Class
  in Contemporary Argentina 46
  LAURA PERELMAN AND PATRICIA VARGAS

4 Continuity and Disruption: The Experiences of Work
  and Employment across Three Generations
  of Steelworkers in Volta Redonda 60
  GONZALO DÍAZ CROVETTO

SECTION II
Continuities and Discontinuities 75

5 Post-Fordist Work Organization and Daily Life from
  a Gender Perspective: The Case of FIAT-SATA in Melfi 77
  FULVIA D'ALOISIO

vi *Contents*

6 Opening the Black Box of Employability: Change
Competence, Masculinity and Identity of Steelworkers
in Germany and the UK   93
VERA TRAPPMANN

7 Employment Precariousness and Social Reproduction
in the Shipbuilding Industry of Piraeus   109
MANOS SPYRIDAKIS

SECTION III
Lives of Worth   121

8 Regimes of Value and Worthlessness: How Two
Subaltern Stories Speak   123
DON KALB

9 Post-industrial Landscape: Space and Place in the Personal
Experiences of Residents of the Former Working-class
Estate of Ksawera in Będzin   137
KAZIMIERA WÓDZ AND MONIKA GNIECIAK

SECTION IV
The Politics of Resistance   155

10 Workers and Populism in Slovakia   157
JURAJ BUZALKA AND MICHAELA FERENCOVÁ

11 'A Trojan Horse in Our Midst': The Saturn Plant
and the Disorganization of Autoworkers in the US   172
SHARRYN KASMIR

12 Getting by Beyond Work, or the Intertwining of Production
and Reproduction among Heavy Industry Workers
and Their Families in Ferrol, Spain   187
IRENE SABATÉ MURIEL

Afterword

203

Making Difference: Concluding Comments on Work and Livelihoods

205

SUSANA NAROTZKY

Index

217

Figures

4.1	Generations at CSN, Volta Redonda.	69
9.1	The ruins of the crèche facilities, Ksawera Estate.	142
9.2	The former mine infrastructure: the canteen and restaurant buildings, Ksawera Estate.	143
9.3	The derelict swimming pool of the "Zagłębianka" sports complex.	143
9.4	Będzin Ksawera railway station.	144
9.5	The new urban landscape: the "Pogoria" hypermarket.	149

Acknowledgments

The chapters in this edited volume were originally presented at a conference held in Barcelona in February 2012, which concluded an EU FP7 funded collaborative research project (MEDEA—Models and their Effects on Development Paths: An Ethnographic and Comparative Approach to Knowledge Transmission and Livelihood Strategies). We wish to thank the European Union's Seventh Framework as well as the University of Barcelona and the ARCS-DGR program of the Generalitat de Catalunya for their support in organizing the conference. We wish to thank the doctoral students at the University of Barcelona who helped organize the conference, in particular Gemma Anton, Jaime Palomera and Diana Sarkis. We would like to thank as well the many colleagues whose participation in the conference enriched the debate. In addition to the contributors to this volume, we would mention Flavia Lessa de Barros, Paz Benito del Pozo, Carmen Bueno, Arianna Dal Forno, Andrea Fumagalli, Enrico Gibellieri, Elena González-Polledo, Rosana Guber, Costis Hadjimichalis, Douglas Holmes, Gustavo Lins Ribeiro, Ubaldo Martínez Veiga, Edoardo Mollona, David Ost, Luis Reygadas, Lydia Morris, Jonathan Parry, and Gavin Smith. We are grateful to the staff at Goldsmiths, University of London and to the University of Barcelona, and the Fundació Bosch Gimpera for the support and assistance they provided the MEDEA project. Finally, we would like to acknowledge the encouragement and guidance offered by staff at the European Commission, in particular Ronan O'Brien, Maria del Pilar González Pantaleón, Marie Ramot and Ivkov Stoyan.

We also take this opportunity to thank friends and colleagues for their encouragement, inspiration and critique over years of collaborative work and intense debate. To our families, our gratitude for their understanding when pressing deadlines have diverted our energies away from the support and care they deserve.

Contributors

Juraj Buzalka is Associate Professor of Social Anthropology at the Faculty of Social and Economic Sciences, Comenius University in Bratislava. He is an author of *Nation and Religion: The Politics of Commemoration in South-east Poland* (Münster: Lit 2007). His recent articles include 'Tasting Wine in Slovakia: Post-socialist Elite Consumption of Cultural Particularities' (in *Wine and Culture: Vineyard to Glass*. Rachel E. Black and Robert C. Ulin (eds.), Bloomsbury Publishing, 2013) and 'The Political Lives of Dead Populists in Post-socialist Slovakia' (in *Thinking through Transition. Liberal Democracy, Authoritarian Pasts, and Intellectual History in East Central Europe After 1989*. Michal Kopeček and Piotr Wciślik (eds.), (CEU Press, 2015). He is currently working on a monograph dealing with political movements in East Central Europe.

Fulvia D'Aloisio is Associate Professor at the Second University of Naples (Seconda Università degli Studi di Napoli). She specializes in the anthropology of work and enterprise, urban anthropology, fertility and family in Italy. Her research collaborations include work with Brown University on the ELFI Project (Explaining Low Fertility in Italy, headed by David Kertzer), with LUPT Centre (Laboratorio di Urbanistica e Pianificazione Territoriale) of the Federico II University (Naples); with Officina Emilia Centre, Department of Economics Marco Biagi of the University of Modena-Reggio. Her main publications are *Donne in tuta amaranto* (Guerini & Associati, 2003); *Non son tempi per fare figli. Orientamenti e comportamenti riproduttivi nella bassa fecondità italiana* (ed., Guerini & Associati, 2007); *Vita di fabbrica. Cristina racconta il decollo e la crisi della Fiat-Sata di Melfi* (Franco Angeli, Milano, 2014).

Gonzalo Díaz Crovetto is Docente Investigador in the Department of Anthropology and in the Center of Intercultural and Interethnic Studies at the Catholic University of Temuco. He has done research and published articles about topics relating to rural anthropology, anthropology of globalization, anthropological theory and anthropology of catastrophes, in a number of specialized journals in Argentina, Brazil, Chile and Colombia.

Michaela Ferencová received her Ph.D. in ethnology from Comenius University/Institute of Ethnology, Slovak Academy of Sciences in Bratislava. In her thesis she studied identity politics and commemoration in Slovakia. She worked as researcher and lecturer at the Faculty of Social and Economic Sciences, Comenius University in Bratislava where she participated in a project *Models and their effects on development paths: an ethnographic and comparative approach*. Currently she is a freelance researcher based in Berlin, Germany.

Monika Gnieciak, has an M.A. in sociology, University of Silesia, 2001, Katowice, and M.A. in science of culture, University of Silesia, 2004, Katowice, and a PhD in Humanities, University of Silesia, 2007, Katowice. Her research fields include: urban studies, social space, housing and home space, popular culture, sociology of literature, and gender studies. She is co-editor (with Kazimiera Wódz) of *Restructuring Class and Gender. Six case studies* (Nomos, 2012).

Victoria Goddard is Professor and National Teaching Fellow at the Anthropology Department at Goldsmiths. She has carried out research on informal sector work, households and small-scale industry in Southern Italy and on gender and politics in Argentina. In collaboration with C. Shore and J. Llobera she edited *The Anthropology of Europe: identity and boundaries in conflict*, Berg, 1994. Research on Neapolitan outworkers and petty entrepreneurs is published in a monograph (*Gender, Family and Work in Naples*, Oxford: Berg, 1996) and in a number of articles. Recent publications include the volume co-edited with S. Narotzky *Industry and Work in Contemporary Capitalism* (Routledge, 2015).

Don Kalb is Professor of Sociology and Social Anthropology at Central European University, Budapest, and Senior Researcher at Utrecht University, the Netherlands. His publications include *Expanding Class: Power and Everyday Politics in Industrial Communities, The Netherlands, 1850–1950* (Duke University Press, 1997); (ed.) *The Ends of Globalization. Bringing Society back in*, (Rowman and Littlefield Publishers, 2000); (ed.) *Globalization and Development: Key Issues and Debates* (Kluwer Academic Publishers, 2004); (ed.) *Critical Junctions: Anthropology and History beyond the Cultural Turn* (Berghahn, 2005); (ed.) *Headlines of Nation, Subtexts of Class: Working Class Populism and the Return of the Repressed in Neoliberal Europe*, (Berghahn, 2011); and (ed.) *Anthropologies of Class* (Cambridge U.P, 2015). He is the Founding Editor of *Focaal—Journal of Global and Historical Anthropology* and *FocaalBlog*. He is a Distinguished Visiting Professor at the Max Planck Institute for Social Anthropology, Halle, Germany, where he co-leads the Financialization Program (together with Chris Hann)

Sharryn Kasmir is Professor and Chair of Anthropology at Hofstra University. She has conducted fieldwork among industrial workers in the Basque

xii *Contributors*

region of Spain and in the southern US. Her monograph on the Mondragón cooperatives was the first major critique of the world renowned, worker-owned enterprises (*The 'Myth' of Mondragón: Cooperatives, Politics and Working-Class Life in a Basque Town.* State University of New York Press, 1996. *El mito de Mondragón: cooperativas, política y la clase obrera en una ciudad vasca.* Txalaparta Editorial, 1996.) She has also written about displacement, dispossession and union activism at General Motors' Saturn automobile plant in the US south, and about the importance for anthropology of the purposeful study of global labor. She is co-editor of *Blood and Fire: Toward a Global Anthropology of Labor* (Berghahn, 2014).

Susana Narotzky is Professor of Social Anthropology at the University of Barcelona, Spain. She has been awarded a European Research Council Advanced Grant to study the effects of austerity on Southern European livelihoods (*Grassroots Economics* [GRECO]). Her work is inspired by theories of critical political economy, moral economies and feminist economics. Her recent writing on making a living, political mobilization and class, includes 'The organic intellectual and the production of class in Spain' in James G. Carrier and Don Kalb (eds.) *Anthropologies of Class. Power, Practice and Inequality* (Cambridge University Press, 2015); and (with N. Besnier) 'Crisis, Value, Hope: Rethinking the Economy', *Current Anthropology* V. 55 (S9):4–16, 2014. She co-edited with V. Goddard *Industry and Work in Contemporary Capitalism* (Routledge, 2015).

Frances Pine is a Reader in the Anthropology Department of Goldsmiths, University of London. Before joining Goldsmiths, she was a lecturer and research fellow at Cambridge, and then a senior research fellow at the Max Plank Institute for Social Anthropology in Halle. She has been conducting research in Poland on kinship and gender, local economy, work and deindustrialization, and memory and landscape, since the late 1970s. She is the co-editor of *Surviving Post Socialism, On the Margins of Religion, Transnational Migration and Emerging Inequalities* (Routledge, 1998), among other volumes, and the author of many articles on gender, kinship, migration and informal economies

Laura Perelman is a Research fellow at the Instituto de Desarrollo Económico y Social (IDES). Her areas of interest include the impact of economic policies and labor institutions on the labor market; determinants of salaries and inequality in salaries; structure and patterns of collective bargaining; trade union affiliation; collective action and workers' identities.

Irene Sabaté Muriel is a researcher in Social Anthropology and a lecturer at the Universitat de Barcelona. In 2009 she obtained her PhD with a dissertation on housing provisioning in East Berlin (*Habitar tras el Muro. La cuestión de la vivienda en el este de Berlín*, Icaria, 2012). As a postdoctoral researcher, between 2009 and 2012 she took part in the 7th FP European project MEDEA (Models and their Effects on Development Paths), on industrial work and economic models; and, since 2012, she is investigating mortgage indebtedness and home repossessions in the Barcelona metropolitan area, with a Post-PhD Research Grant from the Wenner Gren Foundation in 2014. She is a member of the *Grup d'Estudis sobre Reciprocitat* (GER) since 2005, and she teaches Economic Anthropology, Anthropology of Consumption and Urban Anthropology. Her research interests include political economy, reciprocity, provisioning, work and social reproduction, housing, debt and credit relations, and financialization.

Manos Spyridakis is Associate Professor of Social Anthropology at the University of Peloponnese, Greece. His main focus is on the anthropology of work, qualitative research methods, and urban transformations as well as medical anthropology. His publications include two monographs in Greek, *Power and Harassment at Work* (Dionikos Publishers, 2009) and *Work and Social Reproduction in the Shipbuilding Industry of Piraeus* (Papazizis Publishers, 2010) and number of articles including 'Between Structure and Action: Contested Legitimacies and Labor Processes in Piraeus', in I. Pardo and G. Prato (eds.) *Citizenship and the Legitimacy of Governance. Anthropology in the Mediterranean Region* (Ashgate Publishers, 2011); M. Spyridakis (ed.) *Unemployment and Employment Precariousness: Perspectives of a Persistent Risk* (Alexandria Publishers, 2013, in Greek) and 'Cosmopolitan Possibilities and Ethnographic Realities in the Workplace: The Case of Struggling Employees in the Mass Media Sector', in A. Marinopoulou (ed.), *Cosmopolitan Modernity* (Peter Lang , 2015). His most recent monograph, published in 2013 by Ashgate, is *The Liminal Worker. An Ethnography of Work, Unemployment and Precariousness in Contemporary Greece.*

Vera Trappmann is Associate Professor of Work and Employment Relations at the Leeds University Business School. Her research focuses on labor relations, restructuring of industries, and Corporate Social Responsibility. She has published the book *Fallen Heroes in Global Capitalism. Workers and the Restructuring of the Polish Steel Industry*, with Palgrave MacMillan in 2013 and *Business Leaders and New Varieties of Capitalism in Post-Communist Europe* in 2014 with Routledge [co-edited with K. Bluhm, B. Martens].

Patricia Vargas is a Research fellow at the Instituto de Desarrollo Económico y Social (IDES). Her areas of interest include the construction, automobile and metallurgical industries; Mixtec designers, artisans and globalization; entrepreneurship, processes of social mobility and the middle classes; methodological issues in ethnography, reflexivity and fieldwork conducted by women in masculine work environments.

Kazimiera Wódz, has a Masters in Psychology, a PhD in Humanities, and a postdoctoral degree in Sociology. She is a Professor of Sociology at the Department of Cultural Studies, University of Silesia, Institute of Sociology, Katowice. Her research covers issues relating to cultural studies, European studies, urban and regional studies, political sociology, social work and social policy. She has worked on several international projects, including CIVGOV, (2003–2006), 5 FP EU, "Identity, Diversity and Citizenship in the European Union", grant founded by James Madison Trust, (2004–2005) and 'SPHERE', 7 FP, EU (2008–2011). Her publications include a SPHERE publication (as editor): *Restructuring Class and Gender. Six case studies* (Nomos, 2012) and *Zapomniane miejsca, zapomniani ludzie. Restrukturyzacja ekonomiczna a zmiana kulturowa (Forgotten places, forgotten people. Economic restructuring and cultural change)* (Wydawnictwo Naukowe Śląsk, 2013).

1 Work and Livelihoods
An Introduction[1]

Victoria Goddard

On the 18th July 2013 the city of Detroit filed for bankruptcy; once the icon of US industrial might, it faced debts in the region of US$20 billion. The city's financial troubles were largely due to long-term processes that were taking place beyond its boundaries, across the US economy.[2] Between 1910 and 1960 the US Steel Belt produced the bulk of the world's steel and was the core and pulse of world capitalism. Detroit's astonishing expansion had once drawn workers from across the world; now it stood as a testament to the end of the American Dream. The Steel Belt became a new kind of wasteland: "America's Rust Belt"(Bowen 2014).

Although the scale of Detroit's spectacular rise and equally spectacular decline is unmatched elsewhere in the US, its fortunes reflect a broader decline in the industrial might of the region. New investment opportunities were identified in non-industrial regions of the US and industrial centers emerged across the globe to challenge Detroit's supremacy. Competition from Japan's flourishing industrial sector was followed by the rise of the Asian Tigers, and by impressive advances in Brazil, India and China. In the 1990s these trends were accelerated and the Steel Belt's difficulties were compounded by the enhanced mobility of capital, itself enabled by ever more efficacious information technologies. The global strategies they facilitated were part of a wider technological revolution underpinning the emergence of a "new economy" that came to eclipse the Fordist model at the heart of Detroit's success. New technologies and globalized market conditions rendered heretofore geographical and historical advantages obsolete and enabled novel strategies by enterprises that were increasingly disengaged from local and national ties. Large US companies abandoned an earlier model of accumulation linked to investment in particular places, which, as Nash (1989) describes, workers from the Pittsfield General Electric plant saw as a betrayal of the very premises of industrial accumulation. When General Electric relocated key phases of production to Canada, seriously undermining the Pittsfield site, workers objected to "the failure to live up to their own code of competitive free enterprise within national boundaries" (Nash 1989: 6). In this volume, Kasmir outlines the ongoing history of General Motors' relocation of production from the unionized north of the USA to

Springhill, Tennessee, where an experiment in worker-management cooperation was intended to provide an alternative to the contracts and conventions achieved by trade union struggles spanning many years. As Detroit continued its decline, Springhill Tennessee expanded as those searching for work—including those escaping the deteriorating conditions and growing unemployment in the North—swelled the town's population.

Similar processes in other industrial regions have invited direct comparison with the US Rust Belt[3] and have prompted debates about the future prospects of industry—and capitalism—in the late 20th and early 21st centuries.[4] Discussion of the changes affecting industrial areas in the last decades is framed in terms of an historical break between the "old" and the "new", the discontinuities across different forms of production, or distinct stages of capitalist accumulation.[5] The debates of the 1980s and 1990s, which variously focused on "flexible accumulation" (Harvey 1990), and the "end of work" (Gorz 1982; Rifkin 1995), or have deciphered signs that appeared to indicate the imminent "end of capitalism (as we know it)" (Gibson-Graham 1996), continued into the early 21st century. The altered social, economic and political landscapes of post-Fordism have been associated with new forms of work or new sources of value; concepts such as "immaterial", "affective" and "cognitive" labor aim to capture a historical shift in the mechanisms and strategic sites of capitalist production and accumulation. Such shifts entail profound reconfigurations of work and of the relationship of workers to capital linked to the emergence of new kinds of workers, new classes or class-like formations and thus new political responses (Hardt and Negri 2000; Vercellone 2007; Codeluppi 2008; Berardi 2009; Fumagalli and Mezzadra 2010; Fumagalli 2011).[6]

While the changes in the global economy require re-calibrations of theoretical constructs and political strategies, it is equally important to recognize those continuities that may underscore such changes and reflect enduring features of the underlying logic of capitalism (Brown 1995; Federici 2012). Caffentzis (2013), for example, takes issue with the tendency to conflate diverse activities within the concept of "cognitive capitalism". While the term is useful in highlighting the centrality of knowledge in the organization and orientation of important sectors of the contemporary economy, its deployment in conjunction with a problematic dichotomy between the "old" and the "new" can result in disguising practices and relationships that may overlap across these different forms.[7] Caffentzis asks:

> Are non-knowledge based industries ignorance-based? What brings together banks, pornographic film companies, software design firms communication corporations, airplane manufacturers under the knowledge-based industry sector rubric that excludes auto companies, real estate firms, restaurants, mines, and farms?
>
> (Caffentzis 2013: 100).[8]

Early on in the debates Gibson-Graham (1996) observed that the profound realignments that took place with the end of the post-Second World War boom, the decline of Fordism and the rise of a post-Fordist analog, were too readily taken to indicate that industry itself was in decline. Considering these issues on a global scale, as we must, it is clear that globalized production strategies have uneven outcomes, producing a complex landscape consisting of diverse forms and particular concentrations of economic activity. Thrift (2011) proposes a focus on trends rather than substitutions, envisaging the co-existence of different forms of production, in different combinations, at different times and in different places. This requires that we abandon a notion of a fixed capitalist identity in favor of a focus on Gibson-Graham's conceptualization in terms of "a site of multiple forms of economy whose relations to each other are only ever partially fixed and always under subversion" (1996: 12).

A greater attention to multiplicity and fluidity is consistent with the accounts of lived realities in contemporary capitalism presented in this volume. The chapters focus on the changing circumstances affecting workers and their communities, and their responses to conditions of uncertainty that erode privileges and render the future problematic. Drawing on examples from North and South America, Western and Central and Eastern Europe, the authors in this volume pay attention to the ways lives unfold in relation to industrial work and its decline. The locations discussed in the volume reflect the histories of work and of livelihoods, as established arrangements are overturned and the experience of work is transformed, illustrating the entanglements of experience, place and spaces of the economy. Mollona et al. (2009) make a strong case for the continuing urgency of researching this sector of the economy, given the enduring significance of industrial work. Breman, too, drawing on his wide-ranging research in India (1996), argues that it is unlikely that large-scale industry will be eclipsed by smaller units, given that demand for high-grade technology and specialized labor continues unabated. Rather, the empirical and conceptual elements arising from the work of Mollona et al., and Breman, contribute to an understanding of combined and co-existing forms, from large to small-scale, encompassing factories, workshops and home-based production, which, across regions and industries, may persist through different kinds of arrangements of complementarity, accommodation and antagonism.

Industrial Landscapes, Old and New

The historical importance of steel as a commodity, the scale of investment required to establish and operate steel plants and the high levels of employment generated by the sector, account for the historical commitment of nation-states to support the industry (ILO 1997). At the height of state-sponsored modernization projects, such as Import Substitution Industrialization where the creation of employment and internal markets was a priority, new ways of life and new environments emerged. From Detroit to

4   Victoria Goddard

Nowa Huta, large-scale industry drew migrants and generated new, often purpose built urbanizations (Trappmann 2013). Rooted in the industrialization of Europe and North America, the company town provided a model for the settlement, incorporation and disciplining of large workforces, based on a projected future that encompassed workers' public and private lives (Mercier 2001; Cowie 2011; Dinius and Vergara 2011; Borges and Torres 2012). The urbanization projects associated with large-scale industrial ventures reflected the contractual obligations that linked workers, families, unions and employers in complex webs of reciprocities and reflected the intention of creating new ties, and new forms of sociality, identity and belonging (cf. Holston 1989; Kotkin 1995). The emerging landscapes reflected the paternalistic ideologies and practices through which workers were included in the projects of capitalism and the state, and seemed to encapsulate a shared commitment to stability and the pursuit of a secure and satisfying way of life. The recession and the oil crises of the early 1970s unsettled long-term projects, such as those embodied in the company town, as global conditions undermined the paternalistic relations that underpin the company town model (Sánchez 2012). Restructuring, privatization and internationalization heightened the vulnerability of plants and jobs to competition, further cutbacks and closure.[9] Today, the industry faces increased levels of global competition, problems of overcapacity, creeping energy costs and pressures from environmental regulators; at the same time, outsourcing grants firms flexibility in the global market at the price of greater uncertainty for households and deeper inequalities across the workforce.[10]

Responding to cumulative pressures, and anxious to cast off lingering associations with smoking chimneys and the landscapes of the Industrial Revolution,[11] the industry has invested in innovation and tuned in to the discourse of the knowledge-based economy.[12] Today, industry leaders claim the sector is future-oriented, innovative and knowledge-rich.[13] It is thought that these innovations will entail a further loss of blue-collar jobs as the much-lauded "breakthrough" or next-generation production technologies are expected to require new skills. A new kind of worker is predicted to supersede the "historical" figure of the steelworker in a workforce dominated by highly trained technicians, engineers, computer scientists, and business graduates— and only the most highly skilled production workers.[14] Yet, anticipating the impact of next-generation technologies, today's steelworkers are very different from their fathers or grandfathers; credentialism, flexibilization and an emphasis on multi-tasking, self-management and the manipulation of knowledge bring the industrial steelworker closer to the "new worker" of the "new economy". In a parallel process, outsourcing has introduced short-term contracts and precarious conditions into the heart of the steel plant while flexibility in the factory is mirrored in the expectation that out-of-work men and women will manage their skills, dispositions and employability (Trappmann, this volume). [15]

Internationalization and redrawn divisions of labor across space also transformed the automobile industry, increasing the vulnerability of factories and undermining workers' bargaining power. The manufacturing core of the car industry in North America and Europe has been shifting steadily away from its original heartlands,[16] while global strategies highlight the pressing issue of scale in shaping both the experience of work and the possibilities of resistance (Kasmir, this volume).[17] Overall, the industrial sector has pioneered technological and organizational revolutions in the world of production, from Ford's application of Taylorist principles to car production, to the model of speeded-up and market-led innovations developed and promoted by Toyota (D'Aloisio, this volume). The industrial sector has pioneered new forms of work and management, albeit at the cost of jobs, job security and continuity across generations and communities. The resilience that is evident in the lives and livelihoods of workers and communities responds to ongoing challenges and ever-changing pressures, highlighting the urgency of studies of industrial work and their critical role in understanding contemporary social and economic systems.[18]

Work in the Context of Growing Inequalities

The English language edition of Thomas Piketty's "Capital in the Twenty-First Century" was widely acclaimed as an important text that demonstrated the structures of inequality of contemporary capitalism. His claim that wealth inequalities were rising to levels not seen in Europe and the US since before the First World War provoked a great deal of debate and controversy. Criticism of his work has focused on the detail of the data, and raised questions about the suitability of statistical measures to capture and represent complex phenomena.[19] Despite these reservations, policy makers increasingly focus on statistical measures and big data sets, finding little use for the detail generated by qualitative research (Okely 2012: 13). In contrast to this trend, this volume privileges the detail of local places, the implications of local histories and the perspectives of workers, their families and their communities. Ethnographic research in different locations in Europe and Latin America supports the contributors' engagement with large-scale processes of capitalist accumulation, and the effects of shifting distributions of investment across different industries and regions. Such research also reveals the ways that ideologies of difference and inequality are experienced in relation to work, to production and reproduction, and how they are understood and resisted by specific social actors.

The cases explored here pay attention to the divisions and inequalities that obtain across workplaces and economies, frequently organized along axes that divide workers and capitalists, male and female, young and old, across a global division of labor that relies on, yet transcends, geographical divisions (Hoogvelt 2001). The differentiation of space and the production of place are entangled with ideologies of difference that are opportunistically deployed to reproduce highly segmented labor markets and differentiated workforces (Sánchez 2012). Such ideologies can render entire categories of workers and sectors of economic activity invisible (Elson and Pearson 1981; Benería and Roldán 1987; Benton 1990; Collins and Giménez 1990; Berman 1996; Weber 2009; Narotzky and Smith 2013) and shape the opportunities of work for men and women, young and old, and the conditions under which they work. Sectors of work that have been historically associated with masculine identities—as breadwinners, providers and heads of household—are woven into the fabric of family life and underpin ideals of masculinity. These have been affected by the scaling down of heavy industry that breaks down the identification between working class jobs and working class men. Men who are displaced by these processes may not adapt, let alone thrive, in the new conditions where their skills are unappreciated and their earning power is diminished (Arnot 2004; Trappmann 2013 and this volume); or they may be driven to defend their accepted roles by intensifying their strategies, perhaps exposing themselves to risks and dangers they might not otherwise contemplate (Spyridakis, this volume).

Although male household heads struggle with the new conditions, the younger generation faces the most serious challenges, not least in relation to achieving personal autonomy. According to the ILO, young people are three times more likely to be unemployed than older workers, and they are over-represented in low-pay, insecure and informal sector work (ILO 2013). Since university graduates also register high unemployment levels, the trends pose a serious challenge for policy makers and for aspiring workers and their families for whom investment in education may have represented a promising strategy for social mobility and improved life chances.[20] The deregulation and rollback of the state promoted by market fundamentalism have aggravated these conditions and left workers and households more exposed to the vicissitudes of life and capitalism.

Divisions between young and old intersect with other distinctions that play out in everyday life on the shop floor, detailed in Parry's ethnography of the Bhilai steel plant, showing how gender, sexuality, region, and class produce tensions and allegiances within a complex tapestry of hierarchies and solidarities (1999). From the perspective of workers, these distinctions translate into highly significant differences in the degree of stability and well-being they can hope to achieve. However, as Parry points out, "privileged" workers may also face difficulties if their pay declines, their job security is threatened or they are confronted by growing discrepancies between their income and their needs and expectations.[21]

Ideologies of gender and sexuality are integral to the discursive construction of entire sectors of the economy, informing the qualities of the ideal worker and supporting specific forms of sociality and networks of solidarity (Elson and Pearson 1981; Kapadia 1999; Mies 1999; Parry 1999, 2012). However, the specificities of these ideologies and their effects cannot be known in advance, as Lee (1998) shows in her study of women workers in Southern China. Her comparison of two sites belonging to the same company, in Hong Kong and Shenzhen, highlights the importance of place and the particular configurations of kinship, class and space within which gender relations and ideologies are expressed.[22] Masculinities may also be interpreted in different or contrasting ways, as Trappmann explores in her comparison of West German and British steelworkers, while Sabaté, also in this volume, shows how men's priorities change in relation to changes in their domestic lives.

Changing Times and Generational Transmission

The fragmentation of the working class is complicated further by temporal ruptures associated with the cycles of capitalist accumulation and transformation. The cases discussed in this volume exemplify the effects of long-term processes, punctuated by particular critical events (Das 1995; Guyer 2007). Privatization and neoliberal reforms in Europe and Latin America in the 1980s and 1990s, the collapse of state socialism in 1989–91 and the imposition of "shock treatment" policies during the transition to a market economy in the case of Central and East European countries, and the fallout from the 2008 crisis across Europe, felt particularly acutely in Southern European countries such as Spain and Greece, are all constitutive of specific places and temporalities that are simultaneously shared and distinctive. These changes go some way to explaining the different conditions of life that are encountered by succeeding generations and that find expression in the different conditions for continuity and rupture affecting generational transmission (Goddard 2014).

Pine unravels the longer-term implications of the cascading effects of the end of State Socialism in 1989 through her account of the temporal disjuncture that affects the generational transmissions of skills, memory and values, and comes to challenge the very possibility of reproduction. The collapse of Polish industry created a lost generation; the young appear to navigate a different world from that of their seniors for whom the ideals of progress are firmly located in the past. The impact of deindustrialization on jobs and livelihoods is linked to a broader overhauling of society. Everything that was familiar has been replaced; space and time intersect and collude to disorient the present and question the future.

Generational discourses (Foster 2013) articulate tensions arising from changes in the economic, social and political landscape in the Latin American examples discussed in the volume. In the case of Brazilian and Argentine steelworkers (Díaz Crovetto and Vargas and Perelman), the histories and circumstances affecting generations of workers, including different traditions of trade unionism, are constituted through local experiences of kinship and family, notions of masculinity and femininity, and concerns with responsibility and reputation, all of which are themselves subject to contestation and change (also Sabaté, Trappmann, this volume). The chapters show how the older generation perseveres in an effort to pass on to the next the capacity to survive and the hope that they will thrive and prosper. They may bind themselves within moral obligations in the attempt to mediate on behalf of sons and daughters, or nephews and nieces to help them enter the factory; they may sacrifice time and money to support their children's training in the context of the new meritocracy. Or they may invest in preparing the next generation for a rupture that is linked to hope: to leave the places of the past behind them (Pine this volume; Pine 2014).

Disposable Places, Disposable People and the Struggle for Value

Giroux suggests that under neoliberal regimes such as those deployed under Ronald Reagan's presidency, particular social groups became "disposable" (Giroux 2009). In her study of work and lives on the Hooghly River, Calcutta, Bear draws on Mbembe's concept of "necropolitics" (2003), making the point that neoliberal practices and ideologies effectively re-signify objects, persons and spaces, emptying them of meaning and placing them "out of time"; they become "evidence of waste" (Bear 2012: 185). Places and environments are path-dependent, just as much as the models that give rise to their specific shape and characteristics. While distinctions between worth and worthlessness, between the respectable working classes and the disgraced poor are entangled in the very constitution of the welfare state (Morris 1994), the erosion of the contract between citizens and the state, forged under Fordism and Keynesianism, increasingly lays bare the contradictions inherent in the dominant value system. Writing in the 1990s, Morris drew attention to shifts in public discourse from a focus on rights to an emphasis on obligation, which was accompanied by a hardening of the work ethic and a growing sense of discomfort in relation to dependence on the state (Morris 1994).[23] Arguably, the ideological and material processes she describes have shifted, not least in relation to growing contradictions between the reliance on commodities and consumption as a claim to respectability and inclusion on the one hand, and, on the other hand, the declining opportunities for secure employment and wages that have affected growing numbers of agricultural and industrial workers since the 1990s.

The connections between things and identities, places and people, imbue such places with meaning so that "the destruction of places is not experienced simply as the loss of replaceable physical landmarks and material property" (Filipucci 2010: 167); it also causes profound emotional responses related to ruptures in social relations and in lives that are reflected in a sense of "place loss" (Filippucci 2010: 168). In our case studies, reflections about value, worth and worthlessness are entangled with sentiments of loss and expressions of mourning for a way of life, and the landscapes in which it unfolded, that are no longer there. Kalb's focus on personal narratives shows how ideologies of waste and worthlessness unfold and "stick" to persons and their objectified lives (Kalb this volume; Skeggs 1997, 2004; Ahmed 2014). Similarly, Wódz and Gnieciak's chapter uncovers the "emotional geographies" that emerge as a result of the closure of a mine. In both instances, the ebb and flow of histories of industry are entangled with the circuits of valorization of capitalism (Kalb, this volume). From this perspective, the emotional geographies outlined in the chapters reflect the topographies produced by the movement of capital, people and resources, by the shifting priorities of capital and of power captured in the built environment's effect of "ossifying in the landscape the social relations extant at the time of their creation" (Herod 2011: 29). The ruins of a socialist utopia described by Wódz and Gnieciak—but also the erasure of alternatives, such as the worker-controlled privatization proposed during Poland's transition to a market economy (see Kalb this volume), mirror the production (and destruction) of space through which the capitalist project is realized (Massey 2005).

Díaz Crovetto's account of Volta Redonda interprets the city as a "state place", which, like the new, modernist capital of Brasilia, reflects the Brazilian state's national development project (Amaral and Calafate 2010). The collapse of utopias—whether socialist or capitalist (see Grandin 2009)— and the shifting strategies of accumulation that make and unmake persons and places, effectively empty out places and remove people from the sphere of value and recognition. In a context where the exchange-value regime is dominant and is entangled with class, privilege and inequality, morality and value are construed in such a way that exclusions follow, rendering persons and things "value-less" (Skeggs 2004: 91). The implications of this for industrial and post-industrial contexts are exacerbated by the narrative shift in the location of value from production to finance, as Kalb notes in his chapter, and the growing centrality of consumption (Friedman 1995; Freeman 2009; Miller 2012; Lutz 2014). Value appears to remain solely within the sphere of exchange, with no apparent need to seek realization within particular relationships, people or places.

Given these changes, Skeggs' proposal to uncover the alternatives "that exist outside of the dominant symbolic [value system]" (Skeggs 2004: 88) is particularly pertinent. Such alternatives might envisage value as an expression of social relations (Strathern 1988),[24] or in terms of what people do and the meanings attributed to their actions (Graeber 2001, 2005). By drawing from a wider range of registers and frameworks, actions can escape the confines of the narrowly defined "economic" and thus engage with moral, symbolic and aesthetic considerations (Graeber 2005: 452). By shifting the focus from narrowly conceived and exclusive notions of value—through consumption and participation in the circulation of exchange-value—towards what people do in pursuit of "living life with a very different set of values" (Skeggs 2004: 91), the terms and limits of the debate are re-defined to enable the imagination, and pursuit, of alternative frameworks through which to approach the persons, things and places that are displaced by the necropolitics of neoliberal capitalism.

Ethnographies of Value

The identification and pursuit of alternative forms of value require an encompassing definition of "labor" such as Kasmir and Carbonella (2014: 7) propose, which enables an approach to industrial work that de-centers factory wage labor and relates it to a wide range of activities, actors, spaces and outcomes. In recognizing the heterogeneity of contemporary social and economic landscapes, this approach provides strategic and analytical opportunities to identify alternative moralities and regimes of value, as Skeggs proposed (also Gibson-Graham 1996). The project of confronting capital and engaging with the complexities of lived capitalism (Barber et al. 2012) makes visible the marginalized alternatives of those engaged in other forms of work and livelihood; it is also well placed to identify new languages and forms of resistance and struggle. The task is likely to require new concepts and frameworks and build on anthropology's long-standing commitment to understanding the relations that constitute the making and unmaking of social life.

In stressing the dialectical relationship between two value systems, Gudeman outlines an approach, from economic anthropology, that addresses the interconnections and the contradictions between what he describes as "community" values and relationships and the values and actions associated with markets (Gudeman 2008). Feminist perspectives tackle a similar issue in their emphasis on the co-constitution of production and reproduction and the range of value regimes that they encompass (Edholm et al 1977; Benería 1979). The economists Ferber and Nelson (1993, 2003) point to the failure of their discipline to address the economic value of household labor (see also Dalla Costa and James 1975; Pine 2002), and omit family and other social relations from their analysis. Furthermore, their emphasis on the connections across different spheres of activity, recognition and value, have led feminist critiques to broaden the debates on rationality, and propose alternatives to the instrumental self-interest of neoliberal ideology and neoclassical economics. Such alternatives abandon the centrality of the individual embodied in the concept of *"homo economicus"* in order to acknowledge the multiple ways in which actions are socially embedded and recognized (Elson 1998). Different kinds of labor may contribute to the reproduction of capitalism, but non-capitalist forms of production and distribution may also represent alternatives that disturb or de-center current locations of value within the domain of exchange value (Odih 2007).

The entanglements of different kinds of labor and different social relations is evident in the livelihood strategies devised in the context of industrial and post-industrial landscapes. Such entanglement includes overlapping relations of kinship and work, whereby kin may support and encourage but also control and discipline other workers, as Pine and Kalb discuss in detail in their chapters. Similarly, the unemployed or the precariously employed rely on family, kinship and neighborhood networks to get by; the young are supported in their efforts to obtain work and develop careers. Kinship relations are a vehicle for gaining access to food, labor and land, and help compensate for insecurity or loss of income, as described for Slovakia by Buzalka and Ferencová and also explored in D'Aloisio's study of Fiat women workers in rural Basilicata. Kinship and friendship networks may provide a crucial resource for employers as well as for workers, when personal networks are deployed to recruit and discipline the workforce, as described in Vargas and Perelman's chapter. Kalb's discussion of "flexible familism" reminds us of the entanglements of patriarchal kinship and capitalist power and how both support and domination can constitute relationships where kinship and work are entwined. Relationships can be fragile and fraught with contradictions and ambiguities. Spyridakis' chapter describes how, in crisis-ridden Piraeus, personal networks are intensified to ensure survival, but also disclose the potential for the amoral exploitation of such relationships. Personal friendships and political allegiances can blend seamlessly with more instrumental considerations as clientelistic networks mediate between workers and the job market (Vargas and Perelman; Spyridakis, this volume).

Armed with an encompassing concept of labor (Edholm et al. 1977; Harris and Young 1981; Kasmir and Carbonella 2014) the analysis of contemporary capitalism would include insiders and outsiders, capitalist and non-capitalist values and activities. The recognition of industry's enduring legacy in terms of livelihoods, landscapes and identities requires an equivalent recognition of the range of relationships, persons and solidarities that sustain them. It is here where we may identify the emerging alliances and invisible forms of action that are postulated and hoped for, by workers and ethnographers (Gorz 1982; Leach 2012).

Protest, for Change or Continuity?

When subjects and their worth are defined through the prism of individual achievement, self-management and self-improvement in the context of "neoliberal agency" (Gershon 2011), workers are conceptualized as—and encouraged to see themselves as—bearers of human capital, to be invested in, accumulated and managed. However, the capacity to maneuver and adapt flexibly to continuous change, improving the self in relation to the market, is unevenly distributed. Trappmann, in this volume, compares steelworkers in West Germany and the United Kingdom and concludes that the experiences accumulated throughout a life trajectory—as well as the specificities of time and place—can converge to shape individuals' ability to adapt, to respond with greater or lesser degrees of resilience when faced with crisis and loss. This raises a question regarding history and context, and whether, alongside the erasures that affect generational transmission of memory and values, broader erasures—of histories of struggle and collective effort—are achieved through ideologies that individualize, and result in "the privatization of public troubles" (Hall and O'Shea 2014: 12). Personal success and personal failure take the place of the stories that speak of collective effort and disclose the effects of structural inequalities in the distribution of wealth and power.

Individualization weakens the legitimacy of workers' organizations by denying them their histories of struggle, success and failure. Added to this, horizontal and vertical fractures dividing labor markets and workplaces, high levels of uncertainty and precarity, unemployment and underemployment, pose many challenges for effective collective action. The globalization of production and markets poses formidable challenges of scale, as Kasmir illustrates in her account of the Saturn autoworkers. Kasmir's chapter provides a detailed account of the unfolding struggle of the Spring Hill Saturn plant workers, where the workforce had been halved by the time the company filed for bankruptcy in 2009. She outlines the implications of changing conditions of work and the struggles over strategy that divided the trade union and finally contributed to deepening the longer-term dispossession of US workers, spreading insecurity across one of the strongest sectors of the US working class.

Buzalka and Ferencová draw attention to the appeal of right wing populist solutions to what appear to be intractable problems regarding the future. The complicities of governments and many conventional political parties with neoliberal agendas across the contemporary world in addition to the weakening of trade unions, subcontracting and loss of jobs, the erosion of the strategic position of large-scale industry in national economies and the effects of globalization, all contribute to a complex and difficult environment for effective political mobilization towards a fair and equitable future. There are also conceptual and methodological considerations to take into account, as Parry points out regarding the tendency for studies of industrial action to focus largely on the formal sector and privilege particular forms of action, such as strikes. One way forward may be to start from everyday experience and from what Gledhill refers to as "actually existing neoliberalism" (Gledhill 2007) while paying attention to people's "everyday struggles" (Barber et al. 2012; also Scott 1987, 2008; Ong 1987) in the factory, in the community and in the home.

The Chapters

In this volume we consider work and livelihoods as interrelated features of individual lives and the multiple patterns of social relationships that sustain them. The reference to livelihoods draws attention to the changing landscapes of public and private, work, family and community that emerge in different ways in the cases discussed in the volume. It also highlights the important interconnections of different kinds of labor and different spheres of work, of the entanglements of production and reproduction. In the first section, on **Past, Present and Future: Generations in Times of Crisis,** the chapters explore the conditions of possibility and impossibility of generational transmission and social reproduction. The chapters by Pine, Perelman and Vargas and Díaz Crovetto provide a comparison of generational dynamics. Pine's chapter invites us to reflect on the question of interrupted life courses and disrupted generational transmission. She poses the question of the implications of encountering the disappearance of what is familiar and known, when it is as yet unclear what is to follow. What happens when generational transmission confronts its own conditions of impossibility? The disruption of lives and the discontinuity of experience provoked by the downfall of socialism in 1989 represent one such moment of radical change, where the experience of different generations is anchored in radically different contexts and realities. She explores these questions through the life experience of men and women who have witnessed these radical alterations in the arrangements and the meanings of everyday life in two different sites: Lublin in the early 2000s prior to Poland's accession to the EU and Łódź, once a stronghold of the textile industry, in the early 1990s, just after the collapse of state socialism.

Perelman and Vargas focus on a social event to explore the overlapping relationships of unionism, work and friendship. These relationships straddle the public and the private, work and community as experienced by workers in the steel plant of San Nicolás, Argentina. The event revealed the importance of the trade union, of belonging and participating in social networks in order to secure—or attempt to secure—a future in the plant for the next generation. Although deep changes in the industry have broken down the generational transmission of jobs that generated "steel families" and replaced it with highly competitive mechanisms based on credentials, personal contacts continue to play a role in the form of "recommendations" from appropriate personnel, including trade union officials. Neither has the introduction of flexible and precarious conditions through outsourcing diminished the immediate importance of the trade unions or the strategic advantages of "belonging" to the union. Indeed, the local branch of the metalworkers' union is a key actor in the reproduction of the firm—by providing education and training, negotiating the recruitment of suitable workers, offering support in times of hardship—and is therefore, potentially, a crucial ally in the reproduction of working class families in the area.

While the steel plant remained a highly valued workplace in San Nicolás, the denser industrial fabric of the area surrounding Volta Redonda in Brazil offered alternatives to young workers with the appropriate training and skills. Díaz Crovetto emphasizes the historical project of the Brazilian state's developmental vision. Comparing the steel town of Volta Redonda (Dinius 2011) and the modernist project of Brasilia, inaugurated in 1960 under the Presidency of Juscelino Kubitschek as Brazil's new capital (Holston 1989). He notes that the utopian vision embodied in the urban landscape of Brasilia reflects one dimension of a longer history of development and future-oriented planning, in which the CSN steel plant in Volta Redonda was a key element. As occurred in Argentina and Poland, the privatization of this mega-structure entailed deep ruptures in the experience of different generations of workers, ranging from the migrants who adapted their agricultural or mining skills to work in the plant, to the stability and status enjoyed by the second generation (who, however, also experienced the repression of the 1964–85 dictatorship) and the young, post-privatization generation for whom formal education and educational training constitute an indispensable—although not necessarily successful—step in the direction of becoming a steelworker.

The second section, **Continuities and Discontinuities,** focuses on the relationships that cut across the spheres of production and reproduction, with a particular emphasis on gender relations. D'Aloisio's chapter is based on long-term research in Melfi, Basilicata, where Fiat established a new plant, based on new organizational strategies and the recruitment of women in a sector that has historically been heavily identified with male workers. In an agricultural area with high unemployment, the Fiat plant offered welcome opportunities, despite lower wages and worse conditions than those offered in Fiat's northern sites. Tracing the trajectory of Fiat Melfi and the women workers over a period of nearly twenty years, D'Aloisio shows continuities and discontinuities in relation to the relationships that support the wage workers' fulfillment of the double burden of factory work and domestic responsibility, as well as the shift of dependencies from agriculture and subsistence activities towards wage-based incomes. Then, when the firm attempts to weather unfavorable markets, workers resort to informal activities to supplement declining wages and thus uphold the levels of consumption—and debt—acquired on the basis of factory wages.

Trappmann's critical, gendered approach to the concept of "employability", a key concept in the European Commission's economic strategy, addresses the entanglement of ideals of masculinity and work identities in the context of deindustrialization. She suggests that these may be a hindrance in situations of crisis, such as those arising from the loss of work and income that challenge the very basis of male identities and the social relations in which they are enmeshed. Trappmann also highlights the ways in which broader experience, in the workplace and beyond, can shape the ability of individuals to respond to critical situations. While her argument is based on a larger comparative research project, she focuses on two biographies to explore how experiences in work and domestic life inform the different responses to redundancy articulated by steelworkers in Britain and in West Germany.

Long-term precarity and crisis are a feature of the stories of workers in the Piraeus shipbuilding industry discussed by Spyridakis. The Greek shipbuilding industry has been affected by long-term decline as production shifted to other regions within the global economy, and by the effects of the European financial crisis, with devastating implications for workers as employment levels fell from 6,000 to 1,000 workers after 2008. Spyridakis describes workers' strategies in securing what work they might, by intensifying and accelerating their use of personal networks. Information is a crucial resource in a context in which jobs arise sporadically and opportunities for obtaining work require prompt responses. Under pressure from the acute precarity affecting workers and their households, work that may have been refused at one time, because it was too dangerous or poorly paid, is now sought after. Risk assessments are revaluated; networks are intensified in the continuous search for work; and the entire social fabric appears to be stretched to breaking point.

The third section, on **Lives of Worth,** explores the tropes of value and worth through narratives that express a sense of loss of worth, regarding people, places and things, as they relate to the circuits of capitalist valorization. Kalb juxtaposes two stories based in working class experience relating to different places and histories: one linked to industrial life in the context of Holland's welfare state between 1950–90, the other revolving around the transition from socialism to a market economy in Poland. The two stories, of a woman worker in Eindhoven and a male worker in Wroclaw, reflect the specificities of their time and place while revealing shared processes of loss, disorientation and devaluation. Like the older generation in Pine's Polish study, Maria van der Velde finds that her story does not resonate with her children and grandchildren and its meaninglessness renders it obsolete, worthless. Krzysztof Zadrony tells a story of struggle and disappointment in which the Polish working class was devalued by the elites leading the transition, who defined them as worthless workers. In Eindhoven, the entanglements of factory relations and families—and patriarchal systems of control—frame Maria's story of loss and personal devaluation. Krzysztof, on the other hand, is conscious of the highly politicized public rhetoric of devaluation that accompanied the decimation of Poland's industry and working class. Both the privatized and internalized devaluation experienced by Maria and the public devaluation of workers in the rhetoric of transition are symptomatic of what Kalb describes as the global "rhythm of capitalist accumulation".

Wódz and Gnieciak focus on social and physical landscapes produced by different and contradictory economic projects through an ethnographic study of the Ksawera estate in Będzin. The depth of the problems and the associated feelings of loss and worthlessness that their informants attach to this diminished urban landscape are due on the one hand to the large-scale investments in extractive and production sectors of the economy in the 19th and 20th centuries and, on the other hand, to the fact that the decline of these historically significant industries is not being addressed by equivalent investments. Furthermore, "new sectors" of the economy demand fewer, and highly specialized workers. The Będzin estate arose through a symbiotic relationship with the Paryż coal mine, which was nationalized after the Second World War and was then closed in 1995. Wódz and Gnieciak trace the history of the mine, from the experience of State Socialism, its collapse in 1989, the struggle for the survival of the mine and its eventual closure. The residents of Będzin express concerns, similar to those recorded by Pine and other contributors to the volume, regarding the failure to pass on knowledge to the next generation, encapsulated in their disquiet about the young generations' lack of knowledge regarding the roots of the mine's name—a serious deficit since the history of the mine's name encompasses the histories of local struggle. Such a detachment from history robs the place of meaning; it becomes a place of ghosts, loss and memories that may never be passed on to the young.

The last section discusses the possibilities of **Politics and Resistance**, focusing on the difficulties faced by workers and their organizations to combat the onslaught of lean production, rising unemployment, the erosion of wages and growing casualization. The divisions of the labor force opportunistically deployed to produce different categories of workers and differentiated regimes of value (of labor, persons and places) intersect with the fragmentation produced by hiring practices, outsourcing and relocation. The divisions of the working class and the weakening of organized labor in the face of the global market are exacerbated by the rollback of the state, withdrawing support for those rendered vulnerable in the new climate, and promoting the deregulation of markets and workplaces, freeing powerful corporations from local obligations to place and from both moral and contractual commitments to local workforces. The overall shift in the economic and political climate witnessed in the last two decades undermines the organizational bases of trade unions and produces a kind of disorientation as described by Pine and Wódz and Gnieciak in their chapters.

Following the discussion in earlier chapters of the disillusion provoked by the failure of capitalism and socialism—or as Kalb's Polish informant explained, the experience of the worst of socialism and the worst of capitalism that followed the reorganization of life and work after 1989—to deliver the prosperous modernity they promised, Buzalka and Ferencová' argue that socialism and post-socialism have served to undermine the effectiveness and status of workers' organizations. At the same time, enduring links to the land, predating socialism and surviving, to a greater or lesser extent, through the networks of kinship and family that subsidize fluctuating wages, produce "post-peasant" identities and strategies. They argue that the ability to rely on kinship networks and subsistence activities weakens the resolve of workers to fight for better wages or conditions. In some cases, the trade unions are entangled in the everyday life of the firm and come to play a strategic role in the reproduction of the labor force, through recruitment, training and monitoring both safety and performance. At the same time, workers feel threatened, as changes in technology have enabled the recruitment of workers from outside the steel industry, introducing an unprecedented level of competition for jobs and heightened the difficulties in securing favorable conditions in the workplace.

Kasmir's chapter addresses "the long dispossession of US autoworkers" by tracking General Motors' restructuring and relocation strategies, supported by the US government, in relation to the Saturn auto plant in Tennessee. The Saturn plant was established as an innovative site of production based on workers' participation, teamwork and cooperation between management and workers and was intended as the US industry's response to Japanese competition. The cooperation of Saturn's local trade union meant that the national contract was suspended in favor of participation, with a view to developing a different kind of firm and a different kind of autoworker. However, over an extended process of dispossession, the privileged status of this powerful sector of the working class was neutralized. The chapter gives a detailed account of the unfolding struggle of the Spring Hill Saturn plant workers, the decimation of the workforce and the impact of bankruptcy in 2009. Her analysis raises important questions about the implications of scale and of the spatio-temporalities of contemporary capitalism for workers' organizations. In the case of the Saturn plant, the strategies pursued by the local branch of the AUW caused divisions that weakened the workers' position, contributing to further dispossession and widespread insecurity among one of the strongest sectors of the US working class.

Sabaté's chapter returns the discussion to questions raised in earlier sections, regarding the interconnections of public and private, production and reproduction. Her case study of workers in a steel plant in Galicia, Spain, illustrates the complexities of these links and connections, and show how changes in the organization of household labor affect the sphere of production. As increasing numbers of women enter the workforce, new demands arise in the household regarding the allocation of responsibilities, particularly where childcare is concerned. These changes redraw the priorities of male steelworkers whose "class interests" become entangled with "gender interests" (Molyneux 1998), prompted by changing evaluations of domestic roles. In seeking to harmonize the rhythms of work and family life, they privilege what Sabaté calls "social" demands over the trade unions' traditional focus on "economic" priorities. She notes that there is no perceived contradiction between being a "good father" and being a "good worker". Some of the workers in her study adopt a pragmatic acceptance of tedium at work in exchange for stability and security—important conditions for their role as fathers. Others saw no contradiction between their responsibilities as a father and their commitment to political militancy.

The social, spatial and cultural landscapes of the places of work and livelihood examined in this volume reflect the ongoing process of capitalist accumulation and their intersections with local struggles over value and meaning. As such, they reveal the profound effects of the necropolitics of capitalism, while also shedding light on the forms of resilience and resistance that contest, however tentatively, contemporary capitalism's hegemonic project. The path-dependency of industrial landscapes encompasses the entanglements of work, gender, kinship and place, expressed in histories and experiences that reflect individual and collective aspirations and hopes, the utopias of state and industry, and processes of abandonment and decline. In the widely shared context of pervasive "cultural ecologies of the precarious" (Weston 2012), the uncertainties that afflict the world of industrial work concentrate the contradictions faced by the industrial project in the 21st century: the tensions between regulation and deregulation, health and jobs, the present and the future that shape the lives of workers and communities. In this respect, the emphasis on the interconnections between production and reproduction, factory and family, adaptation and resistance, speak to the need for new political and economic paradigms and for broader alliances across scale, sectors and organizations to effectively address the effects of global capitalist strategies.[25] While exploring the ways that stories of people and places unfold in relation to broad trajectories of capitalism and power, the chapters in this volume also propose encompassing approaches to labor and struggle that recognize and enable new ideals, values and languages of work, worth and value.

Notes

1 Research on the steel industry was supported by the European Commission within the Seventh Framework Programme under Grant Agreement No. 225670 in relation to the project 'MEDEA—Models and their Effects on Development Paths: An Ethnographic and Comparative Approach to Knowledge Transmission and Livelihood Strategies' (2009–12).
2 The problems of Detroit were many and complex. The city suffered from long-term decline after the Second World War, with suburbanization depleting the city center of jobs and population, as well as poor administration and racial inequality, which culminated in the 1967 riots (Binelli 2014).
3 This is the case with the United Kingdom where erstwhile thriving communities are struggling to find alternatives that may lead to a reversal of the decline suffered since the 1980s ('The Urban Ghosts. Rustbelt Britain', The Economist, 12th October 2013, www.economist.com. Accessed 20th October 2015).
4 In addition to a range of academic texts regarding the new capitalism (e.g., Boltanski and Chiapello 2005, Sennet 2006) there have been a number of volumes aimed at a wider audience, including the work of Piketty (2014).
5 These include early reflections and proposals from Offe and Keane (1985), Lash and Urry (1987), Piore and Sabel (1984), to more recent contributions from Sennett (2006) who proposes the term of "new capitalism", Boltanski and Chiapello (2005) who refer to the "new spirit of capitalism", Codeluppi's "biocapitalism" (2008), "cognitive capitalism (Vercellone 2007; Moulier Boutang 2011) and "cognitive biocapitalism" (Fumagalli 2011).
6 Autonomist Marxists, who have led the theoretical and political innovations regarding the implications of a transformed and transforming capitalist system suggest a potentially positive outcome to the conditions of life that affect workers in contemporary capitalism (see Procoli 2004), and propose a new focus for worker identity as in the notion of the "cognitariat" proposed by Berardi (2009) and Vercellone (2007); from a different perspective, Huws (2003) stresses the exploitative conditions of work of what she calls the "cybertariat", while Guy Standing highlights the hardships experienced by what he calls the "precariat" and the implications of these conditions of work for political action (2011).
7 Some theorists recognize the changing contours of contemporary capitalism and address this by proposing vigorous debates and re-evaluations of core concepts such as class (Carrier and Kalb 2015) and labor (Kasmir and Carbonella 2014), while others emphasize the implications of changing models of economic development in the histories of different regions of the global economy (Goddard and Narotzky 2015).
8 Kath Weston raises a parallel critique of simplistic oppositions between old and new, Fordist and post-Fordist, from the perspective of sensorial and affective experience in relation to mass-produced commodities. In her discussion of the automobile she asks: "How different is post-Fordist from Fordist production? If people can readily distinguish mass-produced vehicles when apprehending them through another register, that is to say, through touch, there is a kind of customization in the absence of design that customers produce when they take a car out for a spin. The sameness that undergirds mass production may be partially an optical effect. Not all aspects of mass production, in Ford's time or ours, occur en masse." (Weston 2012: 440).

9 In the 1990s, USIMINAS in Brazil reduced its workforce by 79 percent (D'Costa 1999). Over a longer period, between 1975 and 1995, there were significant job losses in the European Union (over 65 percent, with France and the United Kingdom registering rates of 75 percent) (ILO 1997).
10 In October 2015 the question of the immediate and the long-term future of the British steel industry came to public attention as a number of plants were threatened with closure or with mothballing. The Redcar steel plant was bought from Corus by SSI, a Thai company that invested in the plant as a supplier for that country's growing car industry. However, it was forced to scale down production and eventually to close in 2015. The closure was a blow to workers and the wider economy, given the high levels of unemployment affecting the region of Teeside. At a meeting in the UK Parliament the Business, Innovation and Skills Committee met with representatives of the UK steel industry (representatives of Tata Steel Europe, Celsa Steel UK, UK Steel and the Community Trade Union) to discuss what is seen as a deep crisis in the industry. There was widespread agreement that the downturn in China had caused that country to export increasing volumes of Chinese steel, undercutting prices in Europe. The UK is thought to also suffer from high energy costs and other government-induced costs that affect its viability in the current market (www.parliament.uk: Commons Select Committee: "Industry representatives and MPs questioned on UK steel" 27 October 2015; accessed 27th November 2015). Other European countries and industry representatives have appealed to the EU regarding the need for intervention to protect European producers from Chinese imports. Indian producers have also suffered from local manifestations of global problems: a slowdown in demand of local market for steel exacerbated by a lack of working capital to weather the storm. Here, too, China is seen as a threat, since it can produce steel at lower prices. Consequently, Chinese imports have trebled (also imports from Japan and Korea. For the background to Teeside's current struggles, see Beynon et al 1994).
11 This is despite the industry's very uneven record regarding worker and environmental health and numerous struggles and tensions regarding the apparently contradictory demands for healthy communities and for secure jobs. The European Environmental Agency identified the top 30 polluters, amongst which were three iron and steel production facilities. At No. 12 on the list was Thyssen Krupp Steel's facility in Duisburg, Germany; this was followed by Redcar in Teeside, United Kingdom at No. 27 and No. 29 was the ILVA steel plant in Taranto, Southern Italy (EEA - European Environment Agency 2014).

Taranto has witnessed a number of state and EU interventions, and given rise to trade union protests in Taranto and ILVA sites in the north of the country against job losses and in response to the "solidarity contract", which reduced pay and hours of work as many sectors of the plant were closed down. The Riva family, who owned the plant until it was intervened by the Italian government, were found guilty of failing to prevent high levels of toxic emissions and the plant was placed under "extraordinary administration" in an attempt to resolve the environmental problems and bolster the plant's recovery from a period of losses.
12 The knowledge economy is highlighted not only in the radical perspectives proposed in particular by the Italian Autonomist theorists; a parallel variant of the concept is proposed by the World Bank. It is the latter version of the knowledge economy that has been embraced by the industry.
13 Global giants such as Tata Steel, US Steel and Thyssen Krupp define their enterprises in terms of the creation of value and of intelligent steel products for future innovations (thyssenkrupp.com.cn. Accessed 10th October 2015)[13]. Arcelor Mittal, the world's largest steel producer, sets its sights on "transforming tomorrow", producing "safe, sustainable steel" through a clean and

sustainable industry (http://corporate.arcelormittal.com). The World Steel Association emphasizes the capacity of steel to be recycled, as a central element in the sustainability claims of the industry. They also stress improvements made in the area of energy efficiency, the implementation of management schemes for extraction and use of raw materials and the application of life-cycle assessments by the industry (worldsteel.org). See also the 2009 document produced by the European Steel Technology Platform (cordis.europa.eu/pub/estep/docs/steelpaper_en.pdf. Accessed 10th October 2015 and 23rd September 2016).

14 The industry's own figures (www.worldsteel.org) suggest that between 1972 and 2012, employment decreased globally by approximately 50 percent (accessed October 12th, 2015).

15 According to Oleg Korzhov: "Currently state aid is the main drivers of growth as with the US policy of quantitative easing" . . . "Only with a change in the economic growth model and the emergence of radically new industries will the situation alter to any degree. So far, we see no reasons for, or signs of, such a change, but nor could anyone have predicted 30 years ago just how important information technologies would become" (Korzhov 2014: 9).

16 European producers are at greatest risk. It is expected that producers in emerging markets will overtake them in terms of volume, sales and profits. See Mckinsey & Company's 2015 report at www.mckinsey.com "The road to 2020 and beyond. What's driving the global automotive industry?" (accessed October 16th, 2015).

17 Illustrated by the Saturn plant's aim to develop a radically new organizational framework, the car industry has a historical link with experimentation and innovation, from the adaptation of Taylorism by Ford to the Just-in-Time system developed in Japan in the 1960s and 1970s (Kasmir and D'Aloisio, this volume). Also known as the Toyota Production System (TPS), the model was exported to car producers throughout the world and adapted by a wide range of other industries, including steel (see Díaz Crovetto's chapter) and the IT sector. Anticipating many features of the "new" capitalism, this demand-led model made new demands on workers, requiring broadly based skills flexibly applied to different tasks and processes. While this flexibility is often claimed to empower workers, granting them control over the work process, the association of flexibility with precarious working conditions, short-term contracts and shift work in many sectors of industry has raised concerns about the implications of such innovative management and production practices for workers' individual and social well-being (Mehri 2005; Odih 2007).

18 In 2015 the German car manufacturer Volkswagen was rocked by a scandal regarding the deliberate rigging of VW cars to salvage their power and speed yet pass emissions tests in the US and elsewhere. The contradictions experienced in the steel industry between profits and environmental regulation—or indeed between environmental impact of the industry and its products and jobs and livelihoods— are perhaps more complex in the case of the automobile industry given the emotional, sensorial and practical entanglements linking the automobile to everyday life (see Weston 2012).

19 See, for example, the criticisms of Chris Giles based on inaccuracies he claims to have identified in the transcription of Piketty's data sets ('Picketty findings undercut by errors', Financial Times, May 23, 2014, amp.ft.com; accessed May 26 2014).

20 In the countries covered by the chapters in this volume there is considerable variation, both in the official figures for general unemployment and for youth unemployment. For 2014, at the lower end of the scale the United Kingdom has an unemployment rate of 6.1 percent with a youth unemployment rate of 16.9 percent; the US with 6.2 percent unemployed and 13.4 percent youth unemployed; Netherlands, with 7.4 percent unemployment and 12.7 percent youth unemployment; Brazil, with 6.8 percent unemployment and 16.1 percent youth

unemployment; Argentina with 7 percent unemployment and 18.8 percent youth unemployment. Italy and Slovakia are in the middle group with 12.7 percent. Slovakia has an unemployment level of 13.2 percent and a youth unemployment rate of 29.7 percent; Rates of unemployment and in particular youth unemployment are especially high in Southern European countries: Spain's rate is 53.2 percent (with a general level of 24.5 percent), Italy has a youth unemployment rate of 42.7 percent (and 12.7 percent overall unemployment) and Greece has a rate of 52.4 percent for youth unemployment (and an overall rate of unemployment of 26.5 percent) (Country Profiles. ILOSTAT Database 2015 (ilo.org) (Accessed on 16th October 2015.

21 In the Indian steel industry formal sector workers are increasingly forced to supplement their livelihoods by working in the informal sector (Parry 1999; also Sánchez 2012). D'Aloisio, in this volume, also describes how Fiat women workers resort to informal sources of income when their work at the car plant is affected by the company's declining market performance.

22 Lee's comparison of two electrical good factories that, while belonging to the same firm are located in two very different sites, in Shenzhen and Hong Kong, shows that place-specific entanglements of gender, age and kinship, and different histories of migration and class, produce different kinds of gendered workers. Interestingly, she attributes the contrasting management styles of the two factories to the differences arising from the social context of each place and the different expectations towards and responses of the "maiden workers" of Shenzhen on the one hand, and the "matron workers" in Hong Kong on the other (Lee 1998). These variations cannot be separated from the question of desire and aspiration, whether this is directed towards the self or towards family and dependents, illustrated by Freeman's study of Barbadian office workers (2009) and D'Aloisio's discussion of Fiat workers in this volume.

23 Morris points out that changing ideological trends went hand in hand with a general lack of analysis of the implications of migration, gender, ethnicity and other complexities that constitute social structures (Morris 1994).

24 Strathern's discussion is more complex and weaves together work, social relations and value. Taking work in Mt. Hagen as "purposeful activity" that produces things (such as pigs), and given that things such as pigs are multiply produced, by husbands and wives but also incorporating transactions and connections with many categories of kin, we can see the connections between value and social relations as embodied in the product of work: "To think of the work embodied in the pig is to think of the value husband and wife have for each other. A man takes a fattened animal as a sign of his wife's care (it is when he does not that conflict arises)" (Strathern 1988: 160). Similarly, in the case of exchange, the circulation of things and persons cannot take place without reference to the social relations that are entangled in such things and persons (Strathern 1988: 161).

25 The creation of Europe based IndustryALL Global Union is an important step in the direction of multi-sectorial and multi-scalar organization. See Gibellieri (2015) and industriall-union.org. For thoughtful discussions on these issues, see Kasmir and Carbonell (2008, 2014) and Barber, Leach and Lem (2012).

References

Ahmed, S. (2014). *The Cultural Politics of Emotion*. London: Routledge.

Amaral, A., and Calafate, F. (2010). 'Country Profile: The Brazilian Steel Industry'. *MEDEA Project*. Mimeo.

Arnot, M. (2004). 'Male Working-Class Identities and Social Justice: A Reconsideration of Paul Willis's Learning to Labor in Light of Contemporary Research', in N.

Dolby, G. Dimitriadis, P. Willis and S. Aronowitz (eds) *Learning to Labor in New Times* (Critical Social Thought). New York: RoutledgeFalmer, pp. 17–40.

Barber, P.G., Leach, B., and Lem, W. (2012). *Confronting Capital: Critique and Engagement in Anthropology*. New York: Routledge.

Bear, L. (2012). 'Sympathy and its Boundaries: Necropolitics, Labour and Waste on the Hooghly River', in C. Alexander and J. Reno (eds) *Economies of Recycling: The Global Transformation of Materials, Values and Social Relations*. London: Zed Books, pp. 185–203.

Benería, L. (1979). 'Reproduction, production and the sexual division of labour'. *Cambridge Journal of Economics* 3: 203–225.

Benería, L., and Roldán, M. (1987). *The Cross-Roads of Class and Gender: Industrial Homework, Subcontracting and Household Dynamics in Mexico City*. Chicago and London: Chicago University Press.

Benton, L. (1990). *Invisible Factories: The Informal Economy and Industrial Development in Spain*. Albany: State University of New York Press.

Berardi, F. (2009). *The Soul at Work: From Alienation to Autonomy*. Los Angeles, CA: Semiotext(e).

Beynon, H., Hudson, R., and Sadler, D. (1994). *A Place Called Teesside: A Locality in a Global Economy*. Edinburgh: Edinburgh University Press.

Binelli, M. (2014) [2013]. *The Last Days of Detroit: Motor Cars, Motown and the Collapse of an Industrial Giant*. London: Vintage Books.

Boltanski, L., and Chiapello, E. (2005). *The New Spirit of Capitalism*. London and New York: Verso.

Borges, M., and Torres, S. (2012). *Company Towns: Labor, Space, and Power Relations across Time and Continents*. New York: Palgrave Macmillan.

Bowen, W.M. (2014). *The Road through the Rust Belt: From Preeminence to Decline to Prosperity*. Kalamazoo, MI: W.E. Upjohn Institute for Employment Research.

Breman, J. (1996). *Footloose Labor: Working in India's Informal Economy* (Contemporary South Asia). Cambridge, New York, and Melbourne: Cambridge University Press.

Brown, W. (1995). *States of Injury: Power and Freedom in Late Modernity*. Princeton, NJ: Princeton University Press.

Caffentzis, G. (2013). *In Letters of Blood and Fire: Work, Machines and the Crisis of Capitalism*. Oakland, CA and Brooklyn, NY: PM Press.

Carrier, J., and Kalb D. (2015). *Anthropologies of Class: Power and inequality*. Cambridge: Cambridge University Press.

Codeluppi, V. (2008). *Il Biocapitalismo: Verso lo Sfruttamento Integrale di Corpi, Cervelli ed Emozioni*. Torino: Bollati Borighieri.

Collins, J.L., and Giménez, M. (eds). (1990). *Work without Wages: Comparative Studies of Domestic Labor and Self-employment*. New York: State University of New York Press.

Commons Select Committee. (2015). 'Industry representatives and MPs questioned on UK steel' (27th October 2015). Available at www.parliament.uk. Accessed November 27, 2015.

Cowie, S. (2011). 'Working Communities and the Victoria-American Company Town', in S. Cowie (ed) *The Plurality of Power: An Archaeology of Industrial Capitalism*. New York: Springer, pp. 11–30.

D'Costa, A. (2013) [1999]. *The Global Restructuring of the Steel Industry: Innovation, Institutions and Industrial Change*. London and New York: Routledge.

Dalla Costa, M., and James, S. (1975). *The Power of Women and the Subversion of the Community*. Bristol: Falling Wall Press.
Das, V. (1995). *Critical Events: An Anthropological Perspective on Contemporary India*. Delhi and Oxford: Oxford University Press.
Dinius, O.J., and Vergara, A. (eds) (2011). *Company Towns in the Americas: Landscape, Power and Working-Class Communities*. Athens, GA: University of Georgia Press.
Edholm, F., Harris, O., and Young, K. (1977). 'Conceptualizing Women'. *Critique of Anthropology* 3(9–10): 101–130.
EEA. (2014). Industrial Facilities Causing the Highest Damage Costs to Health and the Environment. 6th November 2014, eea.europa.eu. October 15, 2015.
Elson, D. (1998). 'Talking to the Boys: Gender and Economic Growth Models', in C. Jackson and R. Pearson (eds) *Feminist Visions of Development: Gender Analysis and Policy*. London and New York: Routledge, pp. 155–170.
Elson, D. and Pearson, R. (1981). 'Nimble fingers make cheap workers'. *Feminist Review* No. 7 (Spring): 87–107.
ESTEP. (2009). Steel. A Key Partner in the European Low-Carbon Economy of Tomorrow, March 2009, cordis.europea.eu/pub/estep/docs/steelpaper_en.pdf. October 10, 2015 and September 23, 2016.
Federici, S. (2012). *Revolution at Point Zero: Housework, Reproduction, and Feminist Struggle*. Oakland; New York: PM Press.
Ferber, M.A., and Nelson, J.A. (1993). 'Introduction: The Social Construction of Economics and the Social Construction of Gender', in M. Ferber and J.A. Nelson (eds) *Beyond Economic Man: Feminist Theory and Economics*. Chicago and London: The University of Chicago Press, pp. 1–22.
Ferber, M.A., and Nelson, J.A. (eds) (2003). *Feminist Economics Today: Beyond Economic Man*. Chicago and London: University of Chicago Press.
Filippucci, P. (2010). 'In a Ruined Country: Place and the Memory of War Destruction in Argonne, France', in N. Argenti and K. Schramm (eds) *Remembering Violence: Anthropological Perspectives on Intergenerational Transmission*. New York, Oxford: Berghahn Books, pp. 165–189.
Foster, K. (2013). *Generations, Discourse, and Social Change*. New York: Routledge.
Freeman, C. (2009). 'Femininity and Flexible Labor: Fashioning Class Through Gender on the Global Assembly Line', in M. Mollona, G. De Neve and J. Parry (eds) *Industrial Work and Life: An Anthropological Reader*. Oxford, New York: Berg, pp. 257–269.
Friedman, J. (ed) (1995). *Consumption and Identity*. London, Durham: Routledge.
Fumagalli, A. (2011). 'Twenty theses on contemporary capitalism (Cognitive Biocapitalism)'. *Angelaki: The Journal of Theoretical Humanities* 16(3): 7–17.
Fumagalli, A., and Mezzadra, S. (2010). *Crisis in the Global Economy: Financial Markets, Social Struggles, and New Political Scenarios*. Los Angeles, Semiotext(e); Cambridge, MA. Distributed by the MIT Press.
Gershon, I. (2011). 'Neoliberal agency'. *Current Anthropology. Special Section: Keywords* 52(4): 537–555.
Gibellieri, E. (2015). 'Reflections on an Industrial Policy for a Sustainable European Steel Industry', in V. Goddard and S. Narotzky (eds) *Industry and Work in Contemporary Capitalism: Global Models, Local Lives?* London and New York: Routledge, pp. 181–185.
Gibson-Graham, J.K. (1996). *The End of Capitalism (as We Know It): A Feminist Critique of Political Economy*. Oxford: Blackwell Publishers.

Giroux, H. (2009). *Youth in a Suspect Society: Democracy or Disposability?* New York: Palgrave Macmillan.

Gledhill, J. (2007). 'Neoliberalism', in D. Nugent and J. Vincent (eds) *A Companion to the Anthropology of Politics*. Oxford: Blackwell, pp. 332–348.

Goddard, V. (2014) 'Trabajo y sustento en una Europa en transformación- lecciones desde una antropología crítica del Mediterráneo'/'Work and Livelihoods in a Changing Europe—Lessons from a Critical Anthropology of the Mediterranean', in K. Schriewer and S. Cayuela (eds) *Perspectivas Antropológicas: Herramientas para el Análisis de las Sociedades Europeas/Anthropological Perspectives: Tools for the Analysis of European Societies*. Murcia: Universidad de Murcia, Waxmann Editores.

Goddard, V., and Narotzky, S. (2015). *Industry and Work in Contemporary Capitalism: Global Models, Local Lives?* Oxon and New York: Routledge.

Gorz, A. (1982). *Farewell to the Working Class: An Essay on Post-Industrial Socialism*. London and Sydney: Pluto Press [1980. *Adieu au Proletariat*, Paris: Éditions Galilée].

Graeber, D. (2001). *Toward an Anthropological Theory of Value: The False Coin of Our Own Dreams*. New York: Palgrave, pp. 439–454.

Graeber, D. (2005). 'Value: Anthropological Theories of Value', in J.G. Carrier (ed) *Handbook of Economic Anthropology*. Aldershot: Edward Elgar.

Grandin, G. (2009). *Fordlândia: The Rise and Fall of Henry Ford's Forgotten Jungle City*. New York: Metropolitan Books.

Gudeman, S. (2008). *Economy's Tension: The Dialectics of Community and Market*. New York; Oxford: Berghahn.

Guyer, J. (2007). 'Prophecy and the near future: Thoughts on macroeconomic, evangelical and punctuated time'. *American Ethnologist* 34(3): 409–421.

Hall, S., and O'Shea, A. (2014). 'Common-sense neoliberalism'. *Soundings*, 55 'Values as Commodities': 8–24.

Hardt, M., and Negri, A. (2000). *Multitude: War and Democracy in the Age of Empire*. Cambridge, MA: Harvard University Press.

Harris, O., and Young, K. (1981). 'Engendered Structures: Some Problems in the Analysis of Reproduction', in J.S. Khan and J.R. Llobera (eds) *The Anthropology of Pre-Capitalist Societies*. London and Basingstoke: Macmillan, pp. 109–147.

Harvey, D. (1990). *The Condition of Postmodernity: An Enquiry into the Origins of Cultural Change*. Malden, MA: Blackwell.

Herod, A. (2011). 'Social Engineering through Spatial Engineering: Company Towns and the Geographical Imagination', in O.J. Dinius and A. Vergara (eds) *Company Towns in the Americas: Landscape, Power and Working-Class Communities*. Athens, GA: University of Georgia Press, pp. 21–44.

Holston, J. (1989). *The Modernist City: An Anthropological Critique of Brasilia*. Chicago; London: University of Chicago Press.

Hoogvelt, A. (2001). *Globalization and the Postcolonial World: The New Political Economy of Development*. Baltimore, MD: The Johns Hopkins University Press.

Huws, U. (2003). *The Making of a Cybertariat: Virtual Work in a Real World*. New York: Monthly Review Press.

ILO. (1997). *The Iron and Steel Workforce of the Twenty-First Century*. Sectoral Activities Programme. Geneva: International Labor Organization.

ILO. (2013). *Global Employment Trends for Youth 2013: A Generation at Risk*. Geneva: International Labor Organization.

ILOSTAT Database. (2015). 'Country Profiles'. Available at www.Ilo.org. Accessed October 16, 2015.
Kapadia, K. (1999). 'Gender Ideologies and the Formation of Rural Industrial Classes in South India Today', in J.P. Parry, J. Breman and K. Kapadia (eds) *The Worlds of Indian Industrial Labour*. New Delhi; Thousand Oaks, CA; London: Sage.
Kasmir, S., and Carbonella, A. (2008). 'Dispossession and the anthropology of labor'. *Critique of Anthropology* 28(1): 5–25.
Kasmir, S., and Carbonella, A. (2014). *Blood and Fire: Toward a Global Anthropology of Labor*. New York; Oxford: Berghahn.
Korzhov, O. (2014). 'Planning to profit from opportunity: Preparing for future demand. Q & A with Mechel and Tata Steel Group'. Ernst & Young: Global Steel 2014: 9.
Kotkin, S. (1995). *Magnetic Mountain: Stalinism as a Civilization*. Berkeleyand Los Angeles, CA: University of California Press.
Lash, S., and Urry, J. (1987). *The End of Organized Capitalism*. Cambridge, MA: Polity Press.
Leach, B. (2012). 'Not the Same Old Stories: Labor Anthropology, Vulnerabilities, and Solidarity Struggles', in P. Gardiner Barber, B. Leach and W. Lem (eds) *Confronting Capital: Critique and Engagement in Anthropology*. New York and London: Routledge, pp. 113–129.
Lee, C.K. (1998). *Gender and the South China Miracle: Two Worlds of Factory Women*. Berkeley, CA: University of California Press.
Lutz, C. (2014). 'The U.S. Car Colossus and the Production of Inequality'. *American Ethnologist* 113(3): 389–407.
Massey, D. (2005). *For Space*. London, Thousand Oaks, CA, New Delhi, IN: Sage Publications.
Mbembe, J.A. (2003). 'Necropolitics'. *Public Culture* 16(1): 11–40.
McKinsey and Company Report. (2015). 'The road to 2020 and beyond. What's driving the global automotive industry?' www.mckinsey.com. Accessed October 16, 2015.
Mehri, D. (2005). *Notes from Toyota-land: An American Engineer in Japan*. Ithaca, NY: Cornell University Press.
Mercier, L. (2001). *Anaconda: Labor, Community and Culture in Montana's Smelter City*. Urbana: University of Illinois Press.
Mies, M. (1999). *Patriarchy and Accumulation on a World Scale: Women in the International Division of Labor*. London and New York: Zed Books.
Miller, D. (2012). *Consumption and its Consequences*. London: Polity.
Mollona, M., Geert de Neve, and Parry, J. (2009). *Industrial Work and Life: An Anthropological Reader*. Oxford, New York: Berg.
Molyneux, M. (1998). 'Analysing Women's Movements', in C. Jackson and R. Pearson (eds) *Feminist Visions of Development: Gender Analysis and Policy*. London and New York: Routledge, pp. 55–88.
Morris, L. (1994). *Dangerous Classes: The Underclass and Social Citizenship*. London and New York: Routledge.
Moulier-Boutang, Y. (2011). *Cognitive Capitalism*. Cambridge, Malden, MA: Polity Press.
Narotzky, S., and Smith, G. (2013). *Immediate Struggles: People, Power, and Place in Rural Spain*. Berkeley, CA, Los Angeles, London: University of California Press.

Nash, J. (1989). *From Tank Town to High Tech: The Clash of Community and Industrial Cycles*. New York: State University of New York Press.

Odih, P. (2007). *Gender and Work in Capitalist Economies* (Issues in Society). Berkshire, New York: Open University Press.

Offe, C., and Keane, J. (1985). *Disorganized Capitalism: Contemporary Transformations of Work and Politics* (Studies in Contemporary German Social Thought). Cambridge, MA: The MIT Press.

Okely, J. (2012). *Anthropological Practice: Fieldwork and the Ethnographic Method*. London and New York: Bloomsbury.

Ong, A. (1987). *Spirits of Resistance and Capitalist Discipline*. Albany, NY: State University of New York Press.

Parry, J. (1999). 'Introduction', in J. Parry, J. Breman and K. Kapadia (eds) *The Worlds of Indian Industrial Labour*. New Delhi, IN, Thousand Oaks, CA, London: Sage, pp. ix-xxxvi.

Parry, J. (2012). 'Industrial Work', in J. Carrier (ed) *A Handbook of Economic Anthropology* (2nd edition). Cheltenham: Edward Elgar, pp. 145–165.

Picketty, T. (2014). *Capital in the Twenty-First century*. Cambridge, MA: President and Fellows of Harvard College.

Pine, F. (2002). 'Retreat to the Household? Gendered Domains in Post-Socialist Poland', in C. Hann (ed) *Post Socialism: Ideals, Ideologies and Practices in Eurasia*. London: Routledge, pp. 95–113.

Pine, F. (2014). 'Migration as Hope'. *Current Anthropology* 55(S9): S95-S104.

Piore, M., and Sabel, C. (1984). *The Second Industrial Divide: Possibilities for Prosperity*. New York: Basic Books.

Procoli, Angela. (2004). *Workers and Narratives of Survival in Europe: The Management of Precariousness at the End of the Twentieth Century*. New York: State University of New York.

Rifkin, J. (1995). *The End of Work: The Decline of the Global Labor Force and the Dawn of the Post-market Era*. New York: Tarcher/Putnam.

Sánchez, A. (2012). 'Deadwood and Paternalism: Rationalizing Casual Labour in an Indian Company Town'. *Journal of the Royal Anthropological Institute* 18(4): 808–827.

Scott, J.C. (1987). *Weapons of the Weak: Everyday Forms of Peasant Resistance*. Yale: Yale University Press.

Scott, J.C. (2008). *Domination and the Acts of Resistance: Hidden Transcripts*. Yale: Yale University Press.

Sennett, R. (2006). *The Culture of the New Capitalism*. New Haven, CT and London: Yale University Press.

Skeggs, B. (1997). *Formations of Class and Gender*. London, Thousand Oaks, CA, New Delhi, IN: Sage.

Skeggs, B. (2004). *Class, Self, Culture*. London and New York: Routledge.

Standing, G. (2011). *The Precariat: The New Dangerous Class*. London and New York: Bloomsbury Academic.

The *Economist* (2013). 'The Urban Ghosts, Rustbelt Britain' (12th October 2013), http://www.economist.com/node/1394179. Accessed October 20, 2015.

Strathern, M. (1988). *The Gender of the Gift: Problems with Women and Problems with Society in Melanesia*. Berkeley, CA and Los Angeles, CA: University of California Press.

Thrift, N. (2011). 'Lifeworld Inc. and what to do about it: Environment and planning D'. *Society and Space* 29: 5–26.
Trappmann, V. (2013). *Fallen Heroes in Global Capitalism: Workers and the Restructuring of the Polish Steel Industry*. Basingstoke, New York: Palgrave Macmillan.
Vercellone, C. (2007). 'From formal subsumption to generali: Elements for a marxist reading of the thesis of cognitive capitalism in historical materialism'. *Historical Materialism* 15(1): 13–36.
Weber, F. (2009). *Le Travail À-côté: Une Ethngraphie des Perceptions*. Paris: Éditions de l'Ecole des Hautes Études en Sciences Sociales.
Weston, K. (2012). 'Political Ecologies of the Precarious'. *Anthropological Quarterly* 85(2) (Spring): 429–455.

Section I
Past, Present and Future
Generations in Times of Crisis

2 Lost Generations? Unemployment, Migration and New Knowledge Regimes in Post EU Poland

Frances Pine

The primary ethnographic setting of this paper is Lublin, a city in southeastern Poland, in 2003–06. In one of the poorest regions of Poland, on the edge of the kresy, the borderlands with Ukraine, Lublin is situated on the edge of the edge.

In the film 'Goodbye Lenin', the main character, a young boy living in the GDR who is in late adolescence when the wall comes down, suddenly finds himself having to hold onto the material world of socialism as capitalism grows all around him. His mother, who was a dedicated and highly respected party member, collapses as the crowds surge onto the streets, and lies in a coma during the entire first stage of the Wende. When she awakens, her son is told that she must not suffer any shocks, as shock could kill her, and so, dutifully, he sets about restoring the world she does not know has been lost. He fills the cupboards with old East German tins and preserves for which he has to scour the countryside, puts back into the flat all of the solid furniture of socialist design, obscures the large Coca Cola ad which can be seen from the bedroom window, and hires some rather entrepreneurially minded local children to dress in old Pioneer uniforms and come and sing socialist songs at his mother's bedside. Like many of the people I talked to in Poland between 1990 and 1996, and even as late as the first decade of the 2000s, his mother has lost her work, her health and her authority within both the state and the family. The son attempts to disguise these enormous losses, to keep her safe. In taking care of her, like the good son he is, however, he must also take over from her the role of adult and provider in the family.

This film, which as we shall see finds many shadowy parallels in the snippets of life stories from Lublin with which I end this chapter, is basically a tale of life courses interrupted by enormous events and changes in the public world. The tension between simultaneously attempting to hold things still, as they were, and to silence or obscure the monumental changes, and desiring to move into a new and different world and life trajectory, is overwhelming. The move forward is potentially destructive for the mother, and both potentially freeing and incredibly painful for her children. The film reveals the core of the problem of such all-encompassing change: generations cannot reproduce themselves as before, and a new direction in the life course for one generation can often only be implemented by the paralysis or experience of extreme loss of the other.

Throughout eastern and central Europe the year 1989, when socialism fell, saw the beginning of an acute and rapid shift in political economy and social life. Here, in this chapter, I write primarily about Lublin, a city near the border between Ukraine and Poland, which has a complicated, powerful and at times troubled political history. The research on which I am drawing was conducted in the first decade of the 2000s,[1] in the periods leading up to and following Poland's accession to the EU in 2004. For comparison, I also refer at times to the process of deindustrialization which took place in the city of Łódź, particularly around the textile industry, in the early 1990s; this was also a decade of remarkable change, but change caused by the demise of the Soviet Union and its empire rather than the expansion of the European Community.

In the years of the early–mid 1990s that followed the regime change, people all over the former socialist bloc had to remake lives and to remap life courses which had seemed settled and, although difficult, in many ways secure. Now, twenty-five years after, and already a decade into Poland's membership in the new Europe, memories and moral assessments of the socialist period still divide generations. The dissonance is between those who grew up and lived their adult working lives under socialism and hold certain memories, expectations and even moralities associated with socialism, and those now just entering adulthood that have very little personal memory of socialist daily life and have experienced very different educations and ideologies. Disrupture here lies not only between a particular past and present, but also between the lived worlds of different generations, and the experiences, dreams and losses associated with these, within regions, communities, neighborhoods and even close families. In terms of the discussion here, this seems to me to be important, because it addresses the most basic level of disrupture, in social, political and above all economic terms. Class is a major component in this discussion, although religion, political affiliation, ethnicity and all of the other usual suspects are also germane, sometimes even within (and dividing) close kin and their families.

In this chapter, I want to consider kinship and labor as two inextricably interwoven concepts. If kinship is transmitted from generation to generation through definitions of personhood (social and biological), stories, accounts of events and moralities, as well as more tangibly through work practices and skills and other embodied acts—knowledge of the world as it is and how it should be—how can this transmission take place in the now empty spaces where what was has gone and what is to be is still emergent or not yet clear? What happens when transmission becomes thwarted, or absent and silenced?

I am concerned here particularly with how, at times of enormous political, economic and social change, transmission can become so problematic that relations between generations are re-mapped. The process of re-mapping creates fallout, in the form of lost generations: generations written out of the meta narrative of national political economy because there is no longer a place for them or a way for them to fulfill the obligations that they had previously undertaken; or generations who choose a new path which takes them away from the practices of kinship reciprocity, although not necessarily from the emotions, ideologies or moralities. In both cases what occurs is an inability of generations, at least in certain classes and contexts, to reproduce: a failure of reproduction.

Historians such as Braudel (1972) and Hareven (1982) have discussed the existence of different temporalities, in terms of both regimes of time—family time, industrial time, ritual time—and different temporal perspectives—the *longue durée*, the rhythm of everyday life from generation to generation, and the short-term interruptions by events which shake or unsettle, or irrevocably change, the lived world and the life course of the individual. It seems to me that in Lublin, the problem of intergenerational reproduction, and here I mean reproduction in the widest sense encompassing household, work/economy and life course rather than the narrower process of biological reproduction, was acute at the time of this research and I suspect still is today.

Sophie Day (2007) interrogates the idea of the life course in her writings on sex workers. The temporalities of the sex worker, she argues, lie in the present, and involve various persons, all of whom are located in one body, as well as a complex negotiation of the body as private and the body as public, in the latter case a commodity; this presentism and the different bodies and persons it entails often results in an inability to reproduce either biologically, in terms of bearing and raising a child, or socially, in terms of replicating a particular social world in the next generation.

If for sex workers the presentism which they occupy makes a particular type of life course difficult or impossible to realize, for others the disrupture is rooted more in memories of fractured pasts. Skultans (1997), for instance, described the life narratives of Latvians whose lives were torn apart by the German occupation and later by Stalinism. Some survived and took up their lives again after the trauma of war and deportation, while others, failing to do so, instead were hospitalized with a mysterious and obscure, very Soviet disease—a form of neurasthenia. The former were those who could give a structured account of their lives, beginning in an innocent childhood in the forest, moving through a dark and dangerous place of hiding, at the onset of a transition journey, which leads to a prison camp in Germany or Siberia or Central Asia, and finally back again to the re-established safety and magic of home and forest. Those who failed to make and own a coherent and resolved narrative were in effect frozen, embodying a paralysis of emotion and memory.

Such accounts, from very different places, times or work practices, have resonance for my material from Lublin in the early 21st century because they address questions about disrupture and discontinuity: what happens between generations when the established legitimate order collapses, and the rules, both official and informal, by which people have conducted or expect to conduct their lives, no longer apply? How are people able to construct coherent life stories, stories to 'live by'? Are they able to do so?

We are all familiar with descriptions of decaying and dilapidated factories and collective farms in former socialist countries. When people lost their jobs in such enterprises, they lost more than work. To use a phrase which has become rather widespread more generally in anthropology (Escobar 1994; Weiss 1996; Kideckel 2002; Humphrey 2002), accounts are rife with descriptions of the literal unmaking of the everyday or lived world, when the fabric and structures of normal known life under socialism, from secure employment to housing and utilities, to subsidized food, childcare and healthcare, unraveled, became severely eroded or disappeared altogether.

But other less tangible and certainly formerly less visible aspects of work have also shifted. For many state workers, whether in agriculture, industry or services, the socialist workplace had been the site from which informal dealings, transactions, exchanges, from small jobs contracted outside the official work time or place to large-scale redistribution of appropriated goods and produce, were built up and developed (see Wedel 1992). Most people moved between their public and private worlds, and formal and informal work and consumption practices, with relative ease during socialism, but often the success or even possibility of informal work, black marketing, shadow economy work, was dependent upon the existence of both official, formal and legal employment and the resources attached to this. These latter comprised, for example, contacts, goods to appropriate and redistribute, access to machinery and vehicles for purposes other than those intended, and networks of kinship and friendship (see Morris 1992; Pahl 1984) and others writing about the context and consequences of long-term unemployment and socio-economic polarization in Britain).

Hareven (1982, 2001) argued that among textile workers in the Amoskeag Mills in 19th century New Hampshire, "the emergent as well as the more established factory system was dependent on kin to recruit workers, to organize or assist in migration, to train young workers or newly arrived immigrants on the factory floor, to act as interpreters and to supervise or discipline the younger members of their kinship group. Workers carried their kin ties and their traditions of reciprocity into the factory" (2001: 23–24).

Similarly, studies of the Lancashire mills in the 19th century link their success to such kin organization, both on the factory floor and in the recruitment of labor through rural urban kin links (e.g., Michael Anderson, 1971). Margaret Grieco's (1987) work on fish canning factories in Aberdeen, and on migration to the steel mills in Colby, tells a similar story placed in the late 20th century. She shows that factory workers recruited, trained and disciplined their junior kin, not only in local factories, but across significant distances involving periodic migration. My own research on textile workers in Łódź revealed the predominance of such processes of kinship recruitment and training, and kin-based networks of rural urban migration, beginning in the 19th century, and lasting throughout the communist period and until the collapse of the factories in the 1990s.

These various accounts are important not only because they demonstrate the impossibility of separating and compartmentalizing the apparently private world of kinship and the apparently public world of work, but also because in making the links and overlaps between the two domains visible they provide us with some clues about what kinship may mean, and what kinship practices may entail, in an industrial political economy. Processes of recruitment, of transfer of skills and of discipline bind junior kin to their elders, making them dependent on their knowledge and contacts, and hence affording the elders significant power and status. This merging of public and private contradicts the more programmatic model of separate or bounded public and private spaces, which ascribes authority to senior kin in the domestic domain, and to employers, bureaucrats, police and civil servants, and/or the state itself in the public. So the question which follows must be, what happens to these hierarchical but strongly binding ties of family and kinship when many members of the middle/senior generations have not only lost their jobs, but the entire economy in which they worked, including the workplaces themselves, has collapsed and disappeared.

Mollona's (2004) sensitive and evocative ethnography of Sheffield after the collapse of the steel industry illustrates the intertwining of the formal and informal economies in the face of deindustrialization and socio-economic marginality. He shows that in many cases middle-aged men, although they themselves occupy increasingly marginal positions in the wider economy, are able to carve out strong bases of local power by controlling labor recruitment and work practices of their junior male kin in the seasonal waged work in small steel enterprises, and of both male and female junior kin in the surrounding sites of informal economic dealing—brothels, pubs, drug dealing and clandestine markets. Different domains, family and work, public and private, formal and informal, overlap and nest within each other. Power structures which subjugate the male workers to exploitation by the capitalist in the formal public economy are mirrored by those which situate the same male workers in the informal, semi-domestic economy as the exploiters, and their wives, sons and daughters as the exploited, alienated and controlled. Kinship is by no means benign or cozy, but it is a source of both (economic) support and control across generations.

In the socialist countries, I would argue, the combination of fear of or hostility to the state and the workings of the "economy of shortage"[2] created a particular paradox. Socialist ideology and state practice devalued the private sphere as antisocial, bourgeois and individualistic, but for most people it became the sphere of trust and morality, and the center for practical kinship and social relatedness. For instance, officially jobs were open to all, through recruitment on an impartial basis by the state; in practice, jobs in both the state economy and the ubiquitous informal sector were arranged through contacts, connections and kin. The senior generation operated as gatekeepers, setting up work opportunities for their grandchildren, children, nieces and nephews in factories and enterprises, teaching them knowledge of the workplace and skills of survival. Here I think that socialist emphasis on the identification of value with labor is important; in socialist economic theory, human value is realized through labor. Although many aspects of socialist ideology were generally rejected, this notion of worth through labor was, I think, widely internalized by the working populations of the socialist states (see also Kalb, Wódz and Gnieciak, this volume).

With the fall of socialism and the collapse of the planned economy, many of the avenues to work, and many of the connections which had been nurtured by the senior generations and passed on to their juniors, closed. After 1989, and most markedly since the early 2000s, the change from socialist ideology of human value defined through work to capitalist ideology of market exchange and possessive individualism has been played out in the collapse of primary sites of employment and production such as agricultural and industrial cooperatives, collectives and factories. The holes which resulted were filled at first by informal work and work sites; over time this unsettled terrain came to be balanced by new economic regimes, manifested in the highly mobile information-based economy and migration networks of late 20th century global capitalism,

Many of those who were most adversely affected by the collapse of socialism relocated themselves exclusively in the informal or gray sector, often although not always out of necessity rather than choice. In the new information- and knowledge-based sector, characterized by both acceleration and extreme mobility, on the other hand, the new Europeans are being formed, and they are most likely to be members of the younger generations, those with no experience of working under socialism but with education, training and social connections in quite different realms.

Ironically, in the accounts I collected in Lublin of working lives of men and women in their 50s and 60s, unemployed or fearful of losing their jobs, progress tends to be associated with the past. It is a memory of socialism, often of the Gierek years (the 1970s), and above all it is a linear memory of growth and development, after the horrors of the war and then Stalinism, a memory of civilized modernity—full employment, good food and services, and a productive industrialized economy characterized by good, stable and safe working conditions and very high standards. To my mind, and drawing on my own memories of socialism in Poland during the Gierek years, this is a rather partial picture.

During socialism, children of factory workers tended to follow their parents and elder kin into the factories; at the time of my research in Lublin the directors of the tobacco and the sugar plants, both of which also draw on seasonal workers from Ukraine, still tried to hire family members of existing or former employees when possible. But where the parents saw this as life work, and as modern work involving sleek technology, skills and knowledge which they had received from their parents and could and should pass down to their own children, the current young employees say that they plan only to work in the factories for a time, or that they work there because there is no other work at the moment. Their longer term plans involve either finding different work, setting up something on their own, or going abroad as migrant laborers or students. In their accounts of their work in the Polish industrial sector, there is no emphasis at all on modernity, modern machines or progress. Rather they talk about bad working conditions, poor pay and antiquated technology. I rarely heard them speak of skills, or transfer of knowledge between generations.

Łukasz (aged 19), for instance, talked about his work history and his plans. He was taken on by the tobacco factory at 17 after his mother was laid off and his father died. He says that he needs the work for now, to support his mother and sisters, but in the long term he plans to become a baker, and make beautiful and expensive designer cakes, after working in the UK for a time. He has no interest in anything his mother can teach him about the world of the factory floor.

The underactive local labor market is divided in various ways that position categories of people differently: younger versus older workers, those with and without education, and those with or without strong and influential ties of kinship and friendship. On the other hand, as a counterpoint, there is a mobile informal labor force, consisting of young and middle-aged people from all backgrounds who travel abroad to work. In their work abroad, they often perform the worst paid or the least valued work: cleaning, nursing and caring for the ill and the elderly, domestic labor, meat packing, agricultural unskilled labor, construction, labor in sweatshops, sex work, protection and various kinds of petty criminal activity. This is work that they are either unable or unwilling (or both) to carry out at home in Poland. In Lublin, in fact, this work is often performed by people from further east, usually Ukrainians, but also Romanians and Bulgarians. (So, a young woman who has just finished her MA in Psychology may be employed by an EU-funded NGO in Lublin, to help to establish the 'know how' of civil society in Ukraine. During the summer she may take two months off, and travel to the UK, to work as a cleaner or a nanny. Meanwhile, her Ukrainian friend from Kiev, who works for the same NGO, takes time off to travel to Lublin and work there as a cleaner).

What this means, of course, is not only that people do different jobs at different points in their lives, but also, as David Harvey (1990) among others has pointed out, that the age of Fordism, the time when people expect to train in one job and then do it in one place for the rest of their lives, is long past. But it also means that individuals move backwards and forwards between different worlds, kinship and friendship relations, localities and work, in their lives. This is not a lineal progression at all, but a set of cycles determined by socio-political space. Psychologists and economists trained in

Ukraine may work as cleaners in Poland, and their Polish counterparts may work as cleaners in London. Both may return to work again as economists and psychologists in their native countries, and they may go backwards and forwards many times, in different work and social relations each time. But it is highly unlikely at the moment at least that the process could be reversed, and that an English economist would work as a nanny in Poland or a Polish psychologist as a nanny in Ukraine.

In the new information- and knowledge-based sector, characterized by both acceleration and extreme mobility, the new Europeans are being formed, and they are most likely to be members of the younger generations, those with no memory of working under socialism but with education, training and social connections in quite different realms. To the older industrial and agricultural workers, their children or grandchildren seem to work within a complicated world system where very few people seem to be involved in the production of tangible objects or produce, but very many in the production and circulation of ideas, words, concepts, and "know-how".

This kind of rupture and backward and forward movement in time and space which occur with temporary migration is a recurrent theme in personal and family stories in Lublin, calling to mind Hareven's distinction between different kinds of timing (1978:100): synchronization of individual with family transitions; interaction involving the relationship between life course transitions and historical change; and integration, the cumulative impact of earlier life course transitions on subsequent ones, are all important here (Hareven 1978:100).

In Lublin after EU accession the interaction between transitions and historical change was unsettled. Patterns of kinship interdependence and reciprocity, established over generations, continued to be important in socio-economic relations and in social imaginings. Everyone I spoke to declared that they relied on their parents and grandparents, or their children and grandchildren, for emotional support and financial aid. In the work histories I recorded in Lublin, the narrators all referred to kinship ties and networks when describing their attempts to find or keep work. But the ways in which work and a working life were understood varied among the generations. For the youngest, in their late teens or early 20s, socialism was a distant memory, a time when their mothers spent a lot of time in queues. For many, work was not life employment but any short-term job, and above all any short-term job abroad. Middle-aged women and men, those who had been working during the socialist period, all experienced some kind of rupture in or shortly after 1989. For most this was expressed as a negative and frightening change, a going backwards; some, particularly those now unemployed, spoke as though there were two distinct work times—"then", when there was work, and stability, and "now", when nothing was certain anymore.

This, a fragment of a conversation I had with Pani Ula, a 55-year-old woman currently unemployed, is typical of many others: "My first job? It was in the sugar plant; my aunt worked there. How did I get it? What do you mean, how did I get it? That was then. Things were different then. You didn't look for jobs, you just went to them after you finished school". She lost her job with the cuts after 1989, and had a period of unemployment, when she was very depressed and confused. "Then I got a new job in a cosmetics outlet, a little shop, but that only lasted eight months because it got robbed . . . it was down near the station . . . and the owner was frightened and closed it down". The owner was a young woman, a friend of her niece, which is how she got the job. Then, after another longer period of unemployment, she got another job in retail. "This was through my daughter, a friend of hers opened a small shop and said to her . . . 'your mother worked in a shop didn't she? Might she want to work for me?' That was nice work, but it didn't last".

This is a fairly typical story for a woman of this generation, that recounts a movement through a life which seems orderly and smooth and predictable, and in which the narrator does all the right things and for the first 20 or so years of adulthood life things carry on as expected. Her personal life and her work life are knitted together, she works with friends and kin, has time off to have her children, and is unworried about the future at least in terms of work because, as she says "that was then. There was always work." Her life was progressing as expected. And then, with the big historical changes of the fall of communism and the economic restructuring which followed, the pattern of her life changed dramatically. Laid off from the factory, she took a series of small temporary jobs. Her links to her work were still formed through kinship, but instead of first following in the steps of her elder kin and being taught and protected by them, and then in her turn leading her daughter's generation, and training her daughter's generation, it was her daughter and her niece who found her work. In other words, the hierarchies of age and generation had, like work itself, been disrupted and even reversed.

In Pani Ula's story we see a world transformed, as security is replaced by an overwhelming sense of a precarious life and shadowed by fear of actual physical danger. For some of the younger generation, the loss of old certainties and the failing efficacy of old networks were equally traumatic.

Josek, for instance, was 24 when I spoke to him at an unemployment center in Lublin. He had finished middle school, and apprenticed to his father and elder brother, both of whom had lost their jobs at the auto factory but were working independently, as auto mechanics. In a way Josek was following the "old" pattern in terms of kinship and generations, although there was at this point no permanent or even regular work for any of them. After his apprenticeship Jozek did his military service, returned to civilian life and had had no formal work since. Sometimes he did a bit of work for his brother. Usually he worked 'on the black', *na czarna*; he was quite open and explicit about this, saying he got his black work from the street, not through kin or acquaintances particularly but through word of mouth. When I ask him what he wanted to do, whether he was planning to go abroad to work as so many of his contemporaries were doing, he responded, unusually for a young man of his generation and class, that all he wanted to do was what he was doing, only legally. But the lack of legal work at that time affected them all, and in this family neither generation was able to help the other in creating steady or formal work.

One person I interviewed made an unusually strong impression on me. When I talked to her in an unemployment center, Anka was 22, and the mother of three children under five. Unlike Josek (see above), who was more or less her age mate, she wanted to leave her origins and to leave the past, in all of its dysfunctionality, behind her. She was born outside Lublin on a Pat stwowe Gospodarstwo Rolne (PGR from hereon), a state farm. The farm was liquidated in 1993, along with most other PGRs. Anka was 10 or 11 then. Her parents both lost their work and like many former PGR workers had nowhere else to go and so stayed on the farm, with no work and no income. Both drank heavily and Anka was cared for by her grandmother, who urged her to study, helped her with her work and generally protected and cared for her. At 17 or 18 she became pregnant and her grandmother encouraged her to move to Lublin to be with her boyfriend. They married, had more children and moved in with his parents. This meant that Anka has the possibility to work, because her mother-in-law who was retired could care for the children. Anka's aim was to study, to gain a qualification in business studies and to set up a small business of her own. She saw her grandmother as the anchor of her life; although she acknowledges the support she received from her parents-in-law, it was her grandmother who helped her to escape from her dysfunctional parents and the dying PGR. Now her grandmother was ill, and she went back as often as she could, to visit and care for her.

In this account Anka was making claims to a proper life course, with proper relations between generations, mutual help at the right time and a carefully planned and realized future. The disruptions were there, however, in the background; the squalor of the former PGR, the dysfunctional parents, and the bleak poverty and privation of her childhood, all appeared almost as fallout from the wider historical changes. Her parents, like so many of their generation as I have already shown, were lost, and she looked to the previous generation, that of her grandmother, for direction and guidance. Through moving away, on her grandmother's advice, she had been able to begin to form a coherent life story.

Other stories also reflect, like Anka's, the way that help is still streamed down from senior to junior generation, even as the old channels have become distorted or disappeared. Irek and Ewa were in their early forties, and had moved to Lublin from a village about 100 kilometers away in the 1990s. She was a trained nurse, while he had no formal training but had worked in security and construction. They had two small children. Irek had two uncles living in Lublin, and one managed to find them a small flat. First of all Ewa worked in the hospital, in her own field of cardiology, and Irek got a job, through his other uncle, as a security guard in a bank. However, former policemen started to take over the all positions in the highly lucrative security business, and he lost his job. Ewa and Irek then took on the franchise of a small general shop, very near the center of the city. Ewa continued to work in the hospital, but also did most of the managing, purchasing and accounts for the shop, as well as the domestic labor and the childcare at home. Irek worked in the shop, and looked after the children when Ewa was on her hospital shifts. In about 2002 they realized they would have to give up the shop, because people were leaving the city center, migrating out to the suburbs or further afield to other parts of Poland and abroad and there was no longer adequate custom, only, they said, local drunks. They had the opportunity to buy a very dilapidated old house, in one of the roughest areas of the city, for a very low price. Again, the uncles came to their aid, and in conjunction with Ewa's parents in the countryside, lent them the money for the down payment. They moved in and Irek, still out of work, began to fix up the house with a lot of help from the uncles and other friends and cousins.

Ewa meanwhile heard from a nursing friend about work abroad, in a meat packing plant in Ipswich, and went with her friend to England. She moved between Lublin and southeast England for some years, in Lublin continuing to work in cardiology, doing the work she loved and excelled at but receiving very low pay, and in the UK taking a variety of jobs, with very poor working and living conditions, in food processing, which were badly paid by local standards but for her represented far more than she could earn nursing in Poland. With what she earned she managed to support the family, and to pay for the renovation of the house. Her children were both studying English and French in school, and she hoped that they would be able to attend university abroad when the time came. Irek had not been formally employed for a good 10 years, although from time to time through the whole period he worked with the uncles as a laborer or builder. He was absolutely clear and explicit about how much they owe the uncles, and how obliged to them he felt; he said repeatedly that they would never let him and his family down, and that he could always turn to them when things were hard, or when he needed practical help. Ewa could turn to her parents, but because they were farther away it was more difficult to rely on them for day-to-day help.

Ewa's dream was to learn enough English to be able to work in her profession in the UK, in residential caring if not in nursing. She intended to keep traveling backwards and forwards between countries and between jobs. Irek was anxious about her absences, and the children missed her, but they all realized that they would find it hard to live in the way they wanted to without her UK income. She loved her work in the hospital in Lublin, but wages were so low that it was more lucrative for her to work for low UK wages as a meat packer in Ipswich than as a Nursing Sister on a cardiology ward in Lublin. Although since Poland joined the EU she could work legally in the UK, which she could not do when first she went there, she was unable to get work in her own field because, among other factors, she lacked the necessary language skills.

In this case, we can see continued reciprocal exchanges of help and labor between kin of different generations, as well as the extension of these links between the city and the countryside. To some extent, Irek and Ewa migrated to the city to get away from the countryside and what they saw as the trap of rural poverty. Ewa's mobility between different labor markets in different countries allowed the family to move upward, and not only to imagine but also to plan new possibilities and different trajectories for their children. All acknowledged that the emotional and personal costs were high. Ewa and Irek hoped that their children would move (with them) to the West after secondary school, and move into higher education and later well-paid positions.

In this family we see a pattern repeated over generations. Ewa's and Irek's parents, recognizing that there was nothing for their children except hard work and poverty in the countryside, encouraged them to migrate, from the village to the city first, and then in Ewa's case abroad as a cyclical migrant. The aspirational patterns of the generations can be seen to repeat themselves: Ewa and Irek went on to plan the permanent migration of their own children.

Here in a sense we see the beginnings of what might come to be considered another lost generation, although lost in a very different sense. This is the generation of young who are leaving and seem likely not to return, or who certainly do not intend to return permanently.

At the beginning of this chapter I argued that kinship and work are so closely intertwined that it is often impossible to think of or understand one without the other. I suggested that kinship provides a necessary framework for both the transfer of skills and information, and the transfer of knowledge practices, between generations, particularly in relation to work in factories and on farms. Obviously, this is a highly idealized and rather functionalist picture, but it is, I would argue, one to which many ordinary people subscribed.

The collapse of industry in effect created a lost generation, most strongly represented in the industrial and agricultural working classes. The members of this lost generation were unlikely to find 'normal' work again, or to continue on their 'proper' life course. The source of their power and their authority in relation to their children and successors was unsettled and in many cases undermined. This was a drastic change. One minute there was a right to work, and a workforce or agricultural/industrial working class which reproduced itself in a routine and fairly regular way. The next minute, the relations of production, and the process of production itself, were transformed and even eliminated, and thus the basis for reproduction became distorted or disappeared. In effect, the state's abandonment of a generation of workers also created a crisis in reproduction, not only in terms of work and production, but also in terms of kinship and the unfolding of a proper life course.

I want to end with a reflection on where these new generations may be headed. If we refer back to Hareven's comment that historical changes can alter life courses irrevocably, I think we can make a strong argument for saying that this was what happened Łódź, in Lublin and Świdnik, and in other industrial centers in Poland and beyond, as massive state industries collapsed. This is not by any means a situation unique to socialism, but the degree of radical rupture and change tends to be greater in the post-socialist states. The important question now is what new relations between generations and within kin groups will emerge. One possibility, of course, is that the Parsonian model of increasingly individuated and individualist small family units, and the more post modern variations on this which stress isolation, collapse of intimacy, and breakdown of kinship and family ties, will prove accurate. There are suggestions of this in the Europe of the 21st century, and it is possible to argue that the massive migrations of young people from Poland reflect exactly this breakdown of family ties. However, the pictures evoked by my own work and that of others certainly suggest the continuing importance of kin ties, but kinship expressed in ties which are more elastic, extended over wider spaces than before and perhaps with different time frames. These are reflected in the process of arranging migration, funding fares, paying for education abroad and sending remittances home. While the practical links in the migrant chains seem to me to be, most often, forged between contemporaries and peers, and to involve friends as often as siblings or cousins, the financial exchanges continue to be played out between generations of (close) kin.

One of the most rapidly growing businesses in Lublin, in the mid 2000s, was language schools, particularly English language schools. When I spoke to school directors and to students, I discovered that, just as in the past, parents and, very importantly, grandparents, helped with the procurement of a flat, or furniture, or some sort of marriage settlement, now what was being settled on the young was likely to be a course in English (which is rather expensive) and later perhaps help with a fare to the UK. These might be given as first communion presents, well in anticipation of the event of leaving, or as presents on the successful completion of school, or a 16th or 18th birthday. Further, I found that although many of the young generation who traveled abroad were going half on holiday and half to work, few of them planned to send any their earnings home, to their parents and grandparents. Most, however, anticipated caring for them when they were elderly. I suspect that what will become apparent here, as we have access to more and more studies of migration, is that there are quite different streams of migrants. Some, like Berger's Seventh Man, are going to find work in the face of unemployment, are likely to do the work abroad that they cannot get, any longer, at home, and are likely to live rather excluded and impoverished lives, socially and economically, in the destination country. Others, I think, will be more likely to be young, going abroad either to work and study, or to work in order to fund some professional development at home. Or, of course, to stay abroad, and to create an entirely new life course. At the beginning of this chapter I talked about the way that different times and different orders of events all become inscribed on places and incorporated into the stories people tell, of their lives and their pasts. In Lublin at the moment the stories people tell, particularly the stories of the senior generation who have often lost so much, seem disjointed and fragmented. There are new empty and silenced places in the cityscape and the landscape, dilapidated broken down factories, ruined collective farms, empty city blocks where old socialist statues have been torn down and replaced by nothing. There are new absences as well, caused by the migrants, young and old, moving east. But they are replaced as they go by Ukrainians, Romanians and others. In other words, some borders are becoming more porous and the ties which bind people in dependent kin relations more elastic. If we take a long view, it is possible to see that the history of this area is one of periodic acute change. Some aspects of the past are incorporated into personal and social histories while others are silenced, or even forgotten. As social scientists, we try to describe and analyze processes of immediate and long-term change, and to chart their process and consequences. It is in these situations of extreme rupture and change that we see the emergence of new economic orders, and new formations of kinship, generation and work relations.

Notes

1 The research on which this chapter is based was funded by the Volkswagen Foundation with additional funding from the Max Planck Institute for Social Anthropology. I am grateful to both for their support. The Volkswagen Foundation project was held jointly with Deema Kaneff, and my understanding of these processes owes a great deal to her. Kinga Sekerdej and Ania Witeska were my research assistants; they were also more than equal colleagues and the collaboration with them was invaluable. I have as ever benefited from the insights of Haldis Haukanes, Susana Narotzky and Victoria Goddard; Victoria Goddard has also been a most patient editor.
2 "The economy of shortage" was a phrase coined by the Hungarian economist Janos Kornai (1980), in his book *The Economics of Shortage*, to describe the failure of centralized production and distribution systems in the Soviet Union and its satellite states. Katherine Verdery's (1996) use of the concept brought it into anthropological thinking, used as a term alluding to flawed distribution, inadequate centrally led production, and over-employment, leading to empty shops and scarce consumer resources.

References

Anderson, M. (1971). *Family Structure in 19th Century Lancashire*. Cambridge: Cambridge University Press.

Braudel, F. (1958) [1972]. 'History and the social sciences: the longue durée'. *Annales: Histoire, Sciences Sociales* 13(4) (October–December 1958): 725–753.
Day, S. (2007). *On the Game: Women and Sex Work*. London. Pluto Press.
Escobar, A. (1994). *Encountering Development: The Making and Unmaking of the Third World*. Princeton, NJ: Princeton University Press.
Grieco, M. (1987). *Keeping It in the Family: Social Networks and Employment Chance*. London: Tavistock Publications.
Hareven, T. (1978). *Transitions: The Family and the Life Course in Historical Perspective*. New York: Academic Press.
Hareven, T. (1982). *Family Time and Industrial Time: The Relationship between the Family and Work in a New England Industrial Community*. Cambridge: Cambridge University Press.
Hareven, T. (2001). 'Familial Behavior', in R.Wall, T. Hareven and J. Ehmer (eds) *Family History Revisited: Historical Perspectives*. London: Associated University Presses, pp. 40–56.
Harvey, David. (1990). *The Condition of Postmodernity: An Enquiry into the Origins of Cultural Change*. Oxford: Blackwell.
Humphrey, Caroline C. (2002). *The Unmaking of Soviet Life: Everyday Economies after Socialism*. Ithaca, NY: University of Cornell Press.
Kideckel, D. (2002). "The Unmaking of an Eastern Central European Working Class", in C. Hann (ed) *Postsocialism: Ideals, Ideologies and Practices in Eurasia*. London and New York: Routledge, pp. 114–132.
Kornai, J. (1980). *Economics of Shortage*. Amsterdam: North-Holland Press.
Mollona, M. (2004). *Made in Sheffield: An Ethnography of Industrial Work and Politics*. Oxford: Berghahn.
Morris, L. (1992). 'The Social Segregation of the Long-Term Unemployed in Hartlepool'. *The Sociological Review* 40(2): 344–369.
Pahl, R. (1984). *Divisions of Labour*. Oxford: Wiley and Blackwell.
Skultans, V. (1997). *Testimony of Lives: Narrative and Memory in Post-Soviet Latvia*. London: Routledge.
Verdery, K. (1996). *What Was Socialism and What Comes Next?* Princeton, NJ: Princeton University Press.
Wedel, J. (ed) (1992). *The Unplanned Society*. New York: Columbia University Press.
Weiss, B. (1996). *The Making and Unmaking of the Haya Living World: Consumption, Commoditization, and Everyday Practice*. Durham, NC: Duke University Press.

3 Credentialism and Recommendations

The Bases of the Reproduction of the Metallurgical Working Class in Contemporary Argentina[1]

Laura Perelman and Patricia Vargas

Introduction

This chapter addresses some of the central processes entailed in the reproduction of the industrial working class in contemporary Argentina. The study focuses on one of the major integrated steelworks of the country, which is the main source of employment in the urban setting in which it is inserted.[2] The company was founded as a state enterprise and continued to be under state stewardship until its privatization at the early 1990s.[3] The plant's transfer into the hands of private capital entailed a drastic reduction in the number of workers who were permanently employed and hired directly by the company. The restructuring associated with privatization had very negative implications for the future possibilities that young working class people would have with regard to continuing their family's tradition of working in the industry, sometimes over several generations. At the point of the plant's foundation workers came from different regions of the country looking for work and harboring the hope of settling down in San Nicolás, the town adjacent to the steel plant. This first generation of workers was drawn from migrants who addressed the company's need for the large numbers of workers needed to build the plant and, subsequently, set it in operation. Coming from a range of work environments, but largely from the agricultural sector, these workers had no significant educational qualifications. Their children benefited from what would come to be seen as an established practice of intergenerational job transfer, which was widespread among state employees, and guaranteed entry into the plant.

This situation changed radically with privatization: minimum educational requirements were raised as the company restructured[4] the organization of management and production. As part of the flexibilization process promoted by neoliberal capitalism, the privatized company, Siderar, came to employ a wide range of workers under different contractual relations. Since the 1990s the number of permanent jobs has decreased, and many work activities that had depended directly on SOMISA were outsourced. Today, workers fulfill these outsourced tasks through precarious and unstable employment contracts. Different work and wage conditions has fragmented the workforce as permanent plant staff ("*los propios*") enjoy different contracts from workers who, although they carry out their work on company premises, are hired through a network of outsourcing companies and employment agencies ("*los de las compañías*").

The chapter explores these changes through the prism of generational change and considers some of the main mechanisms through which younger workers who descend from a line of steelworkers devise novel strategies of reproduction. We focus on two stages in the trajectories of the new workers: their entry into the plant and their advancement and promotion in the workplace. Two factors are central to a successful completion of these stages. On the one hand, formal education and training related to jobs in the steel industry and, on the other hand, access to a range of personal contacts, and *"recommendations"*.

Currently, a secondary level diploma in vocational training is required in order to obtain a permanent job at Siderar. Young people and their families therefore make enormous efforts to ensure that they obtain such qualifications. With increased demand for vocational training, educational opportunities in the town have expanded, coordinated by white and blue-collar trade union organizations. While in the past having a father in the steel industry could in itself put in motion the customary mechanism of generational job transfer, today, family ties alone offer no such guarantees although they continue to be an informal yet crucial resource.

The continuing importance of kinship and other personal relations in accessing work exposes the inequalities that affect would-be workers. The company's hiring policy is expressed exclusively in terms of meritocratic criteria, evaluated in relation to training, work discipline and commitment to the job. And yet, everyone in San Nicolás knows that recommendations facilitate, and in many cases determine, young people's chances of accessing this privileged strategy of working class reproduction. We therefore propose to consider the "recommendation" as a social mechanism of class reproduction that also functions as a location of power, consolidating the status of the trade unions, which play an important role in the operation of these networks[5].

The ethnography of steelworkers and trade unionists in San Nicolás illustrates how contacts are built and how they might be deployed. As researchers we, too, became entangled in the exchange of favors between candidates' families and trade union leaders, which we explore through a thick description (Geertz 1995) of an event that took place on the "Day of the Metalworker". The event reveals how families invest time and resources in support of the younger generation's attempts to find work through networks of recommendations sustained by the trade unions. This ethnographic event illustrates the transformations that have affected the reproduction of an important segment of the Argentine working class since the establishment of the neoliberal model in the 1990s. In considering the reproduction of the industrial working class in the context of flexible capitalism, we draw on critical theories that explore the link between education and social reproduction and theories of patronage and recommendation systems. While the scholarly literature has considered these two factors (educational background and patronage) separately, describing in ample detail how education contributes to, or limits, the reproduction of the working class,[6] or how recommendation networks make entry into specific labor niches possible,[7] we propose that in the case of the steelworkers of San Nicolás these two dynamics operate jointly, reinforcing one another in specific contexts.

"Metalworkers' Day": Networks of Recommendation at Work

On September 7th in 2011 Argentina commemorated Metalworkers' Day.[8] Tigre is a member of the metalworkers' trade union's executive committee, who invited us to participate in the ceremonies and festivities that were organized for the day. We joined union leaders and representatives in laying flowers at the "Monument to the Metalworker Family" and at the "Monument to the memory of those who died at the workplace", located in the grounds of one of the union's educational facilities. We then went to the union's recreational grounds, where we attended the opening ceremony of the soccer championship that is organized every year. Everyone's attention was focused on the soccer field. A woman, with a child in her arms and a teenager by her side, occupied center stage, accompanied by the secretary general and another union official. Tigre explained that the woman was the wife of a fellow worker who had died of cancer. The union's highest authority publically promised that the union would continue to help their colleague's family and invited the youngster to kick off the football tournament. Following the football match, we were taken on a long tour of the facilities and then to "the lab chemists" party because "that's an area where there are more female workers" where we might feel more at ease.

When we arrived at the *quinta* (a weekend retreat owned by a group of SOMISA workmates) where the *asado*[9] was being prepared, Tigre introduced us to "Tincho", our host for the day. Tigre mentioned that we were interested in compiling "family histories and interviewing different generations of steelworkers", adding: "Treat them well, these gals." Obligingly, our new host responded with: "Sure, sure. Don't you worry", and turning to us he said: "With this buddy's help, we'll go for another new generation". He turned to Tigre and asked: "Are you going to come today to meet the 'boy?" At that point he told us that his son had just graduated from the technical school, and that the family hoped he could get a job at the factory.

As the afternoon progressed we found out that the "boy's" grandfather was one of the founders of the *quinta*. Originally from the north of the country, he arrived in San Nicolás in 1964 having only completed elementary school. He "signed up" for work, and the next day he was called to start work at SOMISA. Sitting under the midday sun, he sadly confided that his only son had obtained a job at the factory, but had then migrated to another city. This filled him with anguish, since he was sure that his son would never again find such good employment. Tincho sat down next to his father-in-law, and joined in the conversation. He told us how he had started working two years after receiving his certificate in chemical technology in 1984. As occurred with many of the workers who joined the plant in the 1980s when the plant was state-owned, he got a job when his father retired, according to the custom of inherited jobs.

There were very few women guests; one of them was Florencia, a young woman of 22 years of age, who had been working at the factory for four years: "Three years on a contract, and one year as a permanent employee". While studying for her secondary degree at the trade union's technical school, she had an internship at Siderar. Once she had obtained her certificate in electromechanical technology, she worked for several years, covering for workers on holiday leave through Sesa Select, the employment agency that supposedly serves as a gateway for a permanent job at Siderar. She explained: "I got a job because my father is a supervisor, and he has been working at the steel factory for 27 years. He knows a lot of people, and spoke to someone from the trade union, for them to take me into account [as a candidate]. I went through the entry exams and tests, they went well, and they called me in for work".

She already possessed suitable technical credentials and the company sent her on advanced courses at the trade union's training center. But Florencia pointed out: "You learn your work on the job, with the help of the supervisor, who helps you day after day explaining how to do the job as the boss expects [it to be done]". She added: "As you gain more experience and you are on top of your job, you show an interest in learning. You do your work faster, and in your spare time you learn the other job that you are aiming for". Florencia considered herself really lucky with her job, which was the envy of her friends. "They say 'you got lucky, you got in!' And one feels, oh, yes, I got lucky! Because if you look at it from outside, you feel really important because you are inside. You work at the factory as one of the *"propios"* with benefits, good wages and a stable job".

We counted more than 40 people at the party, preparing the *asado*, playing football, singing in accompaniment to a guitar and a *"bandoneón"*—an Argentine accordion—while small groups were engaged in lively conversations. Over lunch a man referred to as Gardelito[10] was declared the guest of honor because he had just retired. Gardelito thanked them and announced solemnly: "Even though I am retiring, I will still belong to the union . . . no, no, I meant, I will remain a metalworker . . .". We all laughed at this slip that revealed the intimate connection he felt between being a steelworker and a union member. After lunch, Tincho's son ("the boy") arrived and greeted us awkwardly. While he seemed nervous and embarrassed, his father and grandfather were proudly extolling his virtues and made clear the family's expectations that he might get a job at the plant. We continued our conversation and, when we noticed that the women guests were leaving, we, too, took our leave.

Credentialism and the Managerial Revolution

The connection between education and the labor market has been widely studied, with some authors pointing to improved employment opportunities correlated with higher levels of educational achievement (Beccaria and Groisman n.d.). For our purposes, it is more significant that this connection between educational achievement and good employment opportunities is part of a widely shared, common sense view found among contemporary workers in Argentina. In San Nicolás, where the steel industry has been the principal economic institution and employer since the 1960s, the trade union and the steel plant invest in education, supporting institutions that enroll hundreds of young people who, like Florencia and Tincho's son, pursue their dream of finding a job in the industry.[11] Confirming the validity of their strategy, management only hires those in possession of a suitable diploma, emphasizing meritocratic values based on academic excellence, credentials and the work ethic.

Retired workers we encountered during fieldwork told us that things were different when the plant was founded. At that time, large numbers of migrants came to work in the steel town; by the end of the 1980s there were around 10,000 workers employed in production and maintenance (González 1986). Our interviewees explained how, in the early days of the plant, they had obtained jobs immediately, despite their poor education. Like Tincho, their children joined the plant when their fathers retired. The system of generational transmission meant that those working in the state-run company could enjoy stable and secure work, as well as continuity from one generation of male worker to the next, although sons might take on very different tasks to those of their fathers (Colabella, 2012). Tincho benefited from having obtained a technical diploma by joining the quality control department, while his father had worked in the coke oven of the blast furnace. In the 1980s those with no secondary school credentials were still able to get a job in the plant, although the more prestigious tasks might have eluded them. Today, the secondary school diploma is a basic requirement for entry into the firm. As Florencia's story demonstrates, young people of her generation are keen to work in the company. Of the more than 200 young students in technical and vocational training we contacted, the majority agreed that one of their main aspirations was to join the factory and work at its core as permanent employees. However, the demand for labor has declined since the 1980s, and hiring practices have changed substantially.

In the early 1990s, during the Peronist government of Carlos Menem (1989–99), the company fired approximately 7,000 workers. From 1992, the company was privatized and the new owners continued to implement policies aimed at reducing the number of employees. A new legal framework enabled the company to increase the flexibilization of the workforce. The permanent staff was reduced and new workers were hired through outsourcing companies on contracts that were far less favorable, precarious and insecure. It is unsurprising that today's workers consistently point to the company's privatization as the key event that altered the lives and the work of the steelworkers of San Nicolás.

To help us understand the system that emerged after privatization, several interviewees drew what looked like a solar system. The core of the system was the steelworks with its "own" employees; the surrounding planets were the outsourcing companies, with their "on-contract" workers. A hierarchical arrangement of these companies was expressed in terms of their distance from the center of the system. Those that supplied workers were closer to the core, and those that provided services were farther away. At the same time, each of these, called "satellite companies" by the workers, had a subsystem of their "own" workers and outside workers who were "contracted." In contrast with past practice, no worker is hired directly as a member of permanent staff. As Florencia had explained, workers must be promoted from the outsourcing companies into the heart of the plant—and the closer they are to the center, the greater their chances of being "chosen" to enter the core.

When managers were asked about this system, they emphasized credentialist and meritocratic values as the basis for entry to work and mobility across the system. According to these values, young workers are judged on the merits of their educational background and their adherence to the work ethic. The system works as a field of surveillance as well as training, and managers confirm that the circulation of workers enables them to record "the history of the work attitudes of candidates, as they make their way [through the outsourcing companies]." Young workers tend to reflect these values in their own attitudes. They recognize that "finishing secondary school" is a basic prerequisite that must be complemented by attitudes that "show motivation," that they are "ready to learn", "committed to his/her work". These qualities must be demonstrated in the entry exams and subsequently in the conduct of their daily work.

While tests and credentials are important, there are also numerous informal filters that enable supervisors, foremen and eventually trade union representatives to evaluate each aspiring worker and determine whether or not they will be recommended for advancement. Florencia succeeded in passing the trials and tests, after which she was hired by an outsourcing company that was close to the core, supplying the factory with temporary workers. Here she demonstrated her capacity to respect and fulfill orders, to learn new tasks and to show a proactive attitude. After three years of working as a "contract" worker she succeeded in moving to the core, having proved her worth and benefiting from the help provided by her father, who as an ex-supervisor was able to set in motion his networks. She was recommended by one of her supervisors for promotion and became a permanent member of staff in the plant.

Like others who aspire to join the steel plant's permanent workforce, Florencia would not have been able to succeed without her family's support. Particularly during the uncertain years of her trial period, when she was unemployed in the intervals between one temporary contract and the next, it was her family that supported her and enabled her to persevere. But the efforts of individuals and families do not always pay off. Interviewees agreed that only a handful of those employed by the outsourced firms become part of the permanent staff of the plant. The senior manager of the company confirmed that only 20 out of the 400 candidates they hire on temporary contracts become one of the company's "own" employees.

The striving continues after becoming one of the plant's "own" employees. As soon as she was hired, Florencia set about advancing her career. Following a well-established strategy, once she had mastered the tasks related to her job, she endeavored to learn new skills. She watched, asked questions, and attended training sessions, hoping to be promoted to a more highly-qualified job, a better paid position or moved to more desirable areas of work. Many permanent workers attended courses with a view to moving from shift work to fixed working hours, or from repetitive tasks to jobs that entail more creative or less routinized work, regardless of levels of pay.

Unlike the older generations of workers, young people start work with certain technical skills acquired through training in workshops or through internships with the company itself. They enjoy a degree of familiarity with the space, with the timing and the tasks. But young and old agree that the most important learning takes place on the job: the young worker observes, asks questions and is gradually involved in tasks under the guidance of a more experienced worker, such as a supervisor or a boss. The intergenerational transmission through training and learning at the workplace is still the norm; what has changed since privatization is the location of this learning experience. The steel plant defines the employment policies and the educational and behavioral profile that it requires; the satellite companies bear the costs of training the workforce, whilst families take on the economic burden of the instability generated by the system.

The conditions that sustained the critical attitudes towards schooling that Paul Willis encountered among young working class boys in the 1970s (1988 [1977]) have altered dramatically, in Argentina and in the United Kingdom. The radical changes prompted by the expansion of flexible capitalism (Harvey 1990) articulated through the neoliberal model and implemented by government policy, has left an enduring legacy. Twenty-five years on from the publication of Willis' seminal ethnography, (Dolby et al. 2004) show how in the United Kingdom and the US there is little scope for young people to articulate a cultural critique such as that recorded by Willis. Instead, the young try to conform to demands for educational achievement and are forced to rely on their ties with family, kin and neighborhood, and embrace ethnic and national identities, which support them through times of uncertainty

Since privatization and the impact of broader neoliberal reforms, San Nicolás is, like the examples discussed in Dolby and Dimitriadis, a space where there is little scope for conflict or resistance among the young. As we have shown, the young in this steel town are committed to a project that involves working in the industry and they appear to share many of the values of management, for example, relating to credentials, discipline and the work ethic. This convergence reflects their desire to become part of that privileged segment of the working class. However, discipline and conformity do not suffice; other resources, perhaps even "luck" in Florencia's account, are needed. The majority will be frustrated in their quest. The question is how the "model" of credentialism, discipline and devotion to work can persist in the face of its failure to deliver for the majority of those embarking on this particular journey, where a spotless curriculum, excellent grades and good attitude do not translate into a permanent, secure and well-paid job.

Whereas "territory" or place may provide a basis for alternative forms of sociality, as ties based on territory gain an increasingly important role in integrating young people into the social world, in San Nicolás, relations of place highlight the need to conform. Here "contacts" play a decisive role in the efforts of the young to move across the system of core and periphery companies. On the one hand, the importance of these networks exposes the limits of the meritocratic discourse and uncovers the importance of family and of histories of lineages of steelworkers. While revealing the shortcomings of the model of individual achievement and credentialist competition, the entanglement of the young in networks of requests and favor, gifts and debt, also ties them to a model of privilege through the desire to be "chosen" and to the need for social conformity.

Favors and Recommendations: The Search for a Secure Future

Our participation in the celebrations of Metalworkers' Day led us into an entanglement as well as a witnessing of the unfolding webs of reciprocities, through gifting of favors and the ensuing debts these reciprocities produce. As guests at the event where "the kid", his family and Tigre stated and restated the case for support of the young man's future, we became implicated in the performance. When the grandfather made the *quinta* available for the *asado* and Tincho added the trade union leader and his "protégées" (us), (whom the host agreed to entertain in exchange for a "recommendation" for his son) to his guest list, they were engaged in weaving a chain of favors and of reciprocal support with which we were implicated.

But what this performance of hospitality and favors illustrates is not the success, but the limitations of the recommendation system. Up until the celebrations of Metalworkers' Day, we had been presented with a coherent account of how a trade union might intercede with management on behalf of a candidate. The trade union representatives described how workers hand them their children's CVs, and might even approach them if they are not hired. At the same time, young students from the trade union's training centers told us how they wander around the center, hoping to come across the secretary general and ask for a recommendation that would weigh heavily in the eyes of their instructors. The *asado* revealed the incompleteness of the official version of the recommendation system and showed the wealth of resources that are needed to secure a recommendation; integral to the success of this quest is the relative power and the status of those engaged in making and receiving the request. Although the "boy" at the center of the *asado* had already complied with the indispensable prerequisite of obtaining a technical degree, his family had deployed a unique resource in his favor: 40 years in the factory, which provided the opportunity to develop personal ties with managers and trade unionists. Now those ties were put to work to improve the youngster's chances of success on the long road towards the heart of the company.

Our "contact", Tigre, is a trade union representative of the local branch of the metalworkers' union. Following a well-established tradition in Argentina, the union fulfills multiple functions, which go well beyond workplace issues (Perelman 2006; Marshall and Perelman 2008). The union provides a number of services to its affiliates, to the extent that Tigre often paraphrased the lyrics of a soccer song for our benefit: "with this good-hearted trade union, we accompany you from the cradle to the grave". The facilities managed by the trade union reflect the union's involvement with all stages of the life cycle: the hospital, schools (kindergarten, primary and secondary school, tertiary education, trade school, library and language center), housing, monuments to honor metalworkers and their families, the recreational complex and tourist centers, the amphitheater with its heliport and the funeral services. In addition, the trade union is seen as a central agent in the company's recruitment mechanisms, although this role is in actual fact not set down in any formal agreement. The exchange that took place between Tincho and Tigre at the *asado* can be understood to work through principles of asymmetrical and hierarchical reciprocity, sustained by workers' support for their trade union representatives. It is for this reason that Gardelito revealed, through a slip of the tongue, the importance of "establishing ties with the trade union" in order to "be a good metalworker". Alongside the trade union staff, supervisors, foremen and managers may be approached for help. Here too, the outcome of this informal mechanism depends on the relationship that obtains between the two parties rather than on the relative merits of the candidate.

Despite the obstacles, hundreds of young people continue to enroll on courses and attend educational institutions, striving to learn and to excel. Personal recommendations are considered to be unfair by those who firmly believe in the superiority of meritocracy. Because access to strategic connections is unevenly distributed, such "deals" normally provoke suspiciousness about the true merits of the recommended worker, while it also provides him or her with a halo of protection conferred by the power of the person who made the recommendation.

Conclusions

For the hundreds of candidates who submit their curriculum to Siderar every year, getting a job at Argentina's most important steel-producing company represents their highest possible career expectations. Their hopes are based on a history that links the town's growth and the progress of the working class in San Nicolás to the foundation of the ex SOMISA plant, now called Siderar (Soul 2002). They also draw on the fact that the company provides high quality, stable employment with relatively higher salaries for those who manage to overcome all the obstacles and gain a permanent job. Aspiring SOMISA workers who manage to join the company—as interns or temporary workers in the satellite companies—make a real effort to comply with the expectations of discipline and hard work.

In San Nicolás, recommendations affect a potential worker's work attitudes and conduct. The recommendation strategy strengthens the control mechanisms that work through the entire network of relations in which the candidates become entangled. A breach of confidence in any one of the links in the network could disrupt the long and winding road that is, in the end, reserved for only a few chosen ones, or the lucky ones. In this sense, "learning to labor" in San Nicolás consists in part in understanding the complex networks of favors and support between union leaders and metallurgical families.

The networks of relations that support the dynamics of give and take, of requesting and granting favors and recommendations involves families, workers, the trade unions and the company. Eric Wolf proposes that in complex societies the institutional systems of political and economic powers coexist and are combined with different types of non-institutional or interstitial structures such as family relations, friendship and patronage (Wolf 1999: 20). He highlights the polyvalent role of the family and its influence on the social prestige of a person and on the types of social resources that are available to him/her outside the family setting (Wolf 1999: 27). Family and friendship relations can be vehicles for exchanges but may give rise to asymmetries.[12] In the case discussed in this chapter, the most notable attribute of the relationship between "those who ask" and "those who give" is that—as James Scott (1986) puts it—it constitutes a dynamic of reciprocity between people of unequal status. Here, "those who ask" are families belonging to a long metallurgical "lineage", who attempt to reestablish the customary mechanism for reproducing the metallurgical working class through the intergenerational transmission of jobs. By deploying personal networks built over years of working in the factory, steelworkers hope to secure the future of their children through their incorporation into the protected, well-paid and prestigious core of the Siderar workforce. "Those who give" the necessary recommendations also seek their own reproduction as the workers' representatives, through a position that enables them to facilitate the reproduction of certain metallurgical families.

Personal recommendations, therefore, make manifest the tension that exists between the managerial discourse based on meritocratic ideals (fundamentally based on academic performance and a demonstrated commitment to work) and how this ideal is disregarded by the very same people who formulate it. By agreeing to the practice of favors and personal support, company and trade union leaders actually contribute to the increasingly restricted reproduction of the stable segment of the metallurgical working class in San Nicolás and, in so doing, also reproduce systems of privilege and inequality. As Ernest Geller perspicaciously points out: "we dislike patronage because it offends our principles of equality and universality" (Gellner 1985:9). This is the sentiment that accompanies those who, while they recognize the importance of recommendations, do not possess the necessary social resources to mobilize them. The case discussed here exposes our naturalized respect for merit and justice: when the recommendation does not depend solely on performance (academic or workwise), it is illegitimate, although not inefficient.

Notes

1 This chapter reports some of the results of a comparative international research project concerning economic models and their implications for the steel industry, carried out as part of an EU FP7 Collaborative project "Models and their Effects on Development paths: An Ethnographic and Comparative Approach to Knowledge Transmission and Livelihood Strategies (MEDEA)" (2009–2012) under grant agreement No. 225670, coordinated by Victoria Goddard (Goldsmiths) and Susana Narotzky (University of Barcelona). In Argentina, the project research team is based at the Instituto de Desarrollo Económico y Social (IDES), in the City of Buenos Aires, with Dr. Rosana Guber as its coordinator.
2 The fieldwork was conducted between April 2010 and April 2012 in San Nicolás de los Arroyos, a city situated 240 km north of the city of Buenos Aires in the main pole of steel production in Argentina, located on the border between the provinces of Buenos Aires and Santa Fe. Not far from the city is the most important factory of Ternium-Siderar, a company that belongs to the Techint Group, which is at present the main steel producer in Argentina. On our multiple visits we interviewed more than 100 people who are—in one way or another—connected to the metallurgical activity of the factory: workers from different generations, supervisors, recruiting staff from subcontracting companies, factory foremen, trade union representatives, educators and students.
3 The national metallurgical industry in Argentina received a strong boost during the decade of the 1940s within the framework of the growth model based on Import Substitution Industrialization. In 1947 the Argentine Congress passed a law called National Metallurgical Plan, and founded SOMISA (Sociedad Mixta Siderúrgica Argentina), an integrated plant for the production of blast-furnace

Credentialism and Recommendations 57

iron, steel, semi-finished products and hot-rolled sheet metal. Although the project was delayed until the early 1960s, SOMISA eventually became the most important steel factory in the hands of the Argentine State. Within the framework of the neoliberal reforms of the 1990s in Argentina, SOMISA was privatized.

4 At its plant in General Savio, Siderar currently employs approximately 3500 workers through direct hiring, who mostly work on the production line. They identify themselves, and are recognized by the rest of the steelworkers, as "*los propios*" (the [company's] *own* [personnel]). The outsourcing companies that offer their services to the plant employ a similar number of workers either on permanent or on temporary contracts; they are generally referred to as "*los de las compañías*" (the [personnel] *of the* [outsourcing] *companies*).

5 The ASIMRA trade union (Asociación de Supervisores de la Industria Metalmecánica de la República Argentina) represents supervisors and management. These workers are not included in the discussion outlined in this chapter.

6 The critical theories of "reproductionist" approaches to education have focused on the relationship between education (or culture) and work, in particular with respect to the role it plays in the reproduction of class (Bourdieu and Passeron 1977; Bowles and Gintis 1986; Baudelot and Establet 1987; Bernstein 1989). Basically, these authors have tried to show the correspondence between levels of education and labor insertion, or the relationship between social class and type of linguistic codes, matching the working class sectors with a command of "restricted" codes, and the middle or higher sectors with the use of "elaborate" codes. In this sense, education acquires an ambiguous potential in that it can help legitimize the knowledge of the subaltern sectors, promote class mobility or foment a revolutionary social transformation through pedagogy of liberation (Freire, 1970). Finally, we must mention the struggle between the hegemonic "cultural arbitrary" and the knowledge of students that are not part of this, given their class extraction, and whose refusal to reproduce these codes has been interpreted either as resistance or as a form of reproduction and domination, inasmuch as they result in the reproduction of their social class (Apple 1986; McLaren 1994; Giroux 1996; McRobbie 2009). Within the context of this discussion we will take up Paul Willis' work, which will be of special importance in this chapter.

7 Social theories concerning the exchange of favors between individuals connected through different kinds of relationship (relatives, neighbors, friends, patronage, boss/subordinate or subalternity) have a long tradition in anthropology. What constituted the center of their inquiry was the type of exchange, reciprocal obligations and power relations and status differences between "patrons" and their "followers" [clients] (Wolf 1999; Gellner 1985), and their fundamental goal was to understand the political practices of "clientelism" and "cronyism". A different take on the issue that considers the concept of networks has been essential for comprehending phenomena related to migration, in particular for understanding processes associated with "giving and getting a job" (Vargas 2005), facilitating entry into a specific labor sector (Bourgois 1989; Wallman 1979) or guaranteeing a particular type of conduct on the part of the workers (Pardo 1996). Finally, we must mention inquiries into the role that social relations play in obtaining resources, studies that were inspired in ideas by Pierre Bourdieu (2000), who investigated those relations and their potential within the economic field, as still another form of capital (symbolic capital).

8 Even though no mention is made of the fact, the celebration marks the birth of Fray Luis Beltrán in 1784, a Franciscan friar, who was recognized for his outstanding work as Chief of the Artillery of the Army of the Andes under the leadership of José San Martín, hero of the Latin American struggle for independence.

9 The word *asado* has a double meaning in Argentina. On the one hand, it refers to the kind of food that is consumed, which consists basically of meat (beef or mutton) and is prepared on an open fire or with charcoal. At the same time, it might come with different innards or viscera of the same animals, as well as other types of meat (such as chicken or pork), which are also placed on the grill where things are cooked. It is a typical Argentine custom, and it requires expertise and patience to execute properly. In general there is a person in charge of the process, who takes on the role of the *asador*. At the same time, "going to an *asado*" (as in our specific case) refers to the social situation that this traditional Argentine setting for a meal implies: people who participate in the *asado* contribute with drinks, bread, salads. It is also usual for those who play the guitar to take along their instruments or for background music to be played. If it is a gathering people might eventually dance, play card games or even a soccer game, depending on the available space and the length of the event. Given that on average preparing an *asado* takes somewhere between 2 and 4 hours, the setting turns into a social situation that foments passing time together, conversation and exchanges such as the ones we will present in this paper.

10 "Gardelito" is a diminutive form of "Gardel", the name of the famous tango singer Carlos Gardel, a nickname given to this particular worker because of his lively manner and his habit of singing tangos and Argentine folk songs.

11 One thing that indicates that the company is interested in the training received by young people is the project dedicated to strengthening certain technical schools in the area, which is part of the company's outreach program to the community. In the framework of this program, the factory provides equipment, improvements in building facilities, teacher training and internships, while offering scholarships to the best students. As far as the trade union of metallurgical workers is concerned, they support technical schools at the secondary and tertiary level, as well as a vocational school, which offers programs and specializations related to the steel/metallurgical industry.

12 Wolf argues that if imbalances emerge, the relationship turns into patronage: while the patron provides economic and legal means or uses his/her influence in favor of the client, the client gives respect, loyalty and political backing in return (Wolf 1999: 34–36).

References

Apple, M. (1986). *Ideología y Currículo*. Madrid: Akal.
Baudelot, Ch. y Establet, R. (1987). *La escuela capitalista en Francia*. México, DF: Siglo XXI Editores.
Beccaria, L. y Groisman, F. (n.d.). *Educación y distribución del ingreso*. Sistema de Información de tendencias educativas en América Latina. Available at: http://www.siteal.iipeoei.org/sites/default/files/siteal_debate_3_beccaria_groisman_articulo.pdf Accessed August 27, 2012.
Bernstein, B. (1989). *Clases, códigos y control I. Estudios teóricos para una sociología del lenguaje*. Madrid: Akal.
Bourdieu, P. (2000). *Poder, derecho y clases sociales*. Bilbao: Editorial Desclée de Brouwer.
Bourdieu, P. and Passeron, J. C. (1977). *La reproducción. Elementos para una teoría del sistema de enseñanza*. Barcelona: Editorial Laia.
Bourgois, P. (1989). *Ethnicity at Work: Divided Labor on a Central American Banana Plantation*. Baltimore: Johns Hopkins University Press.

Bowles, S. and Gintis, H. (1986). *La instrucción escolar en la América capitalista: la reforma educativa y las contradicciones de la vida económica*. México, DF: Siglo XXI Editores.

Colabella, L. (2012). *Los Negros del Congreso. Nombre, filiación y honor en el reclutamiento a la burocracia del Estado argentino*. Buenos Aires: Editorial Antropofagia, CAS-IDES.

Dolby, N., Dimitriadis, G. and Willis, P. (2004). (eds) *Learning to Labor in New Times*. New York: Routledge Falmer.

Freire, P. (1970). *Pedagogía del oprimido*. Buenos Aires: Siglo XXI Editores.

Geertz, C. (1995). *La interpretación de las culturas*. Barcelona: Gedisa.

Gellner, E. (1985). 'Introducción', in E. Gellner and J. Waterbury (eds) *Patronos y clientes en las sociedades mediterráneas*. Gijón: Júcar, pp. 9–16.

Giroux, H. (1996). *Placeres inquietantes: Aprendiendo la cultura popular*. Barcelona: Paidós.

González, J.A.E. (1986). SOMISA, una Historia en Reconversión, http://www.buscandohistoria.com.ar/Regional/somisafinal.doc. Accessed on 23rd September 2015.

Harvey, D. (1990). *La condición de la posmodernidad. Investigación sobre los orígenes del cambio cultural*. Buenos Aires: Amorrortu editores.

Marshall, A., and Perelman, L. (2008). 'Estrategias sindicales de afiliación en la Argentina'. *Desarrollo Económico: Revista de Ciencias Sociales. IDES, Buenos Aires* 47(189) April–June: 3–30.

McLaren, P. (1994). *Pedagogía crítica, resistencia cultural y la producción del deseo*. Buenos Aires: Aique.

McRobbie, A. (2009). *The Aftermath of Feminism: Gender, Culture and Social Change*. London: Sage Publications Ltd.

Pardo, I. (1996). *Managing Existence in Naples: Morality, Action and Structure*. New York: Cambridge University Press.

Perelman, L. (2006). Sindicalización y Obras Sociales. *Cuadernos del IDES N° 10*, Julio 2006. Buenos Aires: IDES.

Scott, J. (1986). '¿Patronazgo o explotación?', in E. Gellner and J. Waterbury (eds) *Patronos y clientes en las sociedades mediterráneas*. Gijón: Júcar, pp. 35–61.

Soul, J. (2002). 'Los unos y los otros. La fractura que persiste. Reconversión productiva e identidades colectivas en la ex—somisa, actual siderar'. Tesis de Licenciatura en Antropología, Escuela de Antropología, Facultad de Humanidades y Artes, Universidad Nacional de Rosario, Santa Fe, Argentina.

Vargas, P. (2005). *Bolivianos, paraguayos y argentinos en la obra. Identidades étnico-nacionales entre los trabajadores de la construcción*. Buenos Aires: Editorial Antropofagia, CAS-IDES.

Wallman, S. (1979). (ed) *Ethnicity at Work*. London: The Macmillan Press Ltd.

Willis, P. (1988) [1977]. *Aprendiendo a trabajar. Cómo los chicos de la clase obrera consiguen trabajos de clase obrera*. Madrid: Akal [(1977) Learning to Labour: How Working Class Kids get Working Class Jobs. Aldershot: Ashgate].

Wolf, E. (1999). 'Relaciones de parentesco, de amistad y de patronazgo en las sociedades complejas', in M. Banton and E. Wolf (eds) *Antropología social de las sociedades complejas*. Madrid: Alianza, pp. 19–39.

4 Continuity and Disruption
The Experiences of Work and Employment across Three Generations of Steelworkers in Volta Redonda[1]

Gonzalo Díaz Crovetto

Introduction

This chapter analyzes the history of the relationship between the city of Volta Redonda and the Brazilian National Steel Company (CSN) and also draws a comparison between Volta Redonda and the city of Brasilia. Both cities have been sites for experimentation and implementation of state policies, projects of national development and the manifestation of national ideologies based in notions of work, family and society. Additionally, this chapter considers the consistencies and inconsistencies observed across three generations of CSN workers regarding significant events and changes in the dominant patterns of recruitment, training and administration within CSN. The presented reflections emerge from the systematization of ethnographic fieldwork data, as well as the bibliographic sources available.

Volta Redonda and CSN

The city of Volta Redonda is located in the state of Rio de Janeiro, 130 km from the former capital of the country, the city of Rio de Janeiro, and close to the border of the states of São Paulo and Minas Gerais. The city acquired legal status as an independent district in 1956. Before that date, it was a district of the neighboring city of Barra Mansa. This means that until 1956, basic services were provided by the district's predominant industry: CSN. Nowadays, the city of Volta Redonda, known as the "City of Steel" (*cidade do aço*), has an estimated population of 250,000 inhabitants, and the original village[2] of Volta Redonda has developed as unique urban space with strong links to the steel industry.

In Volta Redonda, the implementation of the company town model (Piquet 1998; Dinius 2011; Dinius & Vergara 2011) supported the expansion of CSN and the reproduction of its labor force.[3] The core of Volta Redonda as a company town was constituted by neighborhoods that were associated with specific categories of employees (workers, technicians and engineers). Hierarchy and social difference among the workers of the company were also geographically displaced and evidenced through the size of the home construction (Piquet 1998). As pointed out by Lask (1991), the home address could reveal the professional position and salary received at CSN. Nevertheless, CSN could never afford to fulfill all of the housing demands. As Piquet (1998) noted, company towns cannot be understood when dissociated from their social and historical background and from the general conditions of production. This particular model of social organization reveals the subordination of the workers and citizens to the company as long as the company owned and controlled the means of production and the housing facilities—regulating, therefore, the employees' lives inside and outside the steel company by providing them with both work and a place to live.

The original city planning of Volta Redonda located CSN's work and production facilities at one end of a main street (Rua 33) and at the other end was the technical school Escola Técnica Pandiá Calógeras (ETPC). To the eastern and western sides of the city, various types of housing and neighborhoods were located and served as the homes of the workforce. We could conclude that this particular map configuration represents a path that many could take from the technical school, where the students developed their abilities, to simply cross the street and directly enter CSN for full-time employment. Over time, new and fragmented neighborhoods appeared, some planned while others were the result of spontaneous occupation caused by new waves of migrants which arrived to the city through familial and friendship ties.

CSN was established on the 9th April of 1941, and although the company started operating in 1946, that initial date has become the national steel commemoration date. Different from the other steel companies developed in the "Steel Valley" (Minas Gerais State), CSN was the only company that was conceived and owned by the state until its privatization 1993. Both CSN and the city of Volta Redonda are part of a project whose gestation predates 1941 and which envisaged the town and the production plant as an important pole of development, strategically significant to Brazil's economic development. In fact, the city and the company can be understood as a testament to the country's industrialization project, initiated in the early twentieth century and which required a national industry for the domestic production of steel (Dinius 2011). This ambitious enterprise also represents a concrete expression of President Getúlio Vargas's ' "new social pact", a labor reform package known as CLT (*Consolidação das Leis do Trabalho*) and regarded as a necessary step toward creating a technical class capable of supporting a massive industrialization process (Dinius 2011; Morel 1989; Lask 1991).

Volta Redonda in-between Contexts

There is a great deal of good material written about the city of Volta Redonda, the plant, the workers and the relationship between them.[4] What this chapter contributes to the literature on Volta Redonda and its relationship to the steel industry is the set of insights generated by a team of *brasilienses*—that is to say, inhabitants of the city of Brasilia, the capital city of Brazil. As someone who is interested in "the anthropology of anthropology" (Díaz Crovetto 2008; 2011), I find this intriguing, as it implies the possibility at least of generating new and different ethnographical insights. Among these are the possibilities offered by a perspective that allows for comparisons between Brasilia and Volta Redonda. Volta Redonda and Brasilia were projects that entailed *total city planning* (Scott 1998), whereby the state embraced an exceptionally large-scale and totalizing urban architectural planning project. By doing so in Volta Redonda and in Brasilia, the state was capable of shaping the *sense* and the representations of such new spaces, although with time newer uses and representations have emerged as the cities' social dynamics have continued to unfold.

In the case of the city of Volta Redonda, we consistently encountered the perception of the city as something relatively *old* that was seen as *new*. This is a "new old" that is not easily visible or recognizable, yet speaks of a city that is still thought of and remembered as new, despite the passing of the different generations. The various facets of Volta Redonda, where the succession of generations marks the passing of time, have produced the subjectivities that lie beneath these conceptions of "new" and "old". This research is not just about the emergence of the city of Volta Redonda, or even about the transformation of the village into a city. It investigates the *lives* and *life trajectories* that were built concomitantly with the implementation of the state's industrial project. In other words, CSN and Volta Redonda together represented new opportunities, new flows and new possibilities for continuity in terms of work, family and livelihoods.

Both in Brasilia and Volta Redonda, the workplace and the living-place emerged in relation to one another. Alongside these places also arose spaces for sociability and spaces which straddled the public and the private sphere, such as hospitals and schools. In the case of Volta Redonda, as previously mentioned, until 1956 there was no provision from the city administration; social care and services were distributed solely by CSN. Therefore, the workplace was a *state-place*, as well as the living space and the place where employees enjoyed their social life. In other words, the state was an integral aspect of their everyday lives—at work, in the public sphere and shaping the private sphere as well.

Brasilia was in a similar situation shortly after its inauguration (1960), although the social segmentation of state employees was mainly evidenced in public service. Both cities were poles of attraction for the waves of immigrants from different regions seeking work that settled and thus established diverse urban populations. Some of the incoming workers found employment in CSN, in the case of Volta Redonda, or in the public sector in Brasilia, but not all were successful in achieving these desirable jobs. Interestingly, both cities were built by *outsiders*,[5] and both came to be characterized by their heterogeneous populations, with a majority of migrants coming from Rio Janeiro but many others who migrated from other parts of Brazil. The growth of these cities and the distinctive social and cultural contributions made by the different waves of internal migrants gave rise to new perspectives and strategies, where informal working arrangements played an important part in adapting to the new environment. Over time, the incorporation of the various migrants gave rise to distinctive cultural, social and linguistic characteristics of these new cities. Thus, regarding the original migration population, it is interesting to note the use of the local term *arigó*, as discussed by Lask. This term, which was originally used to refer to a migratory bird, was given to CSN construction workers to denote their lack of professional qualifications (1991:116). But the term also evokes mobility/dislocation as a practical feature of labor, highlighting the new arrivals and identifying them with a generation of outsiders motivated by specific goals—in this case, to build up the city and CSN. This identification enables a comparison of Volta Redonda and its *arigós* with the case of Brasilia and its *candangos* (i.e., see Ribeiro 2008; Scott 1998; Holton 1993). As with the *candangos* who built the city of Brasília, the local term highlights both the conditions of work and those of migration as inextricably linked features of the labor at the heart of these foundational efforts.

In the case of CSN in Volta Redonda and Brasilia, some common characteristics appear which can be linked to the company town models. These models seem to express the limited capacity to absorb the workforce over time. Hence, by not being able to be inserted into the companies' labor forces, many of the second generation members which were born in these company town cities were forced to migrate in search of work in other cities (i.e., Lucas 2008). Whereas in Volta Redonda, we seem to observe a constant incorporation of labor force between generations, initially motivated by the expansion processes of the CSN, which allowed fulfillment of the work demands of new generations as well as the demands of migrants.

Later, the modernization processes pursued within the plant, linked also to the last expansion processes of the industry, brought about a significant reduction in the total workforce. At the same time, outsourcing was incentivized, especially in the area of maintenance. The reduction of the CSN workforce, a process which was initiated before the privatization of the company (Lima 2010), caused high levels of tension and conflict, leading to a large number of dismissals. However, despite all of those unfavorable conditions for the reproduction of the labor force, the migrant population of the city was not discouraged, as the city continued to attract migrants, converting it into a pole for the services industry. Here, the educational services, specifically those related to technical and professional education, stood out. Furthermore, as I will insist throughout the text, life in Volta Redonda created a territorial identity, incentivized by favorable living conditions, housing, work and health conditions, characteristics which are reflected in the good results obtained by the city in human development and quality of life indexes.[6] Therefore, as CSN gradually ceased to be a particularly interesting place to work, Volta Redonda continued to be an interesting place to live.

In the case of Brasilia, the large number of workers needed to build an entire city planned as the future capital of the country from scratch was not considered to be integrated into the original housing facilities, mainly destined for public employees. Those populations formed the first satellite cities (Ribeiro 2008; Holston 1993; Scott 1998) which expanded over time. Brasilia became famous not only for the public positions offered for people interested in working in the administrative sphere, but also for the plots of land offered to those willing to live in the outlying regions of the suburbs of Brasilia. The movement was incentivized by some populist governments, which led to the emergence of speculative mafias known as *grilheiros*.

The new national capital and the first national steel company were both built from scratch as major projects of the Brazilian state. In their different ways, Volta Redonda and Brasilia were models presented to Brazilian citizens and workers of a new, forthcoming Brazil forged with recourse to an ideology that can be situated within national history in relation to ideas, political processes, workers and citizens. Nevertheless, there are some significant differences, arising from the different historical contexts in which the two centers evolved. On the one hand, through Brasilia and its particular architectural vision, the government intended to build a new Brazilian Modernism, to which the architect Oscar Niemeyer gave its final lines and curves. Brasilia was built not only to expand and develop internal frontiers by moving the previous capital, situated on the eastern coast, further into the center of the country, but it was also a way to show that it could be done, that Brazil was prepared to develop a modern project, raised through the triumph of a political, technological and collective effort. Or as Ribeiro pointed out, Brasilia was constructed as an epic story which was presented, along with a few other projects, for the construction of a national identity (2008: 3). On the other hand, decades before Brasília was built, Volta Redonda and CSN were already projected to be ideological developmental models for a *new Brazil* founded on an industrialized welfare state,[7] this being the most important index of President Getúlio Vargas's abovementioned "CLT". The capacity of materializing ideas through raising up an entire city in a short timeframe is, without a doubt, a remarkable similarity between Volta Redonda and Brasilia. We could think that today these cities stand as a clear reminder of state policies, articulated within a specific landscape and territory. These are policies that have also marked the livelihood of different groups of population through time.

Finally, Volta Redonda, CSN and its workers brought to mind not only the history and character of Brasilia, but also triggered reflections on the different generations of seafarers of the small port town of Corral in southern Chile with whom I worked during my doctoral research. Generations of such mariners have their histories marked by connections between events, policies and interests in the local, regional, national and transnational dimensions, just like those of the CSN. These connections and dislocations across different scales and temporal domains changed the seafaring ways of working, as well as the ways of accessing work. The similarities across these cases relating to generational shifts in relation to training, access to employment and the intensification of the labor process are indicative of deeper and more general transformations of the dominant models of labor and production. With the seamen of Corral, I learned that the arrangements between local, regional, national, global and transnational relations are manifold and can be difficult to track (Díaz Crovetto 2010; 2015). Therefore, as a heuristic device, I focused on the experiences arising from the life histories of three generations of seafarers. Through this I learned that local, regional, national, international and/or transnational projects and processes of development usually leave their mark on life trajectories and concrete communities. In the following section, I discuss the gaps arising between generations as they affect skills, working conditions and community relations.

Some Remarks on Access and Work Conditions between Generations at CSN

A generational perspective on work, access to employment, and institutional and on-the-job training highlights the shifts that have taken place in the dominant models of the state and in the conduct of local industry. It also makes evident that many of these changes are not only local and that it is crucial to explore these local phenomena in relation to other places and broader processes. For the study of Volta Redonda, three generations of CSN employees were considered.[8] People over 55 years of age and who worked until the privatization of the company constitute the *first generation*. The *second generation* is between 30 and 55 years of age and is composed of workers who began their working lives before CSN's privatization.[9] Finally, the *third generation* consists of people who entered the company after privatization and are between 18 and 30 years of age. Such diverse work experiences are reflected in the accounts we gathered from our interviewees.[10]

It is relevant to mention that in order to place the aforementioned workers, CSN had four major stages of planned expansion. The first relates to the beginning of the industry with a production level of 270,000 ingots. The second corresponds to the 1954 plan with a level of production amounting to 680,000 ingots, while the third was divided into two phases: the first phase, in 1960, with 1 million ingots and the second phase in 1962 with 1.4 million ingots. Finally, the fourth and most ambitious plan was divided into three phases, starting in the 1960s. This plan included the construction of Furnace N°3, of different areas for the production and termination of steel, and brought total production up to 4.6 million ingots. On the other hand, as outlined below, the plan envisaged significant changes in the size and composition of the workforce and the conditions of work, as well as changes in the administration of the company (Dinius 2011; Piquet 1998; Morel and Pessanha 1991).

It is also relevant to state that *Escola Técnica Pandiá Calógeras* (ETPC) is still arguably the most important educational center in Volta Redonda, and has been responsible for educating a great part of all three generations of workers. It was founded in 1941 and was envisaged as part of the original plan for the city in order to provide basic courses for the workers involved in the construction of the production plant. It was also intended to generate the technical teams that the plant would require once production got underway. It is interesting to observe the changes ETPC underwent over time, since they coincide with significant points experienced by the different generations of workers in our sample.

As a rule, the *first generation* is composed of people whose parents came to Volta Redonda to work. As former bishop and social activist Waldyr Calheiros pointed out, these workers were "following the smoke that came from the chimneys". Having access to a stable job (that was frequently also a job for a lifetime) was the magnet that drew people to the city. The workers from the first generation offered a great variety of stories about the motivations that drove them and the ways in which they gained access to a job in the plant. From their accounts, it appears that gaining access was an almost random event that depended in part on previously acquired skills (i.e., being a truck driver, a fireman, etc.) that could be useful in a specific department of the General Services Area of CSN. The physical qualities of the prospective workers were an important consideration given the characteristics of the tasks involved in the various steps of steel production; for example, having strong hands and a strong body that could withstand heavy work was an asset. Besides, the plant needed a large number of employees to fulfill a great number of tasks. Another feature that would improve workers' chances of obtaining a job in the plant was the existence of family or friendshipties with company employees. Such contact might well facilitate access to work at the steel plant. In short, previously acquired skills, workers' physical condition and family and friendship ties could facilitate work access. During the first period of expansion, the level of technical training required by the plant was quite low, and people were trained in the plant through on-the-job and institutional training. For this generation, perhaps the most important connection between workers and CSN was the capacity of generating livelihood possibilities and its associated perks: housing and other company benefits that enabled the employee and his/her family to permanently settle in close proximity to the plant. For this generation, becoming a steelworker entailed assurances formalized by CSN job registration; thus, becoming a professional was firmly tied to becoming a CSN employee. As a consequence, at that moment the majority of the CSN workers were trained by ETPC.

The *second generation* is marked by the important status CSN placed on technical abilities, and in doing so, ETPC assumed a vital role in the formation of the workforce. This free and widely recognized institution was known to provide an excellent education and trained a considerable number of people, most of who were employed by CSN. Another segment of CSN workers of this generation were those who wanted to improve their situation but could not access ETPC due to limited capacity within that institution. These workers studied by their own means in other private educational centers. In many cases, these workers studied while they were working in less-qualified positions at CSN, and some of them went on to become engineers or high-profile technicians within CSN. Nevertheless, whether training took place at ETPC or in another educational institution, completing a technical course had a favorable effect on a worker's chances of promotion and achieving better working conditions at CSN.

It is worth noting that the majority of the members of the second generation became CSN employees during the military dictatorship that controlled the state between 1964 and 1985. This was a time of conflict and harsh management practices that had the effect of prompting workers to question their working conditions for the first time. Previously, worker demands had focused on issues such as the construction and allocation of housing by CSN rather than work conditions. This particular generation experienced two important phenomena that marked their daily work practice, training and careers. First, there was the restructuring process that introduced new models of production and management (mainly related to *Toyotism* and Five S Models), both in order to increase the total production and product quality. A second key event relates to the privatization of CSN in 1993 and the period leading up to this event when the plant was preparing for its future sale. The outsourcing of maintenance service within the plant took place before privatization and was in response to the crises experienced by steel production worldwide, and by CSN in particular. All of this can be attributed, particularly in the latter instance, to the second world oil crisis at the end of the 1970s and beginning of the 1980s. Privatization also took place in a context in which the Brazilian state promoted the privatization of other state companies, and which in turn reflects broader global trends that favored privatization of state assets and enterprises (Dal Forno and Mollona 2015).[11] This generation also experienced the effects of a gradual rise in outsourcing, which came to represent an alternative route to accessing a job at CSN. In fact, it was easier to gain access to an outsourcing company than to CSN directly, especially for those who did not have what was considered a good level of formal technical training. This second generation was the last to get high salaries for many different positions, and it was also the last to have access to other social benefits (i.e., to be assigned to a CSN housing plan). The erosion of benefits, salaries and work stability as a result of restructuring, outsourcing and privatization constituted the central claims and principal foci for the strikes that started in the 1980s, before and after the company's privatization. Additionally, the implementation of new phases of the company's expansion[12] meant that workers, technicians and engineers of this generation were engaged in labor challenges of adopting different technologies in the production and administration areas in order to improve the competitiveness of the company. This resulted in processes of concentration and intensification of work. Later, after the restructuring process, employees knew that the situation at CSN would not improve; in fact, they would not even be "as good as before". In fact, in contrast with employment possibilities in other industries in the area, work conditions at CSN were declining. As a consequence, many CSN employees did not want their children to follow their own professions, as neither the wages nor the work conditions seemed to be competitive in relation to other possibilities in nearby manufacturing cities. These workers also developed the perception that there is a marked division between a time in the past and work conditions which are no longer current in the present.

In sum, as I understand it, two key aspects define this generation. First, by restructuring different aspects of CSN, management, production and maintenance, a process of "technification" took shape within the company (Mangabeira 1993) where all job positions became technical, and everybody had at least a technical degree. In most cases, this technical focus was interwoven with processes based on the *automation* of the production line. Such processes were also related to a broader industrial development project in the state of Rio de Janeiro. Thus, to supply the regional demand for technicians, a range of training centers began to offer technical training in different areas of expertise. Moreover, it is noteworthy that many among this generation of workers who became CSN employees were children of previous employees of the plant. These employees had better income and wanted to improve their children's future. Hence, children of previous workers aspired to obtain the available technical or engineering jobs.

It was at the point of completing the major expansion program (D Plan) in 1985 that CSN began outsourcing the workforce on a significant scale, especially in the *maintenance* sector. Those directly employed by CSN were therefore concentrated in production and administration. The second generation, however, had internalized the goal of productivity as a core value, which was inspired by earlier models such as *Toyotism* and especially the Five S Model, also derived from Japanese sources. In the Five S model, training was directed at controlling not only the machine but also the environment surrounding the steelworker, setting patterned orders to be internalized by the worker, and centered around notions of hygiene based on a symbiotic relationship between bodies and the workspace. The Five S model is defined by a disciplinary gaze directed at spotting order and disorder. At the same time, automation intensified the individual workload while reducing the number of workers. Therefore, as an outcome of the aforementioned changes, this generation experienced moments of massive dismissal before and after privatization (Lima 2010).

The ***third generation*** tended to choose technical careers from the rich variety of academic and professional courses offered today in Volta Redonda.[13] Such careers are no longer directed necessarily towards CSN, as they once were, but to many different manufacturing units found in the region today. The increased diversity and number of training courses are not only a consequence of the new requirements for employment, but they also reflect the wider job opportunities that exist not only in the city and at CSN, but in the region as a whole. Interestingly, since the 1980s many of the courses offered have been oriented towards the needs of outsourcing companies. Also, as the city has expanded, the gap between job opportunities at CSN and the number of economically active individuals—especially among the young—is growing so large that access to CSN is becoming more restricted. Despite the fact that wages at CSN are today perceived as being much lower than in the past, and in comparison with other industries in the present, a job at CSN is still considered desirable for a large number of young people, especially those working in unfavorable conditions. This is partly because technical positions are still seen to offer better pay and better prospects than commercial activities. In this sense, outsourcing companies still represent concrete and imaginary possibilities for granting access to CSN.

Today, CSN continues to offer many training programs. After being trainees, some of the students are selected to work inside the former public steel industry. In some cases, CSN is seen as a survival strategy, and in others, as an in-between work possibility prior to finding a better position elsewhere. The perspective of growing old and retiring at CSN is usually absent in the third generation employee's life plans. But taking into consideration that this generation has created ties with the city, and that some in this generation live with their parents, it is fairly common for them to prefer to work in Volta Redonda and earn less than to take up other job opportunities in

GENERATIONS	EMPLOYMENT, ACCESS AND LABOR CONDITIONS.
FIRST GENERATION	Labor skills learned prior to employment in the sector. Importance of physical skills (*força braçal*). Family and friends working at CSN ease hiring. Professional category earned through employment (i.e. one becomes a steelworker when hired as such). Low to medium wages.
SECOND GENERATION	Technical requirements. Increased automation. Work intensification (one person, several functions). Medium to high wages. Outsourcing of some work areas (mainly maintenance).
THIRD GENERATION	Mandatory technical knowledge (every worker is at least a technician). Low wages compared with other sectors. Low levels of work stability. Precarious working conditions.

Figure 4.1 Generations at CSN, Volta Redonda.

the region but further from home. As we can see, this generation feels that they are part of Volta Redonda, with well-established family and friendship ties. As one former ETPC student told us: "this city is still a great place to live, study and work; you have good public health, and it is still a safe city to live in. You have all that you need". The different aspects of work and access to work for the three generations of CSN employees are summarized in Figure 4.1.

Final Remarks

Initially, technical training for CSN workers was offered only by ETPC, which with time solidified its prestige as an important educational center. During the second generation, other centers and training possibilities appeared, but an ETPC student was still considered almost automatically a CSN worker. CSN also used the ETPC as a center for continued training of the labor force, passing on "know-how" linked to different models of production that were introduced over time. After the privatization of CSN, ETPC began to charge for all courses, and the natural link between EPTC's training and hiring at CSN was broken. Thus, with the exception of scholarship holders, those interested in joining CSN had to make considerable financial commitments, either at ETPC or at a different technical school. Today, EPTC is locally recognized not only as a technical school, but also as a good school with high tuition fees. Many middle class families choose to enroll their children there in order to prepare them for university. The old link between the sites of education and of production is now largely severed. Between the three different generations of CSN employees, there is a noticeable shift concerning the high level of skills demanded by the industry and also in the form of knowledge acquisition through work practices. The latter shift evolved from basic "know-how" to a more sophisticated technical emphasis of knowledge. There were also political and administrative changes, such as the changes that followed privatization and then in response to new circumstances, helping to spread to other local businesses the capital that had previously been concentrated in one large entreprise. Additionally, Volta Redonda's city hall assumed a new responsibility: the social distribution of the capital generated through taxes and other indirect sources of revenue coming from CSN. This caused city hall to incorporate once more a parental role—i.e., "taking care" of its citizens—that is evocative of the paternalistic past. Only this time, this *new* form of "care" would not be overseen by CSN.

One ethnographic example of this paternalistic shift, which the research team encountered during our research, occurred during the 2011 Christmas celebration. On the first days of December we witnessed the preparation of the city's Christmas decorations. The public lights are so elaborate and abundant, that power cuts are typical at this time of the year due to the propensity for electric shortages that follow the overcharged public electrical system. But the apex of these decorations centers on the city's main square where a replica of Santa Claus's village is built and where for two weeks, thousands of toys are given for free to the children of Volta Redonda, along with popcorn and bottles of water that were freely distributed to the public.

To conclude, a concise presentation of indicators on training and access to employment among different generations of CSN workers points to certain similarities, such as work intensification, "technification" and a tendency towards decreased income. These similarities, in turn, can be read as evidence of global processes related to changes in the mode of production and in industrial operating practices and strategies. Specifically, in the case of the different generations of CSN workers, the transformation of employment requirements relates to work stability that are mediated by diverse educational possibilities and are marked by a desire to get a better livelihood conditions. And, with the passing of each generation, the possibility of working at CSN has granted the possibility of living in the city of Volta Redonda.

Notes

1 The chapter is based on field research funded by the FP7 Collaborative Project (Grant Agreement No. 225670) MEDEA- Models and their Effects on Development Paths: an Ethnographic and comparative Approach to Knowledge Transmission and Livelihood Strategies and presented at the project's international conference held at the University of Barcelona on 23–24 February. The research was carried out by a core team that was based in the Laboratory for Studies about Globalization and Development of the Department of Anthropology at the University of Brasilia. During that time, this laboratory was directed by professor Gustavo Lins Ribeiro, and it undertook all of the research regarding MEDEA Project in Brasil. The team that studied Volta Redonda was oriented by the Work Package 9 and 10 to deepen understanding concerning livelihood strategies and work experiences through generations of CSN workers. The team was formed by Gonzalo Díaz Crovetto, who acted as coordinator and researcher, and by the researchers Raoni Giraldin and Rafael Lasavitz. The reflections presented here are grounded in the work of systematization and presentation of antecedents and results (Díaz Crovetto et al. 2012). However, the present text and any errors within are my complete responsibility. I'm thankful for the effort put forth by the researchers and the comments that I received from professor Ribeiro.
2 As Ribeiro (2008) pointed out, large-scale-projects are usually built in areas with low population density.
3 This differs from a *sistema-vila-fabrica-operaria* (Lopes 1988), in that the system I describe here incorporates the different classes that compose the factory (workmen, technician and engineers) from the outset.
4 There is interesting bibliographical material about Volta Redonda and CSN; Lima (2010) presents a review of the available bibliography. Especially important are the works of Morel (1989), Lask (1991), Lopes et all (2004), Dias (2010), Graciolli (2007), Dinius (2011) and Mangabeira (1993). Of course, the histories of Volta Redonda and CSN are quite complex, and here I present succinctly only a few points of those—specifically, that which allow me to situate some of the nuances of the workers' work experience.
5 The workers involved in the construction of Brasília are known as *candangos*.

6 For example, according to a report from the PNUD in 2004, its IDH was estimated at 0.815, placing the city in third place among the cities of the state of Rio de Janeiro.
7 The welfare policies also intended to suffocate the power of the anarchist and the communist movements by tightening surveillance over them and bringing labor unions closer to the state.
8 By considering three generations, it is possible to better illustrate the continuities and ruptures from the first to the last, whereas the second can be thought of as a liminal stage between them.
9 As this generation suffers major changes in contrast among the others in terms of working conditions and employment, I discuss this one more than the others.
10 Overall, we interviewed 60 people. The interviewees were chosen among employees occupying different positions within CSN and belong to various generations. Besides these workers, we also interviewed a few educators and technical formation and university students. Additionally, we established various informal conversations with union participants, cultural groups, church groups and social groups, among others.
11 The process of privatization of state companies started at the final period of military government during the 1980s and was continued with the democratically elected government (Matos Filho and Oliveira 1996).
12 There were four: 1) Plan A was established in 1946, 2) Plan B in 1954, 3) Plan C in 1960 and finally, 4) Plan D, the biggest expansion plan, in 1978.
13 Today the city has a public university, two private universities and an endless number of technical training centers.

References

Dal Forno, A., and Mollona, E. (2015). 'Isomorphism and Local Interests in the Diffusion of Global Policies: An Enquiry into Privatization Policy, Adoption using Computer Modeling and Simulation', in Goddard, V. and S. Narotzky (eds) *Industry and Work in Contemporary Capitalism: Global Models, Local Lives?* Abingdon, Oxon and New York: Routledge.

Dias, S. (2010). *Dentro da usina, mas fora da "família": trabalhadores e terceirização na Companhia Siderúrgica Nacional*. Dissertação de Mestrado apresentada ao Programa de Pós Graduação em Sociologia e Antropologia do Instituto de Filosofia e Ciências Sociais da Universidade Federal do Rio de Janeiro (UFRJ). Rio de Janeiro.

Díaz Crovetto, G. (2008). 'Antropologías mundiales en cuestión: diálogos y debates'. *Wan E-Journal*, 3: 131–155. http://ram-wan.net/old/documents/05_e_Journal/jwan-3.pdf. Accessed September 27, 2016.

Díaz Crovetto, G. (2011). 'Antropologías de la Antropologías: situando, ciertas condiciones para su emergencia y consolidación. condiciones para su emergencia y consolidación'. Bogotá, *Antípoda* Revista de Antropología y Arqueología,, 12: 191–210.

Díaz Crovetto, G. (2015). 'Entre lugares y documentos: problematizando el desplazamiento y las condiciones transnacionales del viaje y del trabajo de tripulantes mercantes de Corral (Chile)'. *Antípoda* Revista de Antropología y Arqueología, 23: 23–44.

Díaz Crovetto, G., Lasevitz, R., and Giraldin, R. (2012). 'Situando trajetórias: formação, acesso e trabalho entre diferentes gerações de trabalhadores da Companhia Siderúrgica Nacional (CSN) em Volta Redonda'. *Final Report: WP 9 and WP 10*, Mimeo, Brasilia.

Dinius, O. (2011). *Brazil's Steel City: Developmentalism, Strategic Power, and Industrial Relations in Volta Redonda, 1941–1964*. Stanford: Stanford University Press.
Dinius, O., and Vergara, A. (2011). 'Company Towns in the Americas: An Introduction', in O. Dinius and A. Vergara (eds) *Company Towns in The Americas*. Georgia: The University of Georgia Press, pp. 1–20.
Graciolli, E. (2007). *Privatização da CSN.*, São Paulo: Editora Expressão Popular.
Holston, J. (1993). *A cidade modernista: uma crítica de Brasília e sua utopia*. São Paulo: Companhia das Letras.
Lask, T. (1991). *Ordem e progresso: a estrutura de poder na cidade operária da Companhia Siderúrgica Nacional em Volta Redonda (1941–1964)*. Dissertação de Mestrado. Rio de Janeiro: Museu Nacional/Universidade Federal do Rio de Janeiro.
Lima, R. (2010). 'Novas e velhas questões: revisando a historiografia sobre Volta Redonda (RJ)'. *História Unisinos*, 4(1): 77–87.
Lopes, J.S. (1988). *A tecelagem dos conflitos de classe na "cidade das chaminés"*. São Paulo-Brasília: Marco Zero/Editora da Universidade de Brasília.
Lopes, J.S. (2004). 'Volta Redonda: o percurso entre as chaminés e a curva do rio', in J.S. Lopes (ed) *A ambientalização dos conflitos sociais*. Rio de Janeiro: Relume Dumará Editora, pp. 101–129.
Lucas, R. (2008). *Minetown, Milltown, Railtown*. Oxford: Oxford University Press.
Mangabeira, W. (1993). *Os Dilemas do Novo Sindicalismo: Democracia e Política em Volta Redonda*. Rio de Janeiro: Relume Dumará/ANPOCS.
Matos Filhos, J. and Oliveira, C. (1996). *O Processo de Privatização das Empresas Brasileiras*. Documento de Discussão 422, Brasilia: IPEA.
Morel, R. (1989). *A Ferro e Fogo. Construção da "família siderúrgica": o caso de Volta Redonda (1941–1968)*. Doctoral thesis, Faculdade de Filosofia, Letras e Ciências Humanas da Universidade de São Paulo, São Paulo.
Morel, R.L. de Morais and Pessanha, E.G. da Fonte (1991). Gerações Operárias: Rupturas e Continuidades na Experiência de Metalúrgicos do Rio de Janeiro. *Revista Brasileira de Ciências Sociais*, 6(17): 68–83.
Piquet, R. (1998). *Cidade-Empresa: Presença na paisagem urbana brasileira*. Rio de Janeiro: Jorge Zahar Editor.
Ribeiro, G.L. (2008). *O capital da esperança*. Brasília: Editora Universidade de Brasília.
Scott, J. (1998). *Seeing Like a State*. New Haven: Yale University Press.

Section II
Continuities and Discontinuities

5 Post-Fordist Work Organization and Daily Life from a Gender Perspective
The Case of FIAT-SATA in Melfi

Fulvia D'Aloisio

The Fiat Car Factory in Melfi: The New Integrated Factory and "The Green-Field"

The opening of the integrated FIAT factory in Melfi (Basilicata) in 1994 represented a profound transformation of the Italian automobile industry, with the introduction of highly innovative approaches to production and work. The factory represented the first Italian experimentation of the so-called Japanese model introduced by the Toyota Motor Company of Japan, based on Taichi Ohno's project. During the mid-1990s, Fiat experienced a deep corporate crisis, with a significant drop in sales both on the internal and international markets, in large part due precisely to Japanese competition. Two pillars of the new Japanese model, applied in Melfi's newly constructed factory, were explicitly aimed at overcoming the Fordist production model. First, a "just in time" production strategy that inverted the production cycle, putting on the market only the automobiles for which there was already a demand, and thus eliminating stocks and reducing the costs of production. The second pillar was the so-called "total quality model", which rested on greater expertise and awareness of the workers, and aimed to enable corrective responses to defects at the point of production and on the assembly line. This new model also foresaw improved technology, with increased automation of the productive process (Ohno 1993). More generally, however, the new integrated factory (the Italian translation of the Japanese model: Revelli 1989; Cerruti and Rieser 1991; Bonazzi 1993), was seen as a factory able to launch faster production with less bureaucracy and enhanced quality control. In sum, it was seen as a leaner form of production that benefited from decreased interventions by mid-level professionals, a more agile management structure and greater participation of workers in the decisional processes, leading experts to describe the latter through the metaphor of the "crystal tube" (Bonazzi 1993).

The process of modernizing production proposed by Fiat was, however, impracticable outside of a "green field", that is to say a setting with no tradition in manufacturing or trade union organization. Most significant was the possibility of implementing a new kind of job contract through the establishment of a new company, SATA,[1] which established conditions of work based on lower salaries, more intense work shifts, and a greater percentage of women workers than other FIAT factories (18 percent of the total workforce in the SATA factory).

The opening of the Melfi factory is understandable only if one takes into account the complex PR operation put in place by Fiat, amplified by the role of local institutions, in which the notion of "green field" was used by the Fiat publicists as a symbol of the new industrial plant (Ricci 1993). The term was disseminated by the press to signify the company's intentions to create a completely new corporate and work organization, involving a young (under the age of 32, in line with national law providing tax incentives to those hiring young workers), more highly educated workforce than in the past (workers with a high school degree). The "green field" label was also an accurate description of the vast stretch of agricultural land on which the factory was built. On a symbolic level, the label was reminiscent of local history, or the efforts of famers who worked hard to achieve an abundant harvest, and the well-being and sense of comfort that such a harvest meant for farming families in the years to come. The green field was thus a recognizable and understandable referent for the local inhabitants, closely aligned with a value system within which a prosperous harvest assuring survival and existential serenity were closely linked.

At the time the region of Basilicata was highly underdeveloped from an industrial point of view and suffered from very high levels of unemployment (especially female), in part explaining why the factory was welcomed with great enthusiasm by local administrations. Such enthusiasm should also be contextualized in relation to local and national history. Industrialization had, up until this point, been relatively scarce and sporadic. The period following the earthquake of 1980 stands out, as it involved a large public financing plan for the affected areas (Basilicata and Campania), which, however, ultimately failed (Cuoco 1980; Becchi 1990; Barbagallo 1997). At the national level, Fiat embodied the dreams of thousands of workers who emigrated from the South after the Second World War, to work in the large Fiat factory of Mirafiori in Turin. For this reason, the "landing" of Fiat at Melfi was greeted with only very limited expressions of criticism, which came mostly from the most radical left-leaning local political groups. Such critique went basically unheard, for better or for worse, muffled by majority opinion, which from the very beginning considered the arrival of Fiat as a promising occasion for work and for the development of a relatively depressed and industrially backwards area. Indeed, approximately 9,000 new work positions were opened up by Fiat and its satellite industries. However, a more critical lens reveals that the opening of the factory was in reality an example of industrialization without development (Hitten 1970), or of development without autonomy (Trigilia 1994), in that car manufacturing does not generally provide enough stimulation or have a propulsive effect on the larger local industry. Nor was it able to generate local management skills.

The unconditional acceptance of the Fiat operations, both in terms of the characteristics of the industrial plant and the forms of work, was reflected in the absence of any true negotiation with the labor unions, which occurred before the construction of the factory and in fact approved exhausting work schedules, high levels of productivity, and reduced salaries compared to the factories in northern Italy. On the whole, this was a deal that saw very uneven forces at play, with a strong imbalance in favor of Fiat, which managed to create a working class under unequal and subordinate conditions compared to workers within the same Fiat factories in the North. In fact, with the launching of the factory, when the first workers were sent to Mirafiori in Turin for training and preparation, they were warmly welcomed by the older workers in the North (many of whom were of southern origin) but also with an awareness that a redefinition of both the rights and the security of workers was taking place in Melfi. This awareness resulted in the Melfi workers being labeled by the Northern Mirafiori workers as "the blacks of Basilicata". Indeed, from the very start, the "amaranth overalls",[2] admired as emblematic of a link with the Fiat myth that was seen as very positive in the context of the delayed or absent development of southern Italy (D'Aloisio 2003), were seen outside Melfi as representing the tough and penalizing working conditions of the plant. At the same time, the post-Fordist model promised the arrival of a new kind of worker, different in terms of their skills and the range of their responsibilities. These qualities were less attributable to notions of "class", and related instead to an individualism that was increasingly achieved both in terms of the forms of work and the ever less collective articulation of demands for improvements or basic rights. This new working class, favored in terms of the local context and subordinate from a national point of view, formed the heart of the industrial operation. Quickly nicknamed the "fiatists"[3] of Melfi, they were simultaneously the objects of curiosity and of admiration in the local context, outside of the factory.

An Anthropological Point of View

From an anthropological perspective, the opening of the Fiat factory in Melfi provides an opportunity to interpret cultural changes resulting from what is a significant event of modernization, specifically the introduction of new forms of industrial work (i.e., heavy industry) in an area with a peasant past and, since the 1970s (Ginsborg 1989; 1998) with a growing public service sector. On the one hand, the establishment of the factory responded to processes of economic change on an international scale linked to a general crisis in the automobile industry, Japanese competition, and the need to modernize the manufacture of Fiat cars. On the other hand, the factory inevitably brought about profound changes in local socio-economic structures, creating a new working class and transforming the organization of work, as well as daily life, social and gender relations, and family arrangements.

An anthropological approach aims to elucidate the complex intersections between global processes and local transformations and, through ethnographic methods, to analyze the effects of larger and external economic transformations on daily life. As noted by Kilani, this objective is pursued with an awareness that the terms "local" and "global" do not indicate realities in and of themselves but rather, suggest the ways in which anthropologists correlate different levels of reality in the construction of the anthropological object (Kilani 1994; Appadurai 2001). In Italy, an analytical framework to better understand enterprises and work at different levels and in different ethnographic contexts is being pioneered by influential authors such as Cristina Papa (1999), whose work has been developed further by other scholars interested in local industrial realities (Ghezzi 2007). According to Papa, the anthropology of the enterprise constitutes a specific field of investigation concerned with the dynamics of global capitalism and their effects on local realties. From this perspective, the enterprise is understood not as a closed reality, limited to its internal dynamics, but as a window through which to analyze the interaction between global and local dynamics, which find their own particular articulation within the enterprise. In France, where this line of research has existed for quite some time, Sélim (1996) has highlighted a resistance amongst anthropologists to making the enterprise the object of study, considering this to be a domain more closely associated with sociologists and economists. Already in the 1990s, Sélim argued that the characteristics of the global market were headed towards an increasing loss of social guarantees and a more aggressive commoditization of work, with a consequent weakening of workers' participation in management strategies (Sélim 1996; Althabe and Sélim 2000). According to Sélim, the enterprise represents an ideal observatory of diverse logics and multiple points of view, more or less divergent with respect to the ideology of the enterprise; a field of diversity that allows us to explore larger transformations of the enterprise and of work at the micro-level.

The focus in this chapter on the work of women allows us to extend the investigation of these diverse logics. Historically, high rates of local female unemployment and more generally the subordinate role of women must necessarily first be contextualized within the framework of the lag in the economic structures of southern Italy when compared to northern Italy, and more broadly, of Italy with respect to Europe. Indeed, Italy continues to have one of the lowest rates of female employment in Europe.[4] The work role of women in southern Italy, in areas like Melfi characterized by agricultural pasts and scarce industrialization, has long been marked by job instability and invisibility. Women's work was in fact mainly characterized by agricultural labor carried out for the most part when substituting for the men during periods of war and emigration. Another feature contributing to the invisibility of women's work has been the labor conducted "under the table" that has served to supplement the income of male heads of household (Signorelli 1990; 1993). Employment in the public service sector, in local administration and services, has always been characterized by favoritism and nepotism; this dynamic has more generally characterized the management and allocation of public resources in Italy and especially in the South (Banfield 1961; Piselli 1981; Signorelli 1983; Gribaudi 1999; Zinn 2001). For this reason, work in this large new factory represented a host of novel characteristics for local women regarding their labor, that is to say as legal, recognized, visible, and subject to non-discriminatory hiring. Many female workers described their experiences, having applied to the job "by chance," and being utterly surprised to then receive notification that they had been hired, clearly implying that obtaining work without using some sort of introductory channel was an entirely new experience with respect to local tradition.

This chapter aims to analyze how the Japanese production model, in its Italian incarnation of the integrated factory, influenced the meanings of work and identity and the self-perception of workers, particularly from the perspective of women or, more accurately, from a gender perspective. The particular focus here consists of an analysis of the so-called "double burden" (Balbo 1978), or the dedication of women to both family and work (Ginatempo 1993; Oppo et al 2000.; Facchini 2008), the subsequent transformations in social and family roles, and life strategies aimed at balancing the timing and forms of familial and work organization (Fine-Davis et al. 2007; Naldini and Saraceno 2011). More than 20 years on from the launching of the factory, it is now possible to step back and observe the broader effects of this industrial operation. Beginning with the place of the factory in the context of the global crisis, we can see the implications of the transformations concerning the organization of work, the meaning and value associated with the working class, and the setbacks in the lives of female and male workers of the Fiat factory, and more generally of large-scale industry.

Metalworker Women of SATA in Longitudinal Perspective: Identity, Work and Livelihood Strategies

The case of the Fiat factory in Melfi can be analyzed from a longitudinal perspective or through two phases of field research, through consideration of three key aspects: identity, the meaning of work and subsistence strategies. The first phase of the research was carried out from 1999 to 2002; the second began in 2011 and is still in progress. These periods reflect two very different moments in the life of the factory. During the late 1990s, the factory had been open for only six years, and the memory of an event that marked a break with the past and that had generated great expectations of change was still very much alive. Now the factory is experiencing a phase of decline, constituted by a period of manufacturing instability that began in September 2011 and continued until February 2014, characterized by more or less lengthy interruptions in the work cycle, with recourse to redundancy payments (or short time compensation programs). Subsequently, the plant commenced production of new models (the Jeep Renegade and the 500X) and the compensation programs were brought to an end.

Work identity depends fundamentally on working women's own perceptions of their roles, but it also draws on images that are constructed externally in the local context and in the wider national domain. The meaning of work on the other hand refers to the sense and values attributed to a job, to a role, to status and levels of satisfaction or dissatisfaction derived from such work. When we locate these meanings and values in the context of subsistence strategies we are able to understand whether and how levels of pay, as well as the symbolic value of the work, are inscribed in the organization of women workers' lives. More specifically, it is possible to delineate different scenarios according to the roles and tasks they carry out in the factory; these are necessarily particularized by the existential trajectories of each woman, but there are also strong common elements shared by them.

In the early years of the factory plant workers were locally perceived as having a higher status than other workers (and an even more elevated status when compared to the unemployed). Indeed a job with a permanent contract, guaranteed and protected, marked a break with more unstable forms of work that were common in the area and were a feature of the earlier experiences of most of the workers. For women workers to thus legitimately enter the workplace with full rights and responsibilities, and furthermore to do so in a place of work that was traditionally male, represented a significant gain, especially where they assumed roles with heavy responsibilities, for example, as sprayers, dolly drivers, and quality controllers. At the same time, however, the women assembly line workers experienced, in equal measure as their male counterparts, all the hardship and repetitiveness of this kind of work (as also discussed in classic studies such as that by Walker and Guest 1952), which despite the new organizational model, remained essentially unchanged. Thus, aside from the organizational innovations introduced by the model, the so-called integrated factory drew a sharp distinction between the arduousness and monotony of assembly line work and the work of new professional figures, particularly in quality control. For the latter, a stronger identification with their work was possible; the responsibility of the job brought more gratification, and the sense of motivation and satisfaction was more intense. Consequently, the sense of work and work identity took shape very differently within the factory, on the one hand reproducing traditional working class forms of alienation associated with the Fordist model in the most menial tasks and, on the other hand, opening up new possibilities for satisfaction and upward mobility, higher levels of income and job satisfaction for the more highly-qualified workers, such as quality operators or productive roles out of the assembly line (D'Aloisio 2003, 2014)

For women, the need to reconcile rigid shifts and the toil of the assembly line with the demands of family life was met in the early years by the deployment of an effective syncretism between neighborhood and work networks. Women workers who lived in close proximity to one another and who were employed in the same UTE (Technological Elementary Unit) established a system of support and reciprocal exchange. It was common not only to travel to work together in the same vehicle, but also to exchange the performance of small daily tasks, such as temporarily taking care of a neighbor's or fellow worker's children: fixing one another's hair, going shopping in the city with the same car, all of which resulted in evident savings in terms of time and money. As such, "traditional" support within neighborhoods, very much the object of many anthropological studies in the 1970s and 1980s carried out in small peasant communities (Banfield 1961; Davis 1989), and consisting of reciprocal material and immaterial help was not affected negatively by the anonymous relations of the big factory. On the contrary, social networks were transformed towards fulfilling needs that arose from the difficulties posed by factory life. Positive effects, in this case, were experienced both on a material level through the exchange of goods and services and on a relational level with an enhanced possibility of sharing the rhythm and style of factory life. That said, factory jobs also created tensions and difficulties in the relations of factory workers with workers from other sectors and more generally generated tensions with the rhythms of village life (D'Aloisio 2003). The situation of the factory is very different now, 22 years from its inauguration and 15 years from my first ethnographic field trip. In terms of commercial and residential characteristics the town has grown, and a new neighborhood of single-unit family housing has been developed; many of the homes belong to workers who were able to take out mortgages. A more thorough analysis reveals, however, that the dream of transforming the working class into a middle class remains unfulfilled, even in the years of greatest growth of the automotive industry. This vision thrived in Melfi at the time of the factory's inauguration, somewhat behind national trends, but now appears to be disintegrating.

In this regard, the Fiat merger with Chrysler in 2009 represents an important moment in the so-called "Marchionne era" of Fiat history, which refers to the period initiated when Marchionne became the general manager in 2004. According to a number of scholars, contrary to what was portrayed in the Italian press and in some of the literature,[5] this was a necessary move for Fiat, which found itself forced to leave the confines of the European market for its survival (Berta 2011). Above all, with restructuring and the acquisition by a US firm, Marchionne led a profound reconfiguration of the relations between the corporation and the trade unions (Volpato 2008), in the direction of a strong diminution of representative rights and factory democracy.[6]

As has been documented in the literature, the current Fiat crisis began many years ago. According to several economists (see in particular Comito 2005), among the multiple causes of the crisis of Italian big industry is, foremost, the nature of public intervention, of which Fiat was one of the principal recipients. The significant weight of such intervention was due not so much to the resources made available, sometimes even in too much abundance, but rather to the characteristics of the interventions that were restricted to offering financial support and were completely lacking in terms of economic and industrial policy content. It should also be added that such allocations, which were often granted on the basis of political connections and clientelism, were not driven by long-term policies aimed at encouraging innovation. Currently, different factors suggest that the crisis is deepening, even after the merger with Chrysler, as is evident in the Fiat brand's loss of its lead position in the Brazilian market and further losses in Europe, where Fiat car sales have struggled stagnant market conditions more than their competitors (Berta 2011).

In the period we are considering (2011–2014) there was a marked sense of confusion, worry and uncertainty among the working class of Melfi. The labor unions foresee a period of redundancy payments of at least two years, as Fiat has continued to delay the launch of new automobile models and has not declared a business plan until 2014. Reductions in workers' incomes with the "*cassa integrazione*" (a temporary economic support from the Italian government) vary from 20 to 50 percent, according to periods of stops on production. The long period of "*cassa integrazione*", since 2011 to 2014, has very strongly sapped all the workers, but during the first months they were happy to see their hard work time reduced.

From an "etic" perspective, the workers interviewed 10 years ago have experienced improvements in their overall standard of living over the last decade: some have renovated their homes with lavish furnishings and accessories; others have finally become home owners by taking out a mortgage. All dress fashionably and have well-groomed hair and nails; they go on vacation in the summer and flaunt the occasionally flashy item of expenditure (e.g., birthday parties in clubs), made possible in some cases through loans on income or financing from the bank. Precisely due to this evident increase in overall living standards (which often coincide with rising levels of debt), workers' worries about the future are evident. The signs of the heavy toil of factory work shows clearly: data from the FIOM trade union (National Metalworkers' Federation) show that the number of workers suffering from work-related conditions has increased enormously over the last few years. The women in the FIOM sample complain about problems related to their backs, their necks, tendons, etc.[7] Such suffering has increased their awareness that they have paid for their status as workers on coveted permanent contracts entailing hard work and physical pain. Alongside these observations, interviews carried out 10 years ago suggested a relatively short-term vision of the future, beginning with the awareness that even a factory like Fiat could experience periods of crisis. Now this crisis has clearly arrived and women workers have quickly set up defense mechanisms in the form of small-scale activities, which help supplement their incomes. One woman sells catalogue cleaning products; another returned to her work as a beautician, working from home (and on a cash-in-hand basis). Yet another woman helps her parents in their pizzeria, while another works as a cleaner for a business. Thus, the temporary stoppages in production and recourse to redundancy payments has resulted in the re-emergence of precarious and clandestine labor that characterized the work experience of these women before they entered the factory. In the past, these activities were aimed at guaranteeing survival in the absence of work and a proper income, whereas at present they aim to supplement an income that has diminished significantly and is subject to new threats and uncertainties. In economic terms, this means that there is a parallel informal economy operating alongside the "official" jobs of women workers. In social terms, there seems to be a recovery of a culture of "making do", an ethic of working hard, and a capacity to creatively put together various skills and abilities so as to slip into the small spaces of the labor market: a modality that is typical of the local subsistence strategies that were in place before the changes brought about by the introduction of the Fiat factory into the area.

It is difficult to estimate the significance of these new complementary forms of informal work, both in terms of their nature and the extent of their diffusion, and in terms of their future relevance. That said, the import of these forms of employment is once again both economic and cultural. From an economic point of view, informal jobs are a defense mechanism against the threat of downward mobility as a consequence of stagnant or declining incomes. From a cultural perspective, we may well be observing a form of "female pragmatism" in the sense of the term as it used by Signorelli (1990, 1993). In other words, pragmatism understood not in terms of an abstract "natural" attribute, but rather as the cultural correlation to historically determined material conditions. In this instance, these conditions affect women in rural areas of Southern Italy characterized by high levels of informal agricultural work. This means that in this current historical phase and under the new working conditions characterized by insecure employment in the factory, there is a re-emergence of the ability and willingness to combine small jobs and diverse sources of income. This should not be equated with a simple "survival" of the past, but should be understood as a re-signification of economic and cultural behaviors that draw on past local experience that proves to be useful in the present. They are perceived as strategies for the future precisely at a time when working in Fiat is losing some of its original connotations of stability and safety. Work is thus transformed among the Fiat employees as well, towards more flexible and unstable forms of employment, very much in line with the characteristics of global work (as highlighted by Beck already in the early 2000s). The possibility of fragmenting work and assembling it in response to particular objectives, different phases of productivity and market trends is reinforced. But above all, the vulnerability of workers has increased as they find themselves in a context in which the rules are uncertain and unknown and in which historical mediators such as trade unions are absent or have diminishing influence which means that: "without a collective counterweight, more than ever dependent, they [the workers] work within flexible webs, whose sense and whose rules are by now indecipherable to most of them" (Beck 2000: 123)

Consequently, the meaning of work has undergone profound changes. Notwithstanding the slowdown of production, which translates into three working days per week, the speed of the daily production line has increased, such that toil and stress are still very present and tempered only by the shorter working week. From interviews and discussions with employees, it is clear that this new work regime embodies an effective compromise between a working class with decreased organizational capacity and a company that needs to continue to push production forward, even when confronted with reduced market demand. To all this should be added, as is clearly recounted by the workers, an environment of rigid and pressing controls by management and bosses as well as changed union relations. More specifically, the management personnel have become progressively less open to dialogue and mediation with the result that, with each problem that arises or each need that is expressed by the workers, the response is increasingly: "these are the conditions, if you don't like them, you can leave". It is widely understood that the fear of losing one's job and the lack of alternatives make this an effective and convincing message. At the same time, the role of the union has radically changed, both in terms of new norms that result in the exclusion of an entire section of the organized workforce (the FIOM, the most active and vocal union in the factory) and a generalized system of clientelism, which is already widely diffused within the factory and has produced deep mistrust among many workers and a loss of credibility of their representatives. The sighting of union organizers freely roaming the factory even if they were not engaged in the work process was frequently invoked during conversations with workers, as was the impression that the union organizer was simply a mediator in individual cases. Many workers express a sense of disaffection, of disappointment, of concerns about new job instabilities. These views reflect the increasingly difficult conditions of work at the factory and the growing loss of confidence in what the future might hold. Indeed, at this critical stage of the company's trajectory there is a return to a short-term vision of the future among workers who are unable to predict events beyond a fairly immediate point. Such short-term perceptions were similarly described by a number of Italian scholars as typical of the unemployed youth or those with unstable jobs, especially in the South (Leccardi 1996; Cesareo 2005; Buzzi et al. 2007). This short-term vision of the future now characterizes a working class that is no longer young, living in a relatively underdeveloped area with high unemployment. These workers experienced a phase of employment stability but must now rethink the present, hampered by the impossibility of imagining an alternative work out of the Fiat factory. From being the bearer of certainty and stability, employment at Fiat now presents a new uncertainty that reaches beyond the workers themselves to the local community as a whole. "If Fiat falls here, everything will fall", was the comment of many merchants and long-term residents of the town, who were acutely aware that incomes from Fiat are an element of stability and a driver of the larger economy. Without them, the local economy would certainly suffer.

Conclusion

The case of the Fiat factory, observed over a period of 22 years, illustrates the ascent and decline of an industrial project, the future of which is now dark. The factory was born out of the prospect of reorganizing Italian automobile manufacturing through the importation and tradition of an exogenous (Japanese) organizational model. Local conditions of increased productivity and containment of costs were not sufficient to turn the company around. After only 21 years of activity the company is experiencing faltering production and new forms of work instability. Launched through merger operations at the global scale with the acquisition of Chrysler (2014), Fiat has seemingly shifted its interests away from Italian factories, increasing the risks of exposure of Italian workers to the effects of outsourcing (in part already a reality with plants in Poland and Brazil).

In the 1990s, the opening of the plant in Melfi was welcomed as a dream of economic and modernizing liberation, driven by the largest Italian mechanical engineering company, a protagonist of the post-Second World War economic boom and of the country's modernization. However, the factory disappointed the high expectations of the local population and institutions who had placed such great hopes on a relatively futile myth. New forms of work introduced by the factory divided tasks into those that demanded high levels of skill and worker responsibility more typical of so-called Post-Fordism, and other tasks that were characterized by their heavy, repetitive and alienating nature, which were continuous with the older Fordist assembly line. Ten years ago women workers expressed a stronger or weaker identification with their work depending on the particular tasks they carried out. However, this identification was always set within a clear sense of awareness of having left behind work of a more precarious nature, work that was invisible or poorly paid, which had characterized the work experience of their youth. It is important to note that the new relationships arising from factory work did not eradicate neighborhood relations, including small-scale subsistence activities and the exchange of help and services, or the sharing of shopping. Such exchanges continued to be based in part on face to face relationships and pre-existing neighborhood networks and were partly inspired by new needs linked simultaneously to consumption and to saving, driven by working conditions and an assured income.

The current decline throws a heavy shadow over the future of the Melfi factory and more generally on the place of Fiat in Italy. Women workers today seem to have achieved a new status, become more sophisticated in terms of consumption, and more flexible and modern in terms of lifestyle. At a family level, new conditions have made it easier for couples to separate and for new families to emerge, not least as a result of women's greater economic autonomy. Faced with the possibility that all of this may disappear, women seem able to reorganize and resort to improvised strategies to supplement their income by taking on small jobs and undertaking work that is paid "under the table". At present, such strategies seem to be effective in making up for the loss in income caused by faltering production; from a longer-term perspective, they also appear to represent a kind of partial reassurance in the face of a new and different phase of uncertainty.

Over a period of 21 years, women workers have seemingly passed from an older model of work instability, characterized by invisibility, a lack of guarantees and low incomes to a new uncertainty, whose cloudy future masks a still unknown destination. Generally, the Melfi workers' experience can be situated within a global panorama of a progressive, relentless "disappearance" of the manufacturing industry and the manual labor class in the face of a growing service economy, typical of the post-industrial era. However, as clearly pointed out by Mollona, "old-fashioned" industry has certainly not disappeared. If anything, this subject begs further ethnographic investigation so as to better understand the forms and paths that industry and its workers will take in the future (Mollona 2009). In the Melfi case study, fieldwork reveals a process of cultural hybridization, which mixes historical memories, prior personal experiences of work instability and the ability to combine subsistence strategies and existential readjustments. In this process, the past merges with the present and proves to be a valuable resource in the efforts to reorganize life strategies in the face of a tough future. Memories of a peasant past, of fathers and grandfathers who labored in the fields to earn a day's work, of emigration (to the north of Italy or abroad), and of the very difficult living conditions of migrants, also appears in a number of interviews as a cultural reference driven by a new need, or by the necessity of facing the possible tragedy of losing one's job.

An ethnographic approach reveals points of overlap, cultural syncretism, processes of hybridization between the organizational company model and forms of work on the one hand, and, on the other hand, local practices and cultural horizons. Ethnographic investigation thus allows for a deeper understanding of the problematic developments surrounding the Fiat factory in Melfi which, over the course of 21 years produced, at the local level, at first a turning point in terms of job security and stability and then gradually a transformation towards the current darker phase of uncertainty and instability. In the face of such change, new hybrid cultural processes become strategies of self-defense and a means of coping with present conditions, frequently drawing on their own and their families' histories to provide a framework for the present and the future. Ilaria, a single 38-year-old assembly line worker who is struggling to finish her college degree, pointed out that her family had managed to survive by drawing on their resourcefulness:

> My parents never starved to death. My father built coffins, he worked in an airplane factory, then he studied and became a hairdresser, he learned to work on trees ... my mother worked as baby-sitter, a cashier in a super-market. They were migrants, and so I'm not afraid of moving either.

This phrase reminds us that in the recent past this has been a place characterized by uncertain work, of carrying out several different jobs and different kinds of work, of the need for mobility in the search for work. Perhaps this memory will help the Melfi workers in the task of constructing a cultural horizon that will help them face the crisis.

At the global level, the last vestiges of the Italian myth of Fiat as a giant manufacturer—revived in Melfi in the 1990s in what was an already critical phase—can be seen as an expression of a more general transformation of global industry, set within the crisis currently faced by Western economies. In this context, workers in industrial manufacturing are transforming their identities, their work arrangements, and their life strategies according to ever less self-determined trajectories that are not, however, without forms of resistance, mediations and the search for diverse and original local solutions.

Notes

1 The acronym SATA stands for Automobile Society for Advanced Technologies.
2 Amaranth (reddish-rose) was the color of the Melfi SATA workers' overalls, entirely different from the traditional blue coveralls that have long been symbolic of the metalworkers. The choice of a different coverall, of a more sportive design and vivacious color, explicitly inspired by a casual youthful look, was the sign of an intended break with the past, a symbol of a new working class, born in the spirit of post-Fordism and the new integrated factory. In recent years the overalls have again been modified, this time to a sky-blue, standardized across all the plants. Officially, the change was motivated by economic reasons, but one might legitimately surmise that under new conditions and following a massive strike which took place in Melfi in the Spring of 2004 (Ferrero and Lombardi 2004); maintaining such a different overall, which had become famous in the mass media and the literature, no longer made sense (see also Carrieri et al. 1993).
3 "Fiatist" (*Fiatisti*) is an invented term that, in Italian, denotes protagonists of "Fiatism," a movement with particular characteristics, and specific rules, behaviors and ethic.
4 The 2011 ISTAT (the Italian National Institute of Statistics) reported that in 2010 the rate of Italian female labor force participation was at relatively low levels and experienced a rather slow increase compared to the EU average. At 46.1 percent in 2010, the Italian indicator was 12 percentage points lower that the European average. In the South, rates of female unemployment were twice as high as those in the North (15.8 compared to 7 percent), accompanied by an inactivity rate that was 24 percentage points higher (63.7 compared to 39.6 percent: source ISTAT 2011).
5 A section of the literature celebrates this industrial operation, highlighting that the Chrysler actions did not cost Fiat anything, and that instead the merger paid off with the inputs received regarding technological know-how and new management thus achieving "a brilliant and extremely rapid rescue operation, an out-and-out blitz (...) that would otherwise have been absolutely unworkable and impracticable in an Italian reality" (Varvelli and Varvelli, 2009: 12). There also exists, however, and equally authoritative literature, as delineated below, that is more critical and attentive in its evaluation of the actual results of the operation, which were in fact far from positive. This literature also carefully situates these results within the history of the company and its relationship with national policy.

6 Two crucial events occurred in the restructuring of relations between the company and the labor unions by which Marchionne considerably modified the organization of work with an eye to company "governability": a new agreement for the Fiat plant at Pomigliano (Naples) in June of 2010 and then for Mirafiori (Turin) in the fall of the same year. The next year, with law 238/2011, the exclusion of unions that refused to sign the agreements with the company was ratified. This meant, in substance, the elimination of union representatives from FIOM, the leftwing union with the greatest number of subscribers and votes within the company, and which had long embodied the voice of opposition. Its exclusion walking hand in hand with the introduction of greater work instability and flexibility, both in terms of overtime and in terms of stoppages of production, the start of a more intense work rhythm (e.g., the new Ergo-Uas work time system), and the containment of strikes.

7 Results from a national survey supported by the FIOM trade union in 2008 (Source: Fiom-Cgil 2010) shows that, from a sample of 358 workers who responded to a questionnaire administered in SATA, more than 95 percent reported having backaches, muscular pains in the shoulders and neck, muscular pains in the arms and hands. More than 29 percent declared having never missed a day due to illness. In addition to these results, the first investigation conducted by FIOM and INCA (National Confederate Assistance Institute) between 2009 and 2010 on hidden professional maladies, revealed considerable problems in identifying professional illnesses on-site, combined with the low levels of reporting of professional illness by workers.

References

Althabe, G., and Sélim, M. (2000). *Approcci etnologici della modernità*. Torino: L'Harmattan Italia.

Appadurai, A. (2001). *Modernità in polvere*. Rome: Meltemi.

Balbo, L. (1978). 'La doppia presenza'. *Inchiesta* 32: 3–6.

Banfield, E. C. (1961). *Una comunità del Mezzoggiorno*. Bologna: Il Mulino (*The Moral Basis of a Backward Society*, Glencoe: The Free Press, 1958).

Barbagallo, F. (1997). *Napoli fine Novecento. Politici, camorristi, imprenditor*. Turin: Einaudi.

Becchi, A. (1990). 'Catastrofi, sviluppo e politica del territorio: alcune riflessioni sull'esperienza italiana'. *Archivio di Studi urbani e regionali* XIX:(3): 3–36.

Beck, U. (2000). *Il lavoro nell'epoca della fine del lavoro*. Turin: Einaudi (*Schone neue Arbeitswelt. Vision: Welburgergesellshaft*. Frankfurt am Main: Campus verlag Gmbh).

Berta, G. (2011). *FIAT Chrysler e la deriva dell'Italia industriale*. Bologna: Il Mulino.

Bonazzi, G. (1993). *Il tubo di cristallo. Modello giapponese e fabbrica integrata alla FIAT Auto*. Bologna: Il Mulino.

Buzzi, C., Cavalli, A., and De Lillo, A. (eds) (2007). *Rapporto giovani. Sesta indagine IARD sulla condizione giovanile in Italia*. Bologna: Il Mulino.

Carrieri, M., Cerrutti, G., and Garibaldo, F. (1993). *Fiat Punto e a capo. Problemi e prospettive da Termoli a Melfi*. Rome: Ediesse.

Cerruti, G. and Rieser, V. (1991). Fiat: Qualitá Totale e Fabbrica Integrata. Roma: Ediesse.

Cesareo, V. (ed) (2005). *Ricomporre la vita. Gli adulti giovani in Italia*. Rome: Carocci.

Comito, V. (2005). *L'ultima crisi. La Fiat tra mercato e finanza*. Naples: L'ancora del Mediterraneo.

Cuoco, L. (1980). Rapporto sullo stato e sulle prospettive delle aree terremotate, *Rassegna dell'Economia Lucana* 6: 11–47.

D'Aloisio, F. (2003). *Donne in tuta amaranto. Trasformazione del lavoro e mutamento culturale alla Fiat-Sata di Melfi*. Milan: Guerini & Associati.

D'Aloisio F. (2014). *Vita di fabbrica. Cristina racconta il decollo e la crisi della Fiat-Sata di Melfi*. Milan: Franco Angeli.

Davis, J. (1989) [1973]. *Pisticci. Terra e famiglia*, Castrovillari: Teda Edizioni [(1973) *Land and family in Pisticci*. London: The Athlone Press].

Facchini, C. (ed) (2008). *Conti aperti. Denaro, asimmetrie di coppie e solidarietà tra le generazioni*. Bologna: Il Mulino.

Ferrero, P., and Lombardi, A. (2004). *La primavera di Melfi. Cronaca di una lotta operaia*. Rome: Edizioni Punto Rosso.

Fine-Davis, M., Fagnani, J., Giovannini, D., Hojgaard, L., and Clarke, H. (2007). *Padri e madri: I dilemmi della conciliazione famiglia lavoro*. Bologna: Il Mulino.

Fiom-Cgil (2010). *Il piano industriale Fiat 2010–2014*. Potenza: Osservatorio sull'Industria metalmeccanica.

Ghezzi, S. (2007). *Etnografia storica dell'imprenditorialità in Brianza*. Milan: Franco Angeli.

Ginatempo, N. (ed) (1993). *Donne del Sud. Il prisma femminile sulla questione meridionale*. Palermo: Gelka.

Ginsborg, P. (1989). *Storia d'Italia dal dopoguerra a oggi, Società e politica 1943–1988*. Turin: Einaudi.

Ginsborg, P. (1998). *L'Italia del tempo presente. Famiglia, società civile, stato 1980–1996*. Turin: Einaudi.

Gribaudi, G. (1999). *Donne, Uomini, Famiglie*, Naples: L'Ancora del Mediterraneo.

Hitten, E. (1970). *Industrializzazione senza sviluppo. Gela, una storia meridionale*. Milan: Franco Angeli.

ISTAT. (2011). *Rapporto annuale. La situazione del paese nel 2010*. Rome. Available at: www.istat.it/en/. Accessed September 24, 2012.

Kilani, M. (1994). *Antropologia. Una introduzione*. Bari: Dedalo.

Leccardi, C. (1996). *Futuro breve. Le giovani donne e il futuro*. Torino: Rosenberg & Sellier.

Mollona, M. (2009). 'General Introduction', in M. Mollona, G. De Neeve and J. Parry (ed) *Industrial Work and Life: An Anthropological Reader*. Oxford and New York: Berg, pp. xi–xxviii.

Naldini, M. and Saraceno, C. (2011). *Conciliare famiglia e lavoro. Vecchi e nuovi patti tra i sessi e le generazioni*. Bologna: Il Mulino.

Ohno, T. (1993). *Lo spirito Toyota*. Turin: Einaudi.

Oppo, A., Piccone Stella, S., and Signorelli, A. (ed) (2000). *Maternità, Identità, Scelte. Percorsi dell'emancipazione femminile nel Mezzogiorno*. Naples: Liguori.

Papa, C. (1999). *Antropologia dell'impresa*. Milan: Guerini & Associati.

Piselli, F. (1981). *Parentela e emigrazione. Mutamento e continuità in una comunità calabrese*. Turin: Einaudi.

Revelli, M. (1989). *Lavorare in Fiat*. Milan: Garzanti.

Ricci, A. (1993). 'Operazione Prato verde'. *Dimensione*, 1: 23–24.

Sélim, M. (1996). 'L'enterprise: emprise ideologique, mondialisation et evolution des problématiques'. *Journal des anthropologues*, 66/67: 19–28.

Signorelli, A. (1983). *Chi può e chi aspetta. Giovani e clientelismo in un'area interna del Mezzogiorno*. Naples: Liguori.

Signorelli, A. (1990). 'Il pragmatismo delle donne. La condizione femminile nella trasformazione delle campagne', in P. Bevilacqua (ed) *Storia dell'agricoltura italiana in età contemporanea*, vol. II, *Uomini e classi*, Padova: Marsilio, pp. 625–659.

Signorelli, A. (1993). 'Ancora sul pragmatismo delle donne', in N. Ginatempo (ed) *Donne del Sud. Il prisma femminile sulla questione meridionale*. Palermo: Gelka, pp. 67–77.

Trigilia, C. (1994). *Sviluppo senza autonomia. Effetti perversi delle politiche nel Mezzogiorno*. Bologna: Il Mulino.

Varvelli, R., and Varvelli, M.L. (2009). *Marchionne, la Fiat e gli altri*, Milano: Il Sole 24 ore.

Volpato, G. (2008). *Fiat Group Automobilies. Le nuove sfide*. Bologna: Il Mulino.

Walker, C.R., and Guest, R.H. (1952), *The Man on the Assembly line*, Harvard: Harvard University Press.

Zinn, D.L. (2001), *La raccomandazione. Clientelismo vecchio e nuovo*. Rome: Donzelli

6 Opening the Black Box of Employability

Change Competence, Masculinity and Identity of Steelworkers in Germany and the UK[1]

Vera Trappmann

Introduction

Employability is a highly debated concept. It became prominent during the Lisbon process as a core element of the European Commission's strategy to make the European Union (EU) one of the most competitive knowledge-based societies in the globalized world. The Europe 2020 strategy for more growth and jobs sees employability as a precondition to achieve the targets of an increased employment rate. Against this backdrop an extensive literature has emerged critiquing the relevant merits of employability. Focused at a macro-level, most of the debate has considered questions relating to how to achieve and implement employability. A number of studies have also sought to locate, in an empirical sense, the concept of employability with aspects of qualification, training and career development, yet very little research has been conducted at a micro-level. Significantly, understanding of what employability means for employees or how it may (or may not) be achieved by individuals, remains underdeveloped. In this chapter, employability is deconstructed at the micro-level.

The analysis addresses the question of what employability means for the individual worker and how this may be achieved in daily life. The main argument presented here is that employability should be understood beyond the individual struggle to find new employment or to remain in employment, as it also addresses broader challenges about personal identity. Employability should not be conflated with a person's working life; rather, it should be understood as influenced and shaped by broader life experiences. Consequently, to be employable means more than being well trained as it encompasses "change competence", what I call the successful management of change, the ability to cope with change and new challenges, and the ability to develop an interest in, and enthusiasm for, new forms of knowledge and capabilities, which, I suggest, requires a basic level of self-confidence—a capability that is acquired in the life world.[2]

Furthermore, this chapter reveals the extent to which employability should be understood as a gendered concept[3] analyzing how employability is constituted and achieved over the entire life course. The argument is developed through an actor-oriented analysis of the practices contributing to employability making use of Bourdieu's conceptual tools of field, actor and habitus. Empirically, it draws upon biographies of redundant steelworkers from West Germany[4] and the UK collected in 2002–05.

The chapter is structured as follows. First, in the literature review, the conception of employability is discussed, notions of masculinity and gender are presented, and Bourdieu's concepts of the field, habitus and capital are exposed. Following a presentation of the research design, I will explore the biographical accounts of steelworkers who have recently experienced redundancy and who were struggling in relation to employability and employment. The analysis is structured around the key concerns that assist or constrain the search for employability, namely masculinity, identity and change competence. In conclusion, the role of labor market institutions in West Germany and the UK is evaluated arguing that they do not yet succeed in enhancing employability as they reproduce traditional gender roles, and formation of identity through employment.

Employability: Debates on Policies/Employment, Gender and Bourdieu

The concept of employability became popular as one of the original four pillars of the European Employment Strategy (EES): employability, entrepreneurship, adaptability and equal opportunities. At the EU summit in Lisbon in 2000, the EU set targets for 2010 of 70 percent in employment and 60 percent female participation in the labor market, and employability was seen as one possible way to facilitate this. In 2003, the EES was reformed, and employability then disappeared from the list of priorities, becoming an indirect although still important goal; it is now part of the Europe 2020 initiative, the EU strategy for growth intending to increase employment rates to bring them up to a level of 75 percent. In 2008, the need to increase employability was underscored as part of the European Commission's European Economic Recovery Plan (European Commission 2008). The objective of employability is to ensure that people can develop the right skills to take up job opportunities in a fast-changing world, to "acquire human capital in order to improve their competitive position on the labor market" (Lefresne 1999: 466), and "maintain the ability to participate in the processes of recruitment, selection and career progressing" (Gore 2005: 341–342; see Heyes 2013). Research on employability has analyzed what qualification and skills enable employability, emphasizing soft skills (Marks and Scholarius 2008; McQuaid and Lindsay 2005). However, it is unclear how these soft skills are achieved. Is training a sufficient instrument? Is the reform of labor market policy towards more activating labor market policy an adequate prerequisite, or does employability comprise a still more complex approach?

The concept has thus some substantial weaknesses. First, it has often been (mis)used to threaten workers with the need to be responsible for their own capacity for securing an albeit insecure job, or in other words, for becoming so called self-entrepreneurs (Voß and Pongratz 1998) by marketing and reinvesting in their own labor power. As employment could no longer be guaranteed, only the prospect of employment, in the form of employability, became a political objective. Hence, in politics, employability has for a long time only been perceived as a problem that has primarily concerned disadvantaged groups within the labor market, blaming the victim as individuals are seen as being at risk or as unemployed because they do not possess sufficient levels of human capital (Coffield 1999). In this sense, unemployment is considered to be an individual responsibility, where the unemployed are somehow handicapped and hence excluded from the world of work (Stuart and Greenwood 2006).

The second concern is that employability is a gender-blind concept (Gottschall 2000). As yet, no far-reaching analysis linking the concept to existing gender analysis has been made. But much can be learned about employability by linking it to debates about gender arrangements. With West and Zimmerman (1987) I argue that gender is interactively *produced* (what West and Zimmerman call "doing gender") and can then be understood as an (institutionalized) practice, "a configuration of practice" (Connell 1995: 84). This is important to note in order to understand that gender identity is a relevant element in creating (or more likely, hindering) employability. Gendered practices have an influence on employability, particularly where the gendered division between work and the household is concerned. Pfau-Effinger (1999) distinguishes five different gender arrangements found across Europe that reflect the negotiated gendered division between work and household: (1) the family economy model, (2) the male breadwinner/female home-carer model, (3) the male breadwinner/female part-time-carer model (4) the dual breadwinner/state-carer model where the state is regarded as more competent in providing care than private households, (5) the dual breadwinner/dual carer model (Pfau-Effinger (1999: 63ff). Although the labor markets in the UK and Germany represent different systems—liberal and corporatist capitalisms (Esping-Andersen 2000) according to Pfau-Effinger both countries can be classified as primarily characterized by the strong male breadwinner model, enacted by institutions like schools, taxation systems and parental leave policies, which favor women staying at home to care for the children (Lewis and Ostner 1994; Crompton 2002). While it is middle class political and social values that inform the male breadwinner model, it is also a suitable ideal for the working class, as "In Britain and Germany it became part of the badge of working class respectability to keep a wife" (Crompton 2002: 25). Even if a pure male breadwinner model didn't work out for the working class, post-war governments built up institutions on the assumption that male breadwinner models were the norm (see Daly and Lewis 1998: 9 for the UK and for West Germany see Pfau-Effinger 1999: 68). Although for some, attitudes to gender roles may have changed, the extent of the persistence of gendered models is astonishing (Crompton 2002). Even unemployed young (middle class) men see themselves as the breadwinners, or at least aspire to become so in the future. Against all predictions, waged work remains central to young men's identities, and older notions of masculinity persist (Halford 2005).

A recent study by Charles and James (2005) shows that in regions that have been historically influenced by heavy industry, such as the areas associated with steel industry, such as South Wales or the Ruhr area, the male breadwinning ideology persists, although it may be perceived as old-fashioned (Charles and James 2005). The normative expectations that men will fulfill the role of providers prevail even where women are de facto the main breadwinners.

It is worth recognizing that while women's participation in the labor market has increased, this has not led to changes in the domestic division of labor or in the allocation of caring responsibilities (Duncan et al. 2003: 316, compare also Speakman and Marchington 1999; Singley and Heynes 2005; Pilcher 2000; Crompton et al. 2005). As Yeandle suggests, with the increasing employment of women in the UK and Unified Germany, there occurs a shift away from the male breadwinner/female carer model, towards a sixth model, that of the dual breadwinner/marketized female domestic economy model (Yeandle 1999).[5]

Recently, Bourdieu's work has inspired research in economic sociology (Svendson and Svendson 2004; Widick 2004; Florian and Hildebrandt 2006) and related fields (Swartz and Zolberg 2004), yet labor studies remain a terrain that has been little explored by Bourdieu's disciples (with the exception of Willott and Griffin 2004). Nevertheless, Bourdieu's theoretical perspective offers a very helpful tool, both to understand and to link all the above-mentioned phenomena. In particular, the conceptual devices of field, habitus and capital are relevant to the questions raised here. To define a social field, one needs to know the object that actors contend for in a particular field. According to Bourdieu, actors struggle over the monopoly of naming what constitutes social reality in a field (Bourdieu 1989; 1985).[6] Involvement in a field shapes the habitus and because of the habitus players are disposed to recognize and play the field. Meuser stresses that habitus is gendered in such a way that even if individuals lose capital in a field, the gendered habitus is not put into question. Life within or with a habitus produces security, and people try to sustain this security, thus reproducing the habitus. In a study on skilled workers and managers, Meuser showed men's strategies where the structures to which the habitus referred are being eroded. By a process of "normalization", disturbing factors are integrated into the normative order, often by resorting to claims based on a biologically founded gender order. For example, at times when the role of the breadwinner is threatened by loss of income or by the additional income of wives, the order is still sustained through the intervention of an opposition between breadwinning as a male responsibility and childbearing as a female responsibility. Another strategy, that of "nihilization", implies doubting stated facts, such as not accepting women's labor market discrimination, referring to structural rational economic reasons for their disadvantaged position (Meuser 1998).

Narratives of Work and Unemployment: George and Walter

The following discussion draws on biographical interviews conducted with steelworkers in West Germany and the United Kingdom.[7] I focus on two biographical accounts, that of George from the UK and Walter from Germany, which are supplemented by data drawn from other interviews carried out in these two countries. Of course, the discussion of two cases cannot claim to be representative, but it affords an insight into the complexity of the subject and highlights core aspects of the argument of this chapter.

Walter is German and was 45 years old at the time of the interview in March 2002. He was married and had two sons, who were 18 and 13 years old. Upon leaving school Walter's only career plan was to work in a steel plant. The company (H) that he joined was within a short walking distance from his home. He joined H by chance: a friend of his had already been offered employment there, and he informed Walter about a vacancy. Walter applied and was hired. He was promoted to the position of assistant foreman, and later became shift manager, for which he received two years' training. During these two years, apart from his apprenticeship, he feels he received the most systematic training of all his time at H. In 1995 the plant/factory was taken over by another firm, and together with other workers, Walter was given the opportunity of moving to another production facility. But he decided that, for the sake of his family, he would not relocate. Although production at his plant was continuously being reduced, he did not think he would ever be made redundant. This was because the union had not indicated that it saw the final closure coming and because Walter had faith in the paternalistic nature of the plant, which he thought would prevent his redundancy from taking place. Walter had worked for H all his working life until he was made redundant due to restructuring. At the time of the interview, he had been unemployed for five months.

George is British and was 52 years old at the time of the interview in March 2002, and was employed as a manager for a trade union-based training organization. He has lived in the same steel community in South Wales all his life. He was employed with one and the same steel company since 1974 until his redundancy in 2001. He had already experienced redundancy twice before when he was dismissed because of restructuring. He had lost his job following his craft apprenticeship; he started two new jobs as an unskilled laborer, while applying for several positions in his craft, but with no success. He started to adapt to production work, and worked in a number of different positions until he was able to undertake all the tasks included in an entire shift. His personal life was also full of challenges. He is currently married to his third wife. His first wife took custody of their twins when they divorced, against his wishes. George re-married, but domestic problems followed after his heart attack and his second wife left him. His third and current wife has a 16-year-old daughter from a previous marriage. George had two heart operations in 1996. In 1997 his first wife died and that same year his current wife discovered that she had cancer, which is now in remission. Then his father died in 1999. His son (one of twins from his first marriage) lived with his grandfather (George's father) and was very close to him. Following the death of his grandfather, George's son became depressed and committed suicide.

On the basis of these two cases, I would suggest that employability is linked to three factors: first, to the subjects' concept of masculinity; second, to the dominant gender arrangements they live in, and third, to the extent of change competence they are able to develop. I will discuss each in the following sections more deeply.

Masculinity: Being a 'Real Man'

Steel is a particularly useful identifier for a male professional [employment] career. Steel production is adventurous and dangerous; it interacts with the natural element of fire and serves as a base material for key consumer objects such as cars and aircraft. Steel stands for male values like mobility and dynamism, and its characteristics are often used metaphorically to describe masculinity ("firm as steel"). Maybe we could say that the steel industry is a male industry par excellence, in ways that are similar to what Thomas and Bailey claim for seafaring, in that "it epitomizes the hegemonic masculine image of a 'hero', working in a (predominantly) all male, physically dangerous environment" (2006: 133). Being employed in the steel industry is a social statement that identifies those working in it as a "real man". Indeed, steelworkers almost identify with the product they are producing, and this is true for both countries. Just to give an example from Germany:

> My motto has always been: a steelworker is born a steelworker, and he dies as a steelworker. It's the same with miners. You are born a miner and in most cases, you leave the mill as a miner.
>
> (Dieter)

To "be a real man" means to perform masculine roles in a specific cultural setting. Being a real man is related to doing "real" work, which means engaging in blue-collar work. Although this type of heavy work is disappearing, identification with that traditional type of worker is still very strong

(Hindrichs et al. 1997). A study by Lupton (2006) that compares blue-collar and white-collar jobs for men comes to a similar conclusion. As a librarian in Lupton's study explains: "I know that my step-dad is a real man's man . . . he sees white-collar jobs and managerial positions as women's . . . whereas your blue-collar job is for men. [. . .] I felt probably not like a proper man as result of being a librarian . . . [. . .] A [librarian] is not an accepted role for men. It is not heavy, nor is it hard: it is white-collar, it's something which doesn't take any guts, any danger whatsoever" (Lupton 2006: 116).

When we look at the biographies, workers' worries about the job crisis are less about securing employment, and more about the status of their *male* identity. The men fear losing their masculinity if they lose their jobs. On the other hand, the right kind of work reaffirms these gendered identities. As Walter notes: "Worse than everything is hanging around so uselessly. [. . .] The main thing is I want to work". Walter's attitude is shared by many of his colleagues. Sitting around makes them depressed. To give some examples: "I don't like sitting around. I must do something. I am used to it". "I can't pause". "To be honest, it is very important to me to work until I am 60 years old". Therefore, the experience of redundancy leads to a feeling of superfluousness (see also Franzpötter 2003). However, just being active is not sufficient; the work has to be of a certain status. As Walter clarifies:

> But I won't take just any odd job. Today, now that I'm in this situation myself, I can understand people who are out of work but refuse to do some jobs. I mean, delivering bread or something, I wouldn't do that. If I really can't work in my trade, then the money has at least got to be somewhere near right.

A third aspect is important here: besides the issue of a man's status on the labor market, traditional gender arrangements make him a "real man", too. While he is the breadwinner, his wife stays at home caring for the children. He recalls:

> I met my girlfriend when I was 22, and at 23 we got married. Three years later our first son came into the world, and then after a while, the second one. My wife is Italian and she's two years younger than me. In her job she did what most Italians did then: she worked in a pizzeria where she used to live, and here she worked for a launderette. When our first son was born, she stopped working and never started again.

Having a job allows Walter to care for the basic needs of his family; his earnings mean that his wife can stay at home. This is also relevant for Jason, a British worker, who explained that his main concern in relation to redundancy was to do with the distribution of responsibilities within the family. He said: "I didn't think it was really fair on my missus, she'd be out working and basically she was paying the mortgage and all that kind of stuff and I had nothing".

This reflects the results of an analysis of job insecurity carried out in South Wales by Charles and James (2003). They found that redundancy is particularly difficult for men as it affects their role as providers within the household. Although regarded as old-fashioned, the provider role structures expectations of masculine identity, as expressed by one of their interviewees: "The man is the breadwinner. This is how you're brought up anyway. If the man hasn't got a job it's not just the job insecurity, he feels less of a man, doesn't he". (Charles and James 2003: 547). And the picture is even more complex as illustrated by a study of seafarers on leave that shows that men can experience a loss of role and a threat to their masculine identities while still remaining the breadwinner, if they see themselves as losing power and authority when not performing their job in the public sphere (Thomas and Bailey 2006).

While breadwinning is the predominating role associated with men, it implies a traditional division of domestic labor. Furthermore, providing for the family includes a release from domestic duties at home. As Walter explained: "Sitting at home—what am I meant to do there? Great, then my wife comes and foists the vacuum cleaner on me: 'go and clean up (...)'. But when it comes to it I should actually be providing for my family". Domestic work is not considered to be an activity suited to men, and instead is closely associated with women's work and women's duties. This means that redundancy does not question or challenge the gendered division of domestic labor because a "real man" should be earning an income as the breadwinner *in contrast to* doing domestic work. So Walter would not take any job. Whatever job he takes on needs to be an appropriately "male" job, clearly illustrating how his gender identity hampers his employability by restricting his options.

Identity: A Field and Its Gender Dimension

The relationship between masculinity, home and work constitutes a field in the way that Bourdieu uses the term. The field we are investigating here then would be "a position in society" or more generally "(self-)identity". Although this might not be a distinct, defined field as can be claimed for education, I would still like to call it a field as it is constituted by the struggle of involved actors creating the field. Clearly, Walter fulfilled his job as a way of achieving a position in society:

> I'm actually quite happy with what I've achieved. I only had a secondary school education and then I developed into a foreman and quality controller, I'm actually really proud of that. I've never wanted to do anything else. Alternatives? I've never done my head in thinking about that, everything was all right as it was.

But by losing the job, he also loses his self-identity. George is a contrasting example, as he found new ways to define his masculinity outside the workplace. He committed himself to trade union activities and regained self-confidence and a position in society. As he explained, "Being a union official at the time, it was work that kept me going".[8]

Drawing on these experiences, I propose that by enlarging the field or by extending the location of struggle over identity and social position towards other fields, it is possible to introduce greater stability into social positions.[9] The experiences of steelworkers in Sweden offer an interesting example. Here, redundant ex-steel workers were trained to become male nurses (Randle and Heinemann 2004) and, while huge resistance had to be overcome among the men to perform what they saw as a female profession that would threaten their identities, the men subsequently felt that their lives had been enriched by the experience arising from the training and performance of a new, caring profession. Thus, their male identity became less dependent on being a "real man" in the narrow sense espoused by Walter and George.

The extension of the struggle for oneself or for one's identity towards different fields entails another advantage, that of gaining knowledge and capabilities that can be transformed into resources for employability in the field of working life. Employability, then, would mean not only to be skilled in relation to new challenges. Rather, it suggests that a man's social position is not only defined by the workplace and instead arises from the interplay of societal fields. Identity in the steel sector could also become a 'patchwork identity' (Beck 1992). Employability, in a very broad sense, means building an identity through social fields so it becomes clear that worker's relative adherence to—or flexibility towards—particular forms of masculinity affects their ability (or inability) to respond effectively to the crisis provoked by the loss of a job.

Change Competence

I define change competence as the ability to cope with change and confront new challenges, as well as having the capacity to develop new interests and engage with new knowledge. From the analysis of the biographies it is clear that there is something else, beyond the attainment of qualifications, which enables or hinders an individual's ability to cope with redundancy in a positive way that precludes psychological or other forms of breakdown and, perhaps, results in finding new employment. It seems obvious that George was able to overcome unemployment, most probably because he has had a lot of experience dealing with crisis and change. George's biography shows a propensity to persevere and a strength that dates back to his youth. Also, from very early on, George has been curious, as revealed in his statement about his decision to join the army: "I would join the Navy to get away from round here. At that time I wanted to see the world." From an early age he learned to accept change and make the best of it. As he explained: "In those days you had to take whatever you had, with a family to start looking after, you had no choice really".

In contrast, Walter's employment history has been characterized by stability. Walter claims that it was through the encouragement of the head of his craft guild that he had achieved advancement. Walter can be seen as belonging to what Loer (2003), in a study of the Ruhr area, called a "homebuddy", people who relied mainly on their community of relatives and neighborhood for problem-solving and for building a career (Loer 2003). Rather than formal qualifications, it was the recognition and support of peers (including supervisors) that helped him build a career. Embeddedness in his social milieu gave him a feeling of security that extended to the world of work. His refusal to take a new job at a plant located two hours away can be explained by his ties to the cultural milieu of the Ruhr area, such that a "strong region-specific social capital" (Skrobanek and Jobst 2006: 239) has impeded his mobility. Consequently, Walter seemed less well prepared to face the challenge of redundancy, having had few opportunities during his career to build the qualities associated with what I describe as change competence. What these examples suggest is that, when considering the experience of steelworkers in the current context of global production and high levels of job insecurity, a great deal will depend on their life trajectories and their experience. If, like Walter, redundancy is a man's first experience of change, the difficulties entailed by the loss of his job may well appear to be insurmountable. Like Walter, such workers will have no repertoire of experience from which to draw on in order to interpret their circumstances and elaborate effective strategies to deal with them. It is by having lived through troubled times caused by changes beyond their control that workers learn, and are thus better prepared to face the unexpected and confront the potential loss of work, identity and status, as George's story eloquently shows.

Institutional Support Systems Enhancing Employability

In both the United Kingdom and Germany, institutional support systems were in place to address the employment crisis entailed by restructuring of the steel industry. In West Germany, social partners created so-called transfer agencies to absorb mass redundancies by providing advice for outplacement and offering individual training as preparation for new job opportunities (GIB 2004; Backes and Knuth 2006). The transfer agency drew up individual employment contracts with workers who were under threat of redundancy. The workers received a pay-check of 90 percent of their former salary in the steel company. During the period of "employment" at the transfer agency, workers were supposed to make use of their time to further their professional profiles and redirect them beyond the steel industry, whether through re-training or in searching for a new job. If a worker obtained a new employment contract, there was the option for the new employer to receive co-financing from the transfer agency in support of the worker's salary. In effect, the new employees were given a trainee position in these companies that was financed by the transfer agency. If after two years of employment at a transfer agency no alternative employment was found, workers had to leave the agency and apply to the local labor-exchange office for further work placement services and unemployment benefit, which is equal to 60 percent of the last salary. After 12 months, entitlement to unemployment benefit came to an end, after which it was possible to claim what was referred to as "unemployment benefit 2", which has replaced social aid in recent labor market reforms (Trappmann 2004). In the United Kingdom, it was the steel trade union, the Iron and Steel Trades Confederation (ISTC), now called Community that initiated support through so-called Steel Partnership Training, now called Communitas, established in 1997. ISTC took the decision to facilitate the development of training and learning opportunities, and Communitas was conceived to fulfill this role. Its main objective was to provide training and support at a local level, sometimes directly but more often by facilitating provision of learning opportunities for workers through training projects that enabled partnerships across local employers, colleges and other educational providers (Wallis and Murray 2002).

These institutionalized support structures in both countries aimed at increasing workers' employability record by mobilizing workers *in case of* redundancy. But as this research has shown, critical factors influencing employability occur *prior* to redundancy. George has found new employment because of his personal predisposition of curiosity and due to the change competence he gained during his professional life. Walter has remained unemployed because of his inability to build his identity on any basis other than blue-collar work. For workers like Walter, employment is linked to social expectations about being a breadwinner, and these expectations, particularly the ability to provide for their families, constrain their ability to respond to new and critical events, such as the loss of their jobs. As long as there are no alternatives available to these workers through which they might recognize or appreciate masculinity from other perspectives or identify masculine practices in terrains other than those given by certain kinds of employment, men will continue to search for appropriately masculine jobs at a time when blue-collar work is in decline in the older industrial centers of Europe. It is through changing gender arrangements that men can increase employability—support instruments that only look at the structural challenge of re-employment are doomed to fail.

Learning from this research, a second prerequisite for support structures would be to enable change competence. More instruments have to be found that enable experiences of change while being employed. We could consider the possibility of establishing a temporary exchange of workers between different sites of a company, or training organized through a company network which would imply gaining an acquaintance with other companies' work organizations, etc.[10] The claim that there is a need for greater change competence in individuals' lives, however, should not be read as an endorsement of external flexibilization. Flexibility is only possible if all the risks of the modern market economy are not transferred to the individuals alone.

Labor market policy that only aims to mobilize workers, risks making those workers vulnerable and in particular, those who have little chance of finding alternative employment. However, the experience of change (and internal mobility) during regular employment, would prepare workers for external flexibility in case no other alternative exists.

Conclusion

This chapter has shown the connections that obtain between employment and identity and between displacement and biographical crisis. The role of masculinity as a claim for social struggle over the field of employment has been illustrated, while the relevance of the gender order in enhancing or hindering employability has been unmasked. If an individual is responsible for his own employability or his un-employability, there is a need to recognize the importance of the broader contexts in which employability is achieved. And context is about social structures in working life and private life; it is not about qualifications alone but about change competence, about gender and identity. As a precondition for employability, participation in social life beyond the working life, a better work-life balance and a reconciliation of work and family life is needed, all of which responds to the challenges of a modern, post-industrial world. This inclusive conception calls for a wider understanding of the currently narrow definition of employability in relation to labor market change.

Notes

1 This chapter is based on the project "Learnpartner: Learning in Partnership: Responding to the Restructuring of the European Steel and Metal Sector", funded by the European 5th Framework Programme under the title HPSE-CT2001–00049 (see Stuart 2005). The research was carried out at Sozialforschungsstelle Dortmund and the University of Leeds.
2 Change competence is not to be confused with flexicurity, the new European labor market regulation paradigm aimed at loosening job protection while enhancing employment and income security (Wilthagen 1998, Mufels and Wilthagen 2013).
3 The chapter thus seeks to contribute to recent calls for more gender-sensitive research in industrial relations (Edwards 2005), especially the need to gender "men" (Hanson 2002).
4 In our case, it is important to distinguish between West and East Germany, as the gender attitudes that prevailed in the former GDR differ from those current in the West, as a legacy of state socialism. Female employment participation was the norm and public childcare was universally available.
5 In the UK, dual breadwinner/state-carer model policies were failing due to the diminishing public expenditure for childcare that pushed towards privatized childcare solutions; in Germany, the absence of men's participation in caring activities makes a dual breadwinner/dual carer model incomplete (Yeandle 1999: 99f). An interesting example is provided by the Dutch Equal Opportunities Council's attempt to stimulate men's entry into private life by introducing a full working week of 32 hours instead of 38 hours. But the ambition failed: shorter working hours did not imply another division of domestic labor and caring. (Platenga et al. 1999:103).

6 To give an example, Bourdieu has shown for the field of education that in schools, it is not education that is (re-)produced or fought for, but social class (as in establishing the legitimacy of power and culture, ensuring good careers and so on) (Bourdieu 1988).
7 Interviews were also carried out in Sweden, Norway and Spain, which are not treated directly in this contribution but nevertheless inform the analysis. In total, in all countries 80 biographical interviews were carried out with interviewees who have faced a situation of job crisis, whether because they were at risk of losing their employment or because of having been made redundant. All interviews followed a common topic guideline, were taped, and afterwards transcribed. In the research design we focused on the narrative of a 'told' biography, with a strong interest in the 'realistic' content of the stories told. Following grounded theory (Glaser and Strauss 1967), we treated the life stories as *accounts of fact*, building categories and concepts arising from the interviews and assigning data accordingly. Through constant comparison, categories were continually improved and refined. The analysis was driven by the objective of gaining an understanding of how individuals coped with job loss and how they found new jobs or, alternatively, what factors impeded their employability. Interviews were assessed with the clear aim of identifying those experiences that helped workers to find a new job or to build up employability.
8 Factors leading to change in the field of male work-based identity, such as redundancy or the increasing rate of female employment, might lead to a perceived discrepancy between the normative ideal of a man and the experiences of individual men. As a result we see a growth of the fitness industry that offers new bodily repertoires for performances of masculinity. At the same time that there is evidence for an increase in health problems among men (Böhnisch 2003; Thiele 2002) and a new backlash *vis a vis* feminism (McRobbie 2009).
9 Another study has shown that men gain higher levels of satisfaction from life if they reduce their working hours and spend more time on other activities and interests. However, the study also highlights the extreme difficulties men faced when deciding for and living with part-time jobs. Not only is such a change evaluated as a downturn in their careers, but it is also the case that the traditional concept of masculinity is challenged (Schwerma 2004) as a breadwinner and provider and hard working man.
10 Much stronger support structures have been proposed in a paper by Kruse and Trappmann 2004. There we talk about "fields of intervention" defining social fields in which better support before and after redundancy could enhance employability: these include the life world, the working life, the period of direct displacement, after displacement and trade unions (Trappmann and Kruse 2004). Similar analyses has been made by Knuth, who calls for increased speed of placement on the labor market in order to animate labor mobility (Knuth 2002: 327).

References

Backes, S. and Knuth, M. (2006). Entwicklungslinien des Beschäftligentransfers. Siegfried Backes: Transfergesellschaften: Grundlagen, Instrumente, Praxis. Saarbrücken: VDM Verl Dr. Müller, S., pp. 11–48.
Beck, U. (1992). *Risk Society: Towards a New Modernity*. London: Sage.
Böhnisch, L. (2003). *Die Entgrenzung der Männlichkeit: Verstörungen und Formierungen des Mannseins im gesellschaftlichen Übergang*. Opladen: Leske und Budrich.

Bourdieu, P. (1985). 'Social Space and the Genesis of Groups', *Theory and Society* 14 (November): 723–744.
Bourdieu, P. (1988). *Homo academicus*. Frankfurt am Main: Suhrkamp.
Bourdieu, P. (1989). 'Social Space and Symbolic Power', *Sociological Theory* 7(1): 14–25.
Charles, N., and James, E. (2003). 'The Gender Dimensions of Job Insecurity in a Local Labour Market', *Work Employment Society* 17(3): 531–552.
Charles, N., and James, E. (2005). ' "He earns the bread and butter and I earn the cream": Job insecurity and the male breadwinner family in South Wales', *Work Employment Society* 19(3): 481–502.
Connell, R. (1995). *Masculinities*. Cambridge: Polity Press.
Crompton, R. (2002). 'Employment, flexible working and the family', *The British Journal of Sociology* 53(4): 537–558.
Crompton, R., Brockmann, M., and Lyonette, C. (2005). 'Attitudes, women's employment and the domestic division of labour: a cross-national analysis in two waves', *Work Employment Society* 19(2): 213–233.
Daly, M., and Lewis, J. (1998). 'Introduction: Conceptualising Social Care in the Context of Welfare State Restructuring', in J. Lewis (ed) *Gender, Social Care and Welfare State Restructuring in Europe*. London and Aldershot: Ashgate, pp. 1–24.
Duncan, S., Edwards, R., Reynolds, T., and Alldred, P. (2003) 'Motherhood, paid work and partnering: Values and theories', *Work Employment Society* 17(2): 309–330.
Edwards, P. (2005). 'The challenging but promising future of industrial relations: developing theory and method in context-sensitive research', *Industrial Relations Journal* 36(4): 264–282.
Esping-Andersen, C. (2000). 'Interview on post-industrialism and the future of the welfare state'. *Work Employment Society* 14(4): 757–769.
European Commission. (2008). *Communication from the Commission to the Council: A European Economic Recovery Plan*. COM (2008) 800 Final. Brussels: European Commission. Available at ec.europa.eu/economy_finance/publications/publication13504_en.pdf Accessed 22 April 2012.
Florian, M and Hillebrandt, F. (eds) (2006). Pierre Bourdieu: Neue Perspektiven für die Soziologie der Wirtschaft. Wiesbaden: VS.
Franzpötter, R. (2003) 'Die Disponiblen und die Überflüssigen. Über die dunkle Kehrseite der Employabilitygeselllschaft', *Arbeit* 12(2): 131–146.
GIB - Gesellschaft für Ommpvatove Beschätigungsförderung mbH (2004). Arbeitsmarktpolitische Instrumente zum Beschäftigtentransfer, Arbeitspapiere 8, Bottrop.
Glaser, B., and Strauss, A. (1967). *The Discovery of Grounded Theory*. Chicago: Aldine.
Gore, T. (2005). 'Extending employability or solving employers' recruitment problems? Demand-led approaches as an instrument of labour market policy', *Urban Studies* 42(2): 341–353.
Gottschall, K. (2000). 'The employable European citizen: Beyond gender, class and ethnicity?', paper presented at Centre for Social Policy Research, University of Bremen.
Halford, S. (2005). 'Book Review: Redundant Masculinities? Employment Change and White Working Class Youth', *Work Employment Society* 19(3): 657–660.
Hanson, L.L. (2002). 'Rethinking the industrial relations tradition from a gender perspective: An invitation to integration', *Employee Relations* 24(2): 190–210.

Heyes, J. (2013) 'Vocational training, employability and the post- 2008 jobs crisis: Responses in the European Union', *Economic and Industrial Democracy* 34(2): 291–311.

Hindrichs, W., Jürgenhake, U., Kleinschmidt, C., Kruse, W., Lichte, R., and Martens, H. (1997). *Sozialer Umbruch in der Stahlindustrie. Das "Ende des Malochers" und die Rolle der Betriebsräte von 1960 bis heute*. Final report (funded by Hans-Böckler-Stiftung, Alfried Krupp von Bohlen and Halbach Stiftung), Dortmund.

Knuth, M. (2002). 'Von der "Lebensstellung" zur nachhaltigen Beschäftigungsfähigkeit. Sind wir auf dem Weg zum Hochgeschwindigkeitsarbeitsmarkt?', in G. Bosch (ed) *Zukunft der Erwerbsarbeit: Strategien für Arbeit und Umwelt*. Frankfurt am Main: Campus, pp. 300–331.

Lefresne, F. (1999). 'Employability at the heart of the European employment strategy', *Transfer: European Review of Labour and Research* 5: 460.

Lewis, J., and Ostner, I. (1994) 'Gender and the evolution of European social policies'. ZeS working paper presented at Center for Social Policy Research, University of Bremen.

Loer, T. (2003). *Zum Begriff der Region. Eine soziologische Bestimmung anhand der Rekonstruktion des Falles "Ruhrgebiet"*. Dortmund: Wirtschafts- und Sozialwissenschftliche Fakultät der Universität Dortmund.

Lupton, B. (2006). 'Explaining men's entry into female-concentrated occupations: Issues of masculinity and social class', *Gender, Work and Organization* 13(2): 103–128.

Marks, A., and Scholarius, D. (2008). 'Choreographing a system: Skill and employability in software work', *Economic and Industrial Democracy* 29(1): 96–124.

Meuser, M. (1998). *Geschlecht und Männlichkeit: Soziologische Theorie und kulturelle Deutungsmuster*. Opladen: Leske und Budrich.

McQuaid, R.W., and Lindsay, C. (2005). 'The concept of employability', *Urban Studies* 42(2): 197–219.

McRobbie, A. (2009). *The Aftermath of Feminism: Gender, Culture and Social change*. Los Angeles, London: SAGE.

Muffels, R., and Wilthagen, T. (2013). 'Flexicurity: A New Paradigm for the Analysis of Labor Markets and Policies Challenging the Trade-Off between Flexibility and Security', *Sociology Compass* 7(2): 111–122.

Pfau-Effinger, B. (1999). 'The Modernization of Family and Motherhood in Western Europe', in R. Crompton (ed) *Restructuring Gender Relations and Employment. The Decline of the Male Breadwinner*. Oxford: Oxford University Press, pp. 60–78.

Pilcher, J. (2000). 'Domestic division of labour in twentieth century. Change slow a-coming', *Work Employment Society* 14(4): 771–780.

Plantenga, J., Schippers, J.J., and Siegers, J. (1999). 'Towards an equal division of paid and unpaid work: The case of the Netherlands', *Journal of European Social Policy* 9(2): 99–110.

Randle, H., and Heinemann, A. (2004). *Learning to Cope with Displacement*. Learnpartner report, APel.

Schwerma, K. (2004). 'Veränderungen in der Arbeitswelt. eine Chance für die Neuorientierung männlicher Lebensweisen?', paper presented at project workshop 'Work changes gender'. Available at www.work-changes-gender.org.

Singley, S., and Heynes, K. (2005). 'Transitions to parenthood: Work-family policies, gender and the couple context', *Gender and Society* 19(3): 376–397.

Skrobanek, J., and Jobst, S. (2006). ' "Begrenzung" durch kulturelles Kapital? Zu Bedingungen regionaler Mobilität im Kontext der Kapitalientheorie Pierre Bourdieus', *Berliner Journal für Soziologie* 2: 227–244.

Stuart, M. (2005). Learning in Partnership: Responding to the Restructuring of the European Steel and Metal Sector, Final Report for Fifth Framework Socio-Economic Key Action Award, European Commission DG Research.

Stuart, M., and Greenwood, I. (2006). 'National and European Policies for Lifelong Learning: An Assessment of European Developments', in M. Kuhn and R. G. Sultana (ed) *Homosapiens Europaeus? Creating the European Learning Citizen.* New York: Peter Lang, pp. 131–148.

Svendson, G.L.H. and Svendsen, G.T. (2004). 'The wealth of nations: Bourdieuconomics and social capital', in D.L. Swartz and V.L. Zolberg (ed) *After Bourdieu. Influence, Critique, Elaboration.* Dordrecht: Kluwer Academic Publishers, pp. 239–263.

Swartz, D.L. and Zolberg, V.L. (eds) (2004). *After Bourdieu. Influence, Critique, Elaboration.* Dordrecht: Kluwer Academic Publishers.

Thiele, A. (2002). 'Männlicher Geschlechtsrollenstress über die Lebensspanne', in T. Steffen (ed) *Masculinities—Maskulinitäten: Mythos, Realität, Repräsentation, Rollendruck.* Stuttgart: Metzler Verlag.

Thomas, M. and Bailey, N.J. (2006). 'Square pegs in round holes? Leave periods and role displacement in UK-based seafaring families', *Work, Employment and Society* 20(1): 129–149.

Trappmann, V. (2004). 'Change competence a pre-requisite for employability. Life histories on structural change. Learning to Learn: employability, partnerships and the learning community. The case of Germany', Report for the Learnpartner Project, Dortmund.

Trappmann, V., and Kruse, W. (2004). 'Learning to learn: Employability, partnership and the learning community: A Transnational comparison from Sweden, Norway, Spain, Germany and the U.K.', Report October.

Voß, G. und Pongratz, H.J. (1998). 'Der Arbeitskraftunternehmer. Eine neue Grundform der Ware Arbeitskraft?', *Kölner Zeitschrift für Soziologie und Sozialpsychologie* 50 (1): 131–158.

Wallis, E., and Murray, A. (2002). 'Trade Unions, Partnership and The Learning Agenda: The United Kingdom. The Steel and Metal Sector', Report for the Learnpartner Project, SPT, presented in Rotherham.

West, C., and Zimmerman, D. (1987). 'Doing gender', *Gender and Society* 1: 13–37.

Widick, R. (2004). 'Flesh and the Free Market: (On Taking Bourdieu to the Options Exchange)', in D.L. Swartz and V.L. Zolberg (ed) *After Bourdieu. Influence, Critique, Elaboration.* Dordrecht, Kluwer: Academic Publishers, pp. 193–237.

Willott, S. and Griffin, C. (2004). 'Redundant men: Constraints on identity change', *Journal of Community & Applied Social Psychology* 14(2): 53–69.

Wilthagen, T. (1998). 'Flexicurity: A New Paradigm for Labour Market Policy Reform?' WZB Discussion Paper, FS, pp. I 98–202 presented in Berlin 1998.

7 Employment Precariousness and Social Reproduction in the Shipbuilding Industry of Piraeus

Manos Spyridakis

Introduction

This chapter addresses the ways in which day laborers attempt to cope with precarious employment conditions in the context of informal shipbuilding activities in Perama, a suburb of western Piraeus. I focus on how workers conceive of their involvement in local labor processes and in the social relations that emerge from, or are consolidated through their efforts to make ends meet.

The Greek shipbuilding industry is centered around the Perama region, which accounts for 87 percent of the country's shipbuilding and ship repair activities. It is strategically located at the crossroads of important maritime routes, between the Black Sea and the Suez Canal, the Black Sea and Gibraltar and is close to the route between Gibraltar and Suez. There are approximately 850 small-scale enterprises employing a largely casual workforce. Currently, the area is undergoing a devastating deindustrialization process due to global competition, organizational weaknesses, technological lags and the absence of state policy regarding the shipbuilding industry. The unemployment rates for the economically active population have reached worrying levels and were increasing long before the advent of the recent economic recession, which hit the Greek economy in 2010. Currently, the sector employs fewer than 1,000 workers while in 2008 more than 6,000 workers were employed. Yet, it must be noted that the structure of employment in the area makes it impossible to reach accurate figures for the number of workers employed in the sector. The ethnography of this sector portrays a harsh and insecure context within which workers look for jobs regardless of the employment conditions, for example, where health and safety measures are absent, and earnings are below the minimum wage (what is locally described as a *"broken wage"*) and workers have no job security. In a context of limited and unstable availability of work, re-employment depends on workers' acquiescence to the employer's (often demanding) practices and the contacts each worker has created through local social activities.

The destructive consequences of deindustrialization are clearly exposed in the accounts of workers in the shipbuilding industry. One informant explained that "the area is to the workers what the heart is to man. If it stops ticking, he dies". Considering that in most local households at least one member currently is or has been employed in this industrial activity (Vlachos and Lazopoulos 1997), it becomes clear that changes in the sector will have widespread and profound repercussions for the local community, in both material and social terms. Furthermore, the ethnographic data show that, as far as local workers are concerned, socially meaningful relationships and webs of significance are created in relation to the workplace (Pardo 1996), both in and out of work in the context of a very adverse labor market. Shipbuilding workers devise survival practices and attitudes that can be useful in coping with the harsh conditions by extreme situations (Procoli 2004) in the past or in the present where the gradual downsizing of local industrial activities accelerated the economic recession.

The experience of being in and out of work in the area of Perama is primarily defined by the structure of shipbuilding and ship repair, characterized by two key procedures: contractors bargain for the repair of a part or the whole of a ship and potential employees negotiate for their employment on a daily basis. Depending on market conditions, the relationship between bosses and workers is mediated by commitments stemming from formal and informal contracts that are devised in the context of an employment regime based on subcontracting[1]. The vast majority of workers are employed casually in non-standard forms of employment and it is therefore difficult, if not impossible, to accurately establish the number of workers in this sector. At the same time, there are many who work in jobs other than those they are specialized for, while others try to find jobs in other sectors or occupations as day laborers. In the rare case where formal contracts are agreed, bosses and workers comply with the National Collective Working Agreement, signed on an annual basis. However, the most usual employment arrangements do not follow the National regulatory labor framework, and, instead, they are based on informal arrangements, such as oral ones.

In Perama, the economic recession occurred in the last years under the supervision of international economic organizations, following a longer period of deindustrialization[2] that started in the mid 1990s[3]. These circumstances contribute to the integration of the majority of workers under very unfavorable terms and conditions, with a majority of them in informal economic activities (Mingione 1989; Benton 1990; Vaiou and Chatzimichalis 1997:35). Informal sector work is crucial, sometimes this may be the only kind of work available to support and strategically rearrange the conditions of their social reproduction (Goddard 1996). It also serves as a basis for the creation of cultural capital that sustains a person's symbolic "value" that also constitutes the basis for exchange, whereby economic capital that can be transformed into other forms of benefits or disadvantages (Berger 1995: 45).

Despite recent trends that result in worsening conditions for workers in the sector, these patterns of employment have a longer history and are a more enduring feature of the area. They are not simply an unprecedented consequence of globalization and the pressures that global markets impose on local agents, as the local labor market has always been part of the fluctuations, the recessions and recoveries of global shipping capital[4]. The casual structures of employment preexisted today's crisis and casual work co-exists with strategies to hire a minimum number of full-time (core) workers. The novel element of local employment patterns is one of scale, related to the fact that the casualization of labor is now an everyday, familiar misfortune for a growing number of workers. This is because the current recession has had a broad impact, affecting the entire economy, and therefore affecting a very large sector of the workforce and their families.

Solidarity, "Rabbits" and "Sneaks"

The scarcity of jobs and the hierarchical character of the labor market have intensified competition among workers, who are compelled to engage in antagonistic games of competition that have become more central in the current recession. Charalambos explained that competition between contractors has harmed the relationships among workers and the struggle to secure profitable deals with ship-owners puts pressure on workers to sell their labor power cheaply. He feels that people in the area distrust each other and are skeptical about the other workers' motives and intentions. These, he suggest, respond to the need to compete for jobs, whether one is employed or unemployed. Consequently, workers' efforts support their bosses' interests in making their business competitive and workers have to excel to maintain the reputation of the company for which they work.

Tasos sees himself as a representative of the contractor and therefore has to be productive and, above all, punctual. He knows he is an experienced craftsman, but he must demonstrate his skill and dexterity to his co-workers and to his boss. But he works alongside other craftsmen who also must do likewise. Productivity thus emerges as the sole criterion of performance and the focus for competition among metalworkers. So Tasos pushes himself and his assistant, constantly urging his "right hand" as he calls him, to be quick and to prepare the tools needed faster than the other workers. He is aware that completing a task in a shorter time is good for him and for the enterprise. In fact, he believes that being productive is at the heart of the circulation of money and thus of his own existence as worker, contributing to a constant supply of jobs. For him, as for other a workers, competition is both unavoidable and necessary to survive. Productivity, so central to the competitive process of workers and firms, becomes an aspect of personal status and self-esteem (Cohen 1985), while workers' worthiness is identified with the notion of *"egoismos"* (selfishness)[5].

Nikos, who used to work full-time in the local shipyards, believes that Greeks are by nature selfish and strive constantly to demonstrate their good character. He argued that *"egoismos"* is more than a way of behaving; it is a value inherent in "our people". He told how the foreman of a shipyard where he worked was struggling to find the solution to a problem when Nikos took the initiative and proposed a solution that reduced production time considerably. He received no reward and was not given any credit for his innovation as the foreman considered that it was an integral part of his normal duties. Instead, he was aware of his colleagues' jealous eyes "on his back".

Despite the negative effects of this divisive setting, the majority of workers in the area see this as an inevitable condition of work. For Nikos, this practice is harmful as far as work and social life are concerned and is an aspect of a view that is frequently expressed locally, that the "big fish eats the smaller one; but they do not care so much about the quality of the food". Petros, a local foreman, is one of the "big fishes" in the zone. In his view, competition has the effect of disorganizing working class struggles because everyone is exclusively concerned with their own interests. Petros recognizes the ambiguities of workers' positions regarding work: on the one hand, those who do not perform competitively cannot survive and on the other, those who do behave competitively are benefiting their bosses. In this way a competitive value is created, but on the wrong basis.

The value of competition is best illustrated by the notion of the "rabbit". Petros explains that almost every "shop"[6] in the zone recruits a rabbit. I came to realize that the "rabbit" is the fastest worker, who is indispensable to the enterprise because he provides the benchmark from which others are measured. The rabbit unleashes a competitive struggle that spreads across the workforce, increasing individual productivity and production. One of Petros' duties is to identify and recruit "rabbits" to place them in each part of the labor process. Petros sees the rabbits as a means to increase productivity and to counter the tendency of workers to slow down in the absence of a suitable stimulus. But potentially at least everyone can be a "rabbit", in the workplace and in everyday interactions in the light of widespread fear of losing one's job and the difficulties faced in securing a weekly wage.

Another category to emerge during fieldwork is the category of "sneak". This refers to a person who acts against established ethics and practices by resorting to what are seen as unfair interventions. The category of the sneak includes ship-owners, politicians, trade unionists and all those who in one way or another are seen to "sabotage" working class interests and solidarity.[7] Although the category is stigmatized, metalworkers believe that everyone can become a "sneak" under certain circumstances, and especially in the current conditions of recession. The best example of a "sneak" is someone who accepts a job with what is called a broken day's wage, which means he is willing to sell his labor power at a rate lower than the legal minimum wage.

Mass redundancies and job shortages have made a mockery of workers' struggles according to Panagiotis, the ex-president of the trade union. Panagiotis explains that although rules do exist in Greece, these are ignored by employers and employees. In the local discourse, the law is a mere idea, a fantasy that disguises the real illegalities incurred by all. Contractors fully exploit the economic crisis when searching for labor, seeking personal agreements with individual workers rather than following the law and signing up to collective agreements and thus recruiting workers who agree to lower wages. Panagiotis explains that before the economic crisis, these practices were not widespread because work was readily available and workers could somehow secure proper work conditions and pay in line with the national minimum wage agreement. For him, however, asymmetrical working conditions were almost always the local rule. "Sneaks" have always existed, even during periods of abundant employment, although no one would readily acknowledge that he is a "sneak" or that he violates the ideal of working class solidarity. Because the area is constantly experiencing recessions, much of the local workforce appears to comply with the ideals of working class comradeship while trying to address their own interests. Panagiotis remarks: "That is the way it goes in the system we live in. To change the system, we have to change ourselves first and this is the most difficult issue here, as unemployment entails not only low wages but, above all selling out our class consciousness". Those who sell their labor for "crumbs" are considered to undervalue themselves as workers and human beings. They become "sneaks"' to get a place in the paradise of the daily wage,[8] but this does not ensure the conditions of their reproduction as workers since they are not the only "sneaks" in the area. For Sotiris, the term divides working class men in the existing working conditions. He had become isolated because he refused to engage in the sneak's strategies to secure a job.

Sotiris, a tube maker, worked alongside many who had accepted lower wages. Fellow workers were reluctant to admit this but, while out with a co-worker he had invited for a beer, his friend admitted that none of their colleagues were properly paid. All had made "under-the-table" agreements with the boss, accepting lower wages. Sotiris was not totally surprised. The violation of the national minimum wage agreement is the outcome of job insecurity and of rising unemployment. Consequently, metalworkers provide a source of cheap labor and local firms almost constantly recruit them through local social networks. In the face of uncertainty, workers seek to persuade contractors that they are worthy of employment. Sotiris says that as workers,

> We are not different from the immigrants who have overrun our country. In many aspects I feel like a foreigner, although I have worked here for over ten years. When I mention this to my co-workers they reply: 'so what?' They do not feel responsible for the status they have established in the zone, and they do not realize that by this practice they both facilitate and perpetuate their exploitation. Instead of making the contractors' life difficult, they help them.

Giorgos is an ex foreman who lives in Perama and has worked in the area for 33 years. He gave up the offer of a permanent position because he was not a "sneak". His boss hired workers for lower wages and failed to provide the required safety equipment. Despite frequent inspections, the contractor was never convicted.[9] For Giorgos, the category of "sneak" is inextricably linked to corruption, which is widespread in the area, given the difficulties entailed in controlling the scattered work sites that extend from the port of Piraeus to the western end of Perama bay.

Giorgos says that he is not happy because he did not fully manage to abstain from a system that rewards the insidious, the cunning and the malicious. It is too late for him now, as he is approaching retirement age. He managed, however, to avoid as much as possible the status of self-exploitation and humiliation and the stigma of a sneak; in the last analysis, he explains that this is the blot one should try to avoid.

"Getting by", Risk and Precarity

In Perama it is particularly difficult to track the ways workers are involved in the Marxian processes of relative or absolute surplus value, given the different contracts and the blurred formal and informal conditions of employment. As a metalworker said,

> The smaller the business is, the more difficult the inspection becomes; nobody talks. When the job is short-term it is still difficult to be officially visible. So, 'broken wages' and accidents go together even if the union inspects regularly the workplace. The accident can happen anytime, any hour, an oversight can cause a fatal accident or any other kind of accident. But it isn't only that, people do not just die while working on the ship, there are people crippled and diseased by the nature of the work etc. In essence, for these workers nobody speaks up.

Casual labor affects the vast majority of workers. Due to the structure of employment and to currently low levels of demand, workers look for a way out not only in the local market but beyond, in a search for jobs that may help to increase their income. Thus, it is usual for workers to have several jobs and generate income through these various jobs that are in a way related to the specialties required by the shipbuilding sector. This practice constitutes an alternative way of improving the terms of social reproduction as well as of enhancing choice regarding specific kinds of casual employment, depending on the prevalent conditions. To the degree that employment is qualitatively downgraded through precarious contracts and the expansion of opportunistic subcontracting (Holmes 1986), the critical assessment of survival needs weighed against the conditions of a job informs workers' decisions to either accept or turn down job offers. Indeed, many informants for whom issues of safety and security were a priority might choose to turn down work offered by particular contractors, regardless of the financial difficulties they are faced with.

Local employment patterns have rarely been based on a full-time work model. The local contracts or *"contrata"* are agreed orally (Watson 2001) or, more rarely, officially among the parties involved. Thus, the region is financially embedded in the global division of labor whereas the local division of labor is based on the circulation of information, on everyday encounters, visits to workplaces in search for employment and on workers' relations with local bosses. Consequently, the distribution of information[10] is the key strategic element in the hierarchical organization of the employment structure. Long-term practices of barter and exchange, providing favors, services and mutual support, are part of the local social and historical background, playing a crucial role in coping with daily problems. Social networks conveying information about jobs are central to the management of everyday life, in addition to which social relations provide the means to obtain supplementary income and livelihoods, whether through casual wages or food supplies from workers' places of origin in the countryside and other resources made available through family networks. These forms of provisioning work towards making ends meet by drawing on different sources, like the market, the state, the community or the domestic group.[11] Workers therefore attempt to expand their social contacts through family, friendship and neighborhood relationships, as well as the trade union.

For example, Nikos, an ex-subcontractor, often recruited kin to work in his business. Many friends asked him for assistance in finding employment, both in Perama and in Piraeus, because they were aware that he had an extensive social network.[12] Through Nikos, I met Kostas and Mata. Kostas was forty-five years old and was employed as a foreman. Mata was a forty-year old accountant who was out of work. Mata's brother, Alexandros, used to be sailor in the merchant fleet. He used to "travel", as Mata says, before doing his military service. As soon as he met his wife-to-be he stopped "traveling" and found employment on "shore". Mata helped her brother get a position doing odd-jobs in the enterprise where she worked. Later, Mata's husband hired him as an assistant in the shop where he worked as a foreman. While there was work in the zone all was well. Alexandros built his own house above his sister's flat and the family grew with the birth of two children. When the zone began to decline, he faced serious problems: his brother-in-law could no longer hire him and he faced increasingly precarious conditions. Alexandros desperately needed a permanent job, especially since his wife could not contribute financially to the household and he was not eligible for support from the Unemployment Office, because he had been unable to accumulate the required number of working days in order to qualify. After seven years of working on the mainland he decided to return to sea. Sailors also faced tough conditions, given ship-owners' preference for foreign—and cheaper—seamen. His family supported him again and his godfather, who worked in a shipping company, helped him find work on a merchant ship for a couple of months and eventually he got a full-time contract. Mata is happy with this, as she considers that her brother is a good worker and breadwinner.

The good breadwinner is a widely recognized category among Perama workers. In discussions held at the trade unions' headquarters, Tasos explained that a good breadwinner must pay his debts, be frugal and save as much money as possible. He will then be able to face future economic problems which, considering the current recession, are very likely. Most workers aspire to being good breadwinners and Tasos considers that he qualifies as such because although he experienced long periods of unemployment, his household has never lacked the basic necessities. This he attributes to his sound management of money and his ability to safeguard his savings. Nikos, also a metalworker, also prioritizes his savings. He is 42 years old, married to Evangelia and has two children. The family live in the Ikariotika area of Perama since their parents, like so many other working class people in the zone, are originally from Ikaria. Nikos started work at 16, to contribute to the family's income. By his 20s he had obtained a ship engineer's diploma and went to sea on a merchant ship. However, he decided to stay on the mainland when he became engaged to Evangelia at the age of 24.

In Nikos' view, the zone and Perama are going through the worst recession he can remember. For him and his family there are difficulties in covering daily expenses, taxes, children's expenses and so on. They live in their own home, which they received as Evangelia's dowry. Despite this, and although he has a wide social network in the zone, the situation is becoming harder. Whereas he used to work on a regular basis—almost every month— nowadays he might be unemployed for up to three months. In-between jobs he tries to generate an income, drawing on his extended network. For instance, he set up a metalwork business with a close friend, using another friend's "shop" in Perama as their headquarters. Although they were successful initially, the business closed after a couple of months as a result of the recession. Furthermore, neither had networks that extended beyond Perama, which placed them at a disadvantage as far as building the company was concerned. Nikos decided to return to Ikaria to seek work in the construction industry but found that there, too, there were declining demands for workers. So he returned to Perama and to his trade.

Whenever possible Perama workers try to maximize their opportunities for finding employment, although this usually entails illegal contracts that deprive them of the stamps they need to access pensions. Furthermore, these jobs can be demanding and entail high levels of risk. For example, workers may join a "mission", whereby contractors recruit a crew that is sent to work on a ship in another harbor. While the same hierarchy and conditions of work apply as in Perama, the work on these missions is harder and, above all, is fully deregulated. On a mission workers cannot escape the foreman's gaze and they are forced to work as long as the boss requires and full deregulation is possible because in the majority of cases the repair is carried out while the ship is at sea. This means that workers are exposed to many dangers, exacerbated by the inadequacy of health and safety measures. Nikos is well aware of this but is eager to join a "mission", even if it is for a couple of months, with a view to making good money. Each time Nikos sails to carry out one of these deadly and illegal jobs his wife wonders: "Will I see him again?"

Conclusions

The dominant relations of production in the Perama shipbuilding industry combine with market pressures to create very limited and irregular demands for labor in which local contractors play an important role as mediators between production and market processes. Workers must try to make the right choices and carefully manage their labor and their resources. Casualized labor conditions in the industry mean that shipbuilding workers are continually in-between employment and unemployment. During the golden era of shipbuilding, they could meet their needs through work and through mobilizing their social relations and engaging with local power relations. Now they are faced with the consequences of long-term decline and deindustrialization that began in the mid-1990s, exacerbated by the current economic crisis. Forced to enter a highly informal economic context, they handle— though not always successfully— the conditions of their existence through their social networks. Consequently, peripheral workers coexist with core workers, informal production with formal production, registered employment with unregistered employment, collective struggles with individual ones, legally built houses with illegal ones, employed people with their unemployed counterparts, social solidarity with individualistic interests, vulgar exploitation with bonds of comradeship, competitive emotions with strong networks of friendship, making a living with lethal accidents during work.

These processes are not a new phenomenon in the area, as Perama workers have long been exposed to the vagaries of international shipping capital, global tonnage demand and global supply, EU and governmental policies. So Perama workers have experienced the effects of remote power structures, even in times of affluence, before the current economic recession. They experienced the risks and instabilities of the market economy, along with the tragic irony of the negative effects of "flexible" post-industrial capitalism, which now dominates labor relations. They are, and have always been, employable, struggling in the labor market through their skills, abilities and work experiences. They have always been adaptive and responded to the fluctuations of the market because they have no choice. They have undertaken risks when trying to earn their own living in a harsh and inhumane environment. However, in the last decade there has been a gradual transformation towards permanent insecurity and poverty, with irreversible consequences.

Perama workers are subjected to the rules that govern unequal labor relationships, conscious of their desire to achieve social reproduction negotiating their labor power on their own, developing their own code of values through which they perceive their survival, social relationships and their connection with wider hierarchical institutions and arrangements. From this point of view, the ethnographic case of Perama provides an opportunity to highlight the fact that although agents are seemingly integrated passively into power relations, they perceive these relations and their participation in them from their own perspective, one that is informed by past and present conditions of existence. They reproduce the disciplinary power they are subjected to by managing their accumulated personal experience and their personal and social resources to improve the conditions of their life. In this sense, it is important for future research to investigate the power of those who are seemingly powerless.

Notes

1 Subcontracting has been a historical feature of the regional economy almost since the emergence of the local industrial activities involving casual and non-standard forms of employment for workers. From the perspective of local bosses, it is a very profitable form of employment since the flexibility it introduces provides the opportunity for rapid adaptation to changing market conditions, while also reducing costs and risks. According to Holmes, there are, broadly, three subcontracting categories: capacity subcontracting, specialization subcontracting and supplier subcontracting (Holmes 1986). This system relies heavily upon extended social networks through which information about employment availability is diffused throughout the region. The information circulates among workers and coincides to a great extent with the local social process of work. The local informal system of production is at the same time part and parcel of the local social relationships and of the network within which they are embedded. The informal aspect of employment relationships structures the ways through which the information is disseminated, that is, within a silent and secret framework, a "conspiracy of silence" (Vaiou and Chatzimichalis 1997: 64). Subcontracting relies heavily on this kind of recruitment in order to minimize labor costs. This explains why it is in the interest of local businessmen to create a large local web of acquaintances and connections in order to have alternative sources of labor available. On this issue, see also Zlolniski 2006.
2 A typical example is the closing down of many textile industries previously located in Piraeus as well as many small-scale shipbuilding and repairing industrial units, fertilizer, plastic and metalwork plants, flourmills and foundries (Trade Union of Piraeus 1995).
3 According to a document of the Piraeus Shipbuilders' Association addressed to the Ministry of Development regarding the constitution of a ship constructors' record in the region, the following dimensions are characteristic of the situation: "A basic fact has not been considered, that the small-scale enterprises which we represent are businesses which act periodically and not continuously. And this is due to the fact that repairing a ship is not a stable production process, since the ships are not always in need for repair, nor are they constantly being constructed. Our companies, when there are no active repair contracts, are not operating, are not active, and are not employing workers. When they are active, at specific periods of time, they employ workers with a fixed-term employment contract. The

workers' union has repeatedly stated that the workers in the zone area have the opportunity to earn 100 up to 150 number of day wages per year. It is not possible, therefore, to employ workers with an open-ended work contract, since that would not allow us to continue our operation and, in any case, is not consistent with the nature of our activity" (Piraeus Shipbuilders' Association 1997).
4 For a more detailed account on the issue, see also Spyridakis 2006.
5 On this idiom, see also Herzfeld 1985.
6 It is the name of business in the local idiom.
7 The rules of proper work, in all its aspects, are not only violated by workers and contractors. State officials responsible for inspecting the conditions of work constitute another category of sneaks in local representations simply because, although they are aware of the illegal practices in the zone, they do nothing about it, as is also the case in other ethnographic contexts. For workers, state officials represent the ethic of corruption and unwillingness to challenge illegality. From this point of view, they constitute a group that constantly deviates from its duties and thus helps to perpetuate illegal wages in the zone.
8 Another dimension of the practice of wage hunting through the cultural category of 'sneak' is the recognition of self esteem achieved by taking money for the completion of a certain task. As Willis puts it, "Though it is difficult to obtain stature in work itself, both what work provides and the very sacrifice and strength required to do it provides the materials for an elemental self esteem. This self esteem derives from the achievement of a purpose which not all—particularly women—are held capable of achieving. The wage packet is the provider of freedom, and independence: the particular prize of masculinity in work" (Willis 1993: 150).
9 Before the arrival of the inspection committee, the boss was warned in advance by someone working in the office which bore the responsibility for legal compliance. A few moments before the committee's arrival, the contractor, in collaboration with his foreman, would distribute crash helmets to the workers and would instruct them how to behave in front of the inspectors. Giorgos claims that this example is the norm in the area and believes that he was fired from the '*shop*' because he often commented on this issue.
10 In this line of argument Narotzky, referring to Spain, stresses that "the dominant model of economic development now incorporates the importance of "non-economic" social relations that are deemed increasingly necessary for the local establishment of dynamic entrepreneurial practices and flexible relations of production" (Narotzky 2004: 57).
11 Provisioning includes complex connections between agents in material, social and cultural terms (Narotzky 2005)
12 This kind of interaction has a multidimensional character, not only economic. As Mackee states, 'It is important to stress that the unemployed families evaluated the type of help available not so much in terms of its quantity, extensiveness or frequency, but commented more on the spirit in which it was given' (Mackee1987: 103).

References

Berger, B. (1995). *An Essay on Culture. Symbolic Structure and Social Structure*. Berkeley, CA: University of California Press.

Benton, L. (1990). *Invisible Factories. The Informal Economy and Industrial Development in Spain*. Albany: State University of New York Press.

Cohen, A.P. (1985). *The Symbolic Construction of Community*. London: Routledge.

Goddard, V.A. (1996). *Gender, Family and Work in Naples*. Oxford: Berg.

Herzfeld, M. (1985). *The Poetics of Manhood: Contest and Identity in a Cretan Mountain Village*. Princeton: Princeton University Press.

Holmes, J. (1986). 'The Organization and Locational Structure of Production Subcontracting, in A. Scott and M. Storper (eds) *Production, Work, Territory. The Geographical Anatomy of Industrial Capitalism*, London: Allen and Unwin, pp. 80–106.

McKee, L. (1987). 'Households During Unemployment: The Resourcefulness of the Unemployed', in J. Brannen and G. Wilson (eds), *Give and Take in Families. Studies in Resources Distribution*, London: Allen Unwin, pp. 96–116.

Mingione, E. (1989). "Work and Informal Activities in Urban Southern Italy", in R. Pahl (ed), *On Work: Historical, Comparative and Theoretical Approaches*. Oxford: Basil Blackwell, pp. 548–578.

Narotzky, S. (2004). "The Political Economy of Affects: Community, Friendship, and Family in the Organization of a Spanish Economic Region", in A. Procoli (ed), *Workers and Narratives of Survival in Europe. The Management of Precariousness at the End of the Twentieth Century*. Albany: State University of New York Press, pp. 57–83.

Narotzky, S. (2005). "Provisioning", in J.G. Carrier (ed), *A Handbook of Economic Anthropology*, Cheltenham: Edward Elgar, pp. 78–93.

Pardo, I. (1996). *Managing Existence in Naples*, Cambridge: Cambridge University Press.

Piraeus Shipbuilders' Association. (1997). *Suggestions for the Categorization of Shipbuilding Enterprises*, Piraeus (in Greek).

Procoli, A. (2004). "Introduction", in A. Procoli (ed), *Workers and Narratives of Survival in Europe. The Management of Precariousness at the End of the Twentieth Century*, Albany: State University of New York Press, pp. 1–15.

Spyridakis, M. (2006). 'The political economy of labor relations in the context of Greek Shipbuilding: An Ethnographic Account', *History and Anthropology* 17(2), June: 173–170.

Trade Union of Piraeus. (1995). *Qualitative Research for the Character of Labour Market in Piraeus*, Piraeus. (in Greek).

Vaiou, D., and Chatzimichalis, K. (1997). *Me ti raptomihani stin kouzina kai tous Polonous stous agrous. Poleis, perifereies kai atupi ergasia*, Athens: Exandas (in Greek).

Vlahos, G.P., and Lazopoulos, A.K. (1997). 'Competitiveness of the European shipbuilding and shiprepairing industry and sectorial unemployment. A case study: Crisis and possibilities of Greek enterprises', *European Research Studies*, 1(1): pp. 2–32.

Watson, T. (2001). *Sociology, Work and Industry*. London: Routledge.

Willis, P. (1993). *Learning to Labour: How Working Class Kids Get Working Class Jobs*. Aldershot: Ashgate.

Zlolniski, C. (2006). *Janitors, Street Vendors, and Activists. The Lives of Mexican Immigrants in Silicon Valley*. Los Angeles: University of California Press.

Section III
Lives of Worth

8 Regimes of Value and Worthlessness
How Two Subaltern Stories Speak

Don Kalb

In my earlier work on Poland and the Netherlands I have made extensive use of two longer life stories, one told by Maria van de Velde in Eindhoven, the other by Krisztof Zadrozny in Wroclaw. Against the background of other life interviews I held in these settings, those two exceptionally rich stories helped me to understand in more subtle and complex ways the antagonistic intimate experiences and immediate struggles that were characteristic of—but can never be "read off"—the historical dynamics of class in the places and times in which these histories were lived and narrated. These were working class stories grappling with the locally lived contradictions of the pre and high welfare state period in the Netherlands (1950–90), and the "transition" from "really existing socialism" to really existing capitalism in Poland (1985–2005), respectively.

Both these stories expressed lives unfolding within the proverbially high-pressure relationships of export-oriented mass manufacturing in the light electrical sector. Perhaps more than any other industry, this particular sector, since it emerged in the late 19th century, has been emblematic of "emerging" and "catch up" regions. In this context of perceived local backwardness, it has been surrounded by hopes and ideologies of modernity, welfare, security and middle class consumption. However, in order to secure competitiveness, it often rooted itself deeply within local histories and relationships. In fact, more often than not, the relational logics embedded in those prior histories were magnified, thus turning the promised modernity into an uncomfortably lingering past. Despite its futuristic glamour, electrical production remained mostly based on a big component of low to middle skilled labor, often highly feminized, strong on kinship ties, weak on formal organization and by definition exposed to ruthless competition from emergent sites with even more exploitable proletariats in the making.

I have never before, in any publication, set these stories in relation to each other. They were part of what I thought of as separate projects: one in Western Europe, which I carried out in the early 1990s, the other in post-socialist Eastern Europe (now called Central Europe) conducted in the late 90s and early 2000s. They were also part of apparently separate analyses. What could a socialist/post-socialist case study of industrial privatization and restructuring after the fall of the Wall have to do with a solidly capitalist and Western story of female exploitation and urban-industrial patriarchy in the 1950s? Yet in retrospect the stories, while discontinuous in time and place, are closely implicated in each other and in ways that are, on closer scrutiny, of surprising contemporary anthropological significance.

For one, the Whirlpool "white goods" manufacturing complex in Wroclaw, probably the biggest in the sector in contemporary Europe, was an indirect offspring of the Philips large domestic appliances' sector once headquartered in Eindhoven. Exposed to fierce competition from cheaper Italian manufacturers, in the 1970s Philips sought to move up the ladder of added value, and sold this typically "mid-tech" business to the Italians. Italian capital, similarly moving up in the 1990s, sold its mass-production interests to the US-based Whirlpool. Whirlpool then became the holding around which the entire sector began to consolidate within a re-unified Europe. In 2002 it took over the "Polar" plant in Wroclaw, then one of the biggest in Central and Eastern Europe (CEE), from a failing French investor, and made it the prime European production site for refrigerators, dishwashers, washing machines and so on, marketed under various labels including the old Italian ones. Thus, apparently disconnected in time and territory, these were in fact different sites within one European/global rhythm of capitalist accumulation, a rhythm deeply entangled with a particular combination of "low to middle tech" electronic technologies, consumer products and competitive markets. This was set in motion by capital of an increasingly oligopolistic and transnational nature, in the end traded on the Amsterdam and New York stock exchanges, and hence becoming thoroughly tuned into the global value regime. It is noteworthy that oligopoly in a sector as competitive as this one does not imply major curbs on market competition and hence a relaxation of pressures. Rather, it means that there is a small number of hands-on actors who dictate these pressures.

But what is most fascinating from the point of view of an anthropology of class is that both stories were narratively framed around what I gradually came to understand as an involuntary and perhaps somewhat compulsive conversation, waged both intra-personally, privately and sometimes publicly—not necessarily with a steady voice—on value, or more precisely on personal worth and worthlessness. This alludes to an overwhelmingly urgent contemporary anthropological issue: the question of what is believed to generate value, the competing folk theories on value and its opposite (including those usually represented as "expert theories"), the proponents of those theories, and the struggle among them. While being very different stories about very different local relations, both addressed deep concerns about the possibility of lives being made worthless and hence devalued in the context of particular regimes of value and accumulation.

Ideas of personal worth and worthlessness are in contemporary academic language often evoked through the lofty concept of "dignity". Dignity is a key concept of Catholic-Christian social teaching and theology, as it is of other religions. The coupling of "cultural value" and "dignity" has historically been offered, not only by conservatives, as a more wholesome and ethical rival to the liberal and Marxist notions of "value and interest", rejecting the latter's connotations of pragmatism, individualism, materialism, conflict and struggle as supposedly inescapable facts of modern life. "Value and dignity" were also important notions within the ethical socialisms of Proudhon or Polanyi. The "protection of personal dignity" within mutuality is also a core idea of anarchism, which is presently being resurrected among the anthropological Left. Although both my informants, were Catholic, one of them a schooled Catholic social activist, rather than using the Catholic vocabulary, they spontaneously coined their thoughts in this more down to earth language of "worth and worthlessness", which seems a perhaps intentionally unstable hybrid of value theory and market-speak. While appreciative of the ethical foundations and prefigurative aims of these pre and non-Marxian approaches, I suggest that a more analytic and relational understanding of the origins, meanings and functions of these two compulsive conversations on value and worthlessness might well take its cue from some Marxian reflections.

Investment bankers these days often talk about themselves with a characteristic lack of modesty as "the discoverers and un-lockers of value". They also speak freely about "high worth individuals", the ones that magazines such as *Forbes* and *Fortune* report on. These are people with "heavenly bank-accounts", as Frank Zappa would say. But beyond the dollars, the bankers' notion of "high worth individuals" also suggests that these are people worthy of unrestricted attendance to their needs and wishes by the "discoverers of value". Worthlessness, in contrast, is what describes, mostly in acerbic and strident tones, not only the bank accounts of the plebs but also, and often in the form of a resolute critique, the kind of social relations and practical moralities that are attributed to them: undependable, nonreciprocal, undeserving, volatile, *lumpen*, less than solid and with unpredictable edges: scrap metal rather than gold.

Terence Turner has reminded us recently that Marx built his critique of political economy not only on the labor theory of value, but in no less measure on a value theory of labor under capitalism (Turner 2005). Value under capitalism, Marx argued, was not measured by exchange prices on the market or the application of units of labor power, although the latter was certainly the ultimate source of all value. Rather, value in capitalism was realized only if and when products embodying the cost of "socially necessary labor time" plus the fixed and variable costs of the capitalist could actually be sold with a profit on the market. The value theory of labor demands that living labor can only be allowed to reproduce itself as "valuable" living labor if it reciprocally allows capital a degree of exploitation and competitiveness that, in the end, does not compare unfavorably to the degree of exploitation and competitiveness realized elsewhere in the system. Thus, the value that investment bankers will claim to have discovered has already been produced. Marx used the example of the Yorkshire handloom weavers after the introduction of machine driven looms in Lancashire.

These machine looms doubled the productivity of labor in the area around Manchester. From now on, Marx argued, the value of the labor power of handloom weavers in Yorkshire was only half of what it used to be (Marx 1976: 125–31). It is this unrelenting value regime that is at the root of what Marx called "the dull compulsion" of market-enforced discipline. It is also the origin of alienation.

However, as Marxist anthropologists know, market discipline and the resulting alienation are neither merely abstract categories nor are they always-anonymous forces weighing down invisibly but tangibly upon particular working people. Under capitalism, sometimes very visible impostors are delegated to promote the further alienation of control over one's life. Global regimes of value are often locally enacted with the help of visible financial actors, hands-on managerial power, local status and kinship hierarchies, national political elites, bureaucracies and legal protocols, etc. Capitalism, for Marxist anthropologists, was always already a thickly layered structure, perhaps even more so than was envisaged by Marx himself (see, for example, Barber et al. 2013; Carbonella and Kasmir 2014; Carrier and Kalb 2015; Kalb 1997; Kalb and Halmai 2011; Narotzky and Smith 2006; Sider 1986; Wolf 1982). Hence, the value regime of labor, while ultimately determined globally by the pressure of the system of relationships itself, also tends to announce and implement itself through manifold empirical local agents and social forms. Sometimes it seems more directly induced by the nebulous forces of the hidden hand, while at other times it comes embodied in visible and tangible drivers. The former is perhaps more characteristic of highly advanced locations that are shielded from the greatest pressures arising from global competition by oligopoly, or of very peripheral ones where little local capital accumulation takes place. The latter seems to obtain rather often in the zones in between, those in which sectors such as electrical consumer goods usually appear to represent the royal road to the future. My suggestion is that local vernacular narratives of worthlessness are deployed in both obscuring and revealing what is being alienated, how and why, and on whose behalf.

These stories of "worthlessness", while thus affiliated in their deeper existential concerns and in their global placement within a certain industrial value regime linked to the spaces and times of a certain "backwardness", arose from very different local political conjunctures, actual industrial episodes and social relations. They also reflected very different relationships of gender, and were indeed told by a man and a woman. In particular, they made non-identical connections between pasts, presents and futures and had hugely contrasting repercussions for the possibility and nature of agency. Closely read, one might sense that the one would perhaps incline towards a certain depressive neurosis while the other may have a feel of the paranoid. The neurosis and the paranoia were about the possibility of being or becoming "worthless" in a context of less than abstract capitalist value extraction. In what follows I will place these stories in the context of what are the "critical junctions" (Kalb 2005, 2011) of their emergence and social meaningfulness. I will come back to this.

Worthless Histories

During my interview with her (see Kalb 2005, Kalb 1997), Maria van de Velde regularly exclaimed, "this is my own history, but it is worthless! My kids always tell me 'shut up mother, the past is the past and today is today' ". After a short initial hesitation, she was visibly impatient to tell me a host of small stories, stories of growing up as a working class girl in the Eindhoven of the 1950s, stories of "her people", stories that to me as an anthropologist were of fascinating significance but that to most others might have appeared unconnected, confused even, and without much point. I became puzzled by how precisely the imagined "worthlessness" of her own history connected with what I increasingly started to see as a systematic, hegemonic, although always shifting regime of exploitation of daughters by an unspoken alliance of parents and local industrialists on behalf of capitalist as well as parental accumulation. The contradictions of class on which the whole local electronics boom was based were steadily displaced onto relationships of kinship and gender. It turned the working class family into the site at which the actual contradictions had to be managed, contained, made inhabitable and grown habitual and, ultimately, therefore, rendered "unspeakable".

Maria grew up under the industrial conditions that I tried to capture with the term "flexible familism" (Kalb 1997, 2005). Mass production departments in the Philips plants (1890–1960) relied heavily on girls' labor, just like the Foxconn plants in Malaysia or Guangdong do now. Over time Philips had succeeded by way of state-sponsored selective immigration, psychological selection, social policy and corporate urbanism, to shape working class family structures around its own accumulation imperatives (Kalb 1997). That meant that families tended to be very large (major neighborhoods had average families of over 10 people), and have a disproportionate number of girls of working age. Fathers were rewarded with jobs, status and a certain security for the family as a whole, including housing, health insurance and a pension, in exchange for bringing in a number of unskilled but well socialized and highly disciplined, hence exploitable daughters. This regime changed over time in its particularities. As Philips' mass production departments were increasingly spread to low wage/high population sites first in the Netherlands and Flanders, then Europe and finally, since the 1960s, to the global south and east, local production in Eindhoven became ever more skill and education intensive. Over time Philips families were allowed to climb the ladder of added value more or less in synch with the production processes, run from the headquarters of what was an increasingly global corporation. For example, Philips was heavily involved in adult and professional education (as well as in primary and secondary education), which partly explains the good name Philips had and kept. But in the early 1950s there were still considerable levels of mass production in the Eindhoven premises. And girls like Maria, whose unskilled father worked as an archivist in a Philips warehouse, were exposed to the intricately complex despotic and gendered regimes of production and reproduction, on the shop floor, at home, in their leisure time, on which Philips' profitability was based.

I proposed the concept of flexible familism precisely in order to highlight an ensemble, a key set of interlocking relationships that in characteristic ways shaped not just families and the local industrial relations of the corporation but also the city and the region (1997). I called this ensemble a "critical junction" in order to emphasize the multi-scalar and intersectional nature of the connective mechanisms and relations. The concept of critical junction was intended to do broadly similar work as the 1970s structural Marxist concept of "articulation", but without the baggage of extreme rationalism or Gallic logic chopping as Eric Wolf once called it (1982). The aim was also to provide a stronger sense of the spatiotemporal connections and the actual path-dependent trajectories of development that were rolled out as accumulation was pushed on to higher levels of value creation. I also used flexible familism to mark a contrast with Fordism. Fordism signified mass production for a national market, high male wages, mass private consumption and a family-oriented life. These were what Gramsci in the early 1930s described as the characteristic hegemonic moments of Ford's 10-dollar a day regime in Detroit, and for him it exemplified how capitalist hegemony in advanced locations was secured (Gramsci 1971: 277–316). He then contrasted this with how such hegemony in less advanced locations in Europe, in Italy for example, could not be attained by purely market-based processes and the wage. Productivity, revenues and popular purchasing power were insufficient to achieve this. Instead, hegemony had to be forcefully imposed by repressive counter-revolutions of a conservative or fascist kind: "passive revolution".

Philips and Eindhoven were different from both of these situations, although they did embody a revolution from above, albeit in a weaker sense of the term. Philips was hegemonic, like Ford, but in a female-dominated, low wage, export-oriented production process. The crucial mediating mechanism here was neither high consumption nor state repression. It was the working class family that was set up as its key hegemonic mechanism. The firm did so by thoroughly integrating the social reproduction of workers' families into the rhythms and cycles of its own accumulation. It employed family heads, fathers, and took on more children-workers from within families as demand rose, selectively, but also temporally dismissed workers that mattered less for the status of working class households—girls—as downturns hit the firm. All the while it kept intricate control over an extremely hard working and indeed from the point of view of capitalist accumulation highly valuable and reliable working class. Corporate housing policy was the essential enabling condition for that. Philips families acquired access to affordable and modern company housing, with controlled rents that the corporation could and did temporarily reduce if the business cycle demanded such a measure, as occurred in the early 1930s.

In a sense then this was indeed a managerial revolution from above with "social policy" as its hegemonic banner, facilitated by a state in crisis that was therefore willing to furnish massive loans for housing construction. But it is important to stress that Philips learned about the possible functions of the working class family from the existing peasant-worker relations in South East Brabant, which it found when it started there, in the 1890s. For a generation, until 1925, Philips' lamp production grew on the basis of these organic regional relationships and it was only with the massive expansions into radio set making around 1930 and the associated migrations that it decided to turn its knowledge about local family mechanisms into a large-scale managerial device.

The family thus became a complex overlapping set of relationships of production and reproduction, set up as such by industrial management. Flexible familism thoroughly shaped the properties of the associated urbanism and the everyday ideologies and politics that reigned (for a detailed analysis see Kalb 1997). The straightforward upshot was that Philips made parents complicit in girls' exploitation in ways that were never openly talked about—indeed it remained a local secret overlaid with ideologies of company care and family care—in exchange for a certain durable loyalty the corporation offered to families, including housing and income, plus a set of implicit and explicit guarantees for parental social status and jobs for the next generation. Here was one of the largest concentrated sites of electronics production in the Western world—40 thousand workers in one local complex in the 1950s—but socialism and unionism remained thoroughly tamed forces, even in the conflictive 1930s and 1960s. More than that, politics understood as the public discussion and shaping of social forms was a very small domain indeed. The secret thus remained a secret, and not quite a public one.

As with so many of the older women I talked with in Eindhoven, Maria van de Velde, youngest daughter of a family of nine, had a very contradictory relationship with her parents (see Kalb 1997, 2005 for a full account). Her father appeared in her stories as simultaneously intimate and intimidating, his behavior regularly bordering on violence, and he was nervously imagined as having been capable of rape and incest. Her mother was nice to her youngest daughter and made her nice suits for the Saturday night dances. But Maria recognized in retrospect that precisely because of her mother's attention she had always been ready to exploit herself more than she was capable of enduring. Nor did she trust her mother's perennial "illnesses", which forced her to take over responsibility for household work. Of her lovers, including the one who became her lifelong husband, she was often just as uncertain as she was about her father.

The coming of Philips to this peripheral region of peasant-workers had intensified "traditional" patriarchy and sex segregation, while it simultaneously produced the modern experience of youth clustered together by the hundreds in production departments, workers' neighborhoods and leisure spaces. Contradiction reigned. Local moralists described and deplored the "immoral" distractions of love and consumption and recommended keeping the sexes separate as well as religious. Philips battled the mixing of the sexes within production in order to secure super-efficiency. And parents, dependent on girls' earnings, sought to manage nerves, anxiety and discontent, while collectively pushing up the local marriage age for girls as compared to other Dutch cities. All the while boys and girls were uncertainly seeking intimate and reliable bonds, which always appeared to them as a possibly illicit escape from conservative paternal domination. This conservative domination was popularly believed to be religious and traditional in origin, derived from conservative "values" and ideas of gendered dignity, rather than modern and industrial and derived from the valorization of capital within a global value regime of electrical production. Class contradictions were displaced onto families, generations and gender, and hence exploitation and solidarity, intimacy and intimidation were bundled into an inseparable relational whole that was fraught with fragility and insecurity for local women. While local industry was churning out the consumption items of the future—lamps, radio sets, television screens—it was also producing "worthless histories".

In the early fifties Philips was the quintessential foreign currency earner for an overpopulated Dutch nation-state deeply dependent on foreign purchases of food and raw materials. Flexible familism, and a whole city geared towards sustaining that relationship, helped to secure the necessary hard currencies. "Worthless histories" were the gendered underside of the valorization of the unprecedented mass of capital sunk into an urban-industrial complex geared to electronics production.

Worthless Poles

The second "critical junction" of value and worthlessness that I want to address was broadly situated within the same regime of accumulation around electrical consumer goods in Europe, but constituted very differently with regard to gender and politics. That was not just because of the differences in time and place, this being post-socialist Wroclaw, Poland. It was also because the forces behind alienation and human devaluation here were thoroughly public and expressly political, not abstract and hidden-hand like, nor so confusingly intimate as in the Eindhoven case. The site was also much more equitably gendered. Instead of silence, there were strong public counter-voices, institutional ones such as the Solidarność labor union and its increasingly right wing political alliances, and individual ones, such as Krysztof Zadrozny's.

Originating in the socialist buildup of domestic industry, electrical production in Wroclaw, as in Eindhoven, helped to urbanize rural people in a relatively underdeveloped part of Europe and offered them a way to education and modernity. Unlike Eindhoven, which rose full speed to the highest ranks of added value in the sector, Wroclaw under socialist auspices took the low-to-middle tech road of the "white goods" sector. White goods were a useful and achievable form of import substitution for the COMECON market and offered thousands of jobs to both men and women with primary (still represented by more than 50 percent of employees in the 1990s), secondary, vocational school and university backgrounds.

As in Eindhoven, however, the modernity achieved seemed somehow failed and hollow. It failed in the 1980s because of socialist stagnation and collapse. And it failed in the 1990s—2000s because of the appropriation of value by transnational capital, facilitated by privatization and a new political elite that was keen to set itself up more as what Lenin would have singled out as a "comprador" regime for international capitalists than as anything else. Here, in a sense, was a secret too, although it was a public secret rather than a private one, while often just as misrecognized: sovereignty, parliamentary democracy and the rule of law served to transfer factories that by 1990 were *de facto* and *de jure* worker-controlled, first to the banks, then to the state, and finally to the circuits of transnational capital. So-called successful democratic transition brought freedom of speech, the vote and travel, but also condemned local workers to lifelong stagnation (Ost 2005; Kideckel 2009; Kalb 2009, 2014). What exactly was alienated from them was infinitely more complex and overwhelming than is described by that straightforward material fact.

Socialist forms of industrial organization tended to delegate quite a bit of tactical power to worker constituencies as compared to capitalist forms (Burawoy 1985; Verdery 1996). In Poland, splits in the political and intellectual landscape were deeper than anywhere else in "really existing socialism", which served to further reinforce informal workers' power. Between 1976 and 1980 this ultimately led to the formation of the mass labor movement *Solidarność*, which mobilized more than 10 million people in Poland between 1980 and 1982, a quarter of whom were in fact Communist party members. The "Polar" factory, with a lot of young workers in the late 1970s, was a hotbed of rebellion. Zadrozny and his family and friends were key actors in the making and development of the local Solidarność cells. Zadrozny also became one of the local heroes of the resistance against the military coup of December 1981, but was captured and imprisoned in 1982.

The contradictions of Communist military rule, as it shifted from central planning towards a socialist market mechanism paradoxically meant that the claims for worker self-management that had been made by the now outlawed Solidarność Union were eventually granted (Kalb 2009). Property rights though were shared between the firm and its worker-controlled board on the one hand, and the state on the other. In some regions, such as Wroclaw, clandestine Solidarność groups immediately took up these legal openings offered in 1984 and reconstituted themselves around the workers' councils. By 1989, Zadrozny and his family and friends had rebuilt a network of worker activists that for all practical purposes was running the "white goods" plants and all the social functions attached to them—housing, pensions, leisure, poor relief, health, etc.—with massive local support.

In the years after 1989, a traumatic split occurred between democratic intellectuals now increasingly in control of positions in a state that was incorporated as a periphery in the global capitalist system and worker constituencies that were in *de facto* and *de jure* control of industries in several regions, including Wroclaw (Ost 2005, Kalb 2009). Workers in Wroclaw and elsewhere were demanding a privatization that would allow for worker cooperatives, but the liberal state elite was adamantly against putting labor unions in control of major assets. A long political silence followed while the state began unleashing shock-therapy on an economy that had lost its COMECON links but had not yet gained any access to the markets of Western Europe. As a consequence, industries first became indebted to the state-owned banking system, then were practically bankrupted, then split, and subsequently consolidated via new loans under the wing of the Treasury, and later sold to transnational investors. Privatization was thus, first and foremost, a state-orchestrated appropriation. The whole process took a decade. At the same time new legal and financial protocols reduced activist worker councils and labor unions to defensive struggles in trying to secure their very own factory communities. In Polar, for example, they were forced to make large investments of their own funds in new production lines in order to survive. By 1993 the cooperative movement had failed catastrophically. By 2000 worker management had been dismantled by legal process and through the concessions demanded by the state and the new international owners. None of them, however, failed for lack of support on the ground or for lack of good arguments. By the late 1990s there was still a palpable moral sense of popular ownership, but the legal reality had been thoroughly transformed.

From the standpoint of transnational capital there was a specific logic at work here. Polar was an attractive option for Whirlpool because local wages were some 70 percent below any of the standards obtaining for semi-skilled work in the European West or South. Furthermore, it was located in Poland, the post-socialist EU accession country with the largest home-market, and bordering Germany; also, white goods were simply too big to be profitably made in China and then shipped to Europe. The local plant, however, while viable within the wider value regime, was exposed to fierce competition. Also accounting for the management, marketing and technology rents it would have to pay Whirlpool for, it was forced into an efficiency drive that drove up productivity by 700 percent in a few years. A low wage, despotic and increasingly hierarchical production regime emerged that combined, as Zadrozny concluded, "the worst of socialism and the worst of capitalism".

While Maria van de Velde in Eindhoven talked about her "worthless history", Zadrozny and his fellow activists were exposed to a dominant public discourse emanating from the mouthpieces of liberal politics and to some extent from international capital, that loudly claimed that "Polish workers were worthless", in Zadrozny's straightforward summary (Kalb 2009). In the first decade after 1989, while the liberal state was crushing worker sodalities, expropriating collectively claimed industrial assets and repressing wages and unionism, workers and peasants were systematically depicted as ossified remnants of an Asiatic socialist despotism, a version of *Homo Sovieticus*, and therefore a huge civilizational liability for Poland's desperately sought middle class status within the West (Buchowski 2006, Kalb 2009). Workers and peasants were energetically debunked on the grounds of an educational deficit, habits of alcoholism and lack of initiative and responsibility. Humiliated, their only role for the new Poland they had helped to establish, often at great personal risk, was hard work under an unforgiving regime of capitalist supervision.

Solidarność unions, thus abandoned by their former liberal allies, inverted the verdict. They claimed the nation's recently gained sovereignty as their own exclusive achievement, pictured the new liberal elite as traitors of the nation and shifted to a nationalist position that celebrated Poland and the Poles against the ongoing liberal cosmopolitan "theft from the people" (see also Kalb 2011).

Zadrozny was keenly aware that the liberal-capitalist alienation of newly won sovereignty had been forced upon them via a double dispossession. Material assets had been alienated surreptitiously by obscure legal-financial means and in political backroom deals. At the same time, but now in full daylight, the reputations of workers had been relentlessly attacked and devalued by narratives about "worthless Poles". Transnational capital had acquired Polish assets "for nothing" he concluded, while capital and the state were claiming that they were doing this "for the people". Zadrozny emphasized (in 2006) that "we cannot undo what was done. But it would be psychologically important to find out whether this company was sold for less than its real value. Then it could become easier to enforce something now, like better wages. It is all a question of honor. I myself never believed that this was how it had to be, that Poles are such that they cannot do this or that . . . it was a big mistake to say that Poles were worthless" (Kalb 2009, 2014).

Capitalist value regimes, the reputations of the Polish state elite within the new European neoliberal order, and the value of Polish labor, both in terms of its dignity and as market exchange, had been massively at odds. There was no doubt that Polish workers had dramatically lost out. The forces which they were up against were far more coherent than the Communist Party, the generals or the Soviets had been in the 1970s and 1980s. While the old enemies did control the national state, by 1989 they were transparently out of synch with world time and global value regimes; neither could they anymore rely on their local cadres. Capitalist global-national-local levels, however, worked perfectly in unison. Zadrozny and his cohort of freedom fighters for a democratic labor-based Polish sovereignty now actively helped to launch a broad neo-nationalist mobilization against transnational capital and the cosmopolitanized state class. In the end they succeeded to put the Kaczynskis in power for a couple of years in the mid-2000s, the "terrible twins", in the expression frequently used by *The Economist*. And, with wider alliances, and now emboldened by Hungary's Victor Orban, they brought Lech Kaczynski back to power again in 2015. But while post-socialist conservative identity politics had a field day and European liberals and multiculturalists were shocked in anger, little changed in the global position or bargaining power of Polish labor. What they did get, though, were much increased child benefits and a definite end to "the Poles are worthless" narrative.

Conclusion

In Capital, Karl Marx strove for an abstract analysis of the workings of capitalist value regimes, arguing that abstract modeling was the only way to get to an empirically concrete understanding of "the real" because under capitalism the real tended to show itself in inverted ways. This is a necessary insight but not a sufficient one. In my two accounts here I have therefore emphasized that the actual pressures of global value regimes on concrete labor are often delegated to local actors, relationships and histories. These relationships and histories, including their insertion in or capture by global systemic processes of value generation, can be described by the notion of critical junctions, a notion that serves both an exploratory and an explanatory function not unlike the more rationalist idea of "articulation" in the Marxist anthropologies of the 1970s. Local vernacular narrative themes of worth and worthlessness in the context of global value regimes serve to both obscure and reveal the relational mechanisms of alienation, dispossession and devaluation of labor upon which capitalist valorization is based. The analysis of the critical junctions that structure such regimes in concrete territorial cases becomes necessary and indeed possibly sufficient, in order to show what such notions obscure and reveal, and why.

My two accounts show a woman and a man whose lives have unfolded within the rhythms of industrial accumulation associated with electrical production, and who see their life and labor confronted by forces that appear to reduce them to an ontological "worthlessness". This common experience is happening for very different and very particular reasons springing from the very different logic of their time, place, gender and politics. But there is a more general cause, too, located within the rhythms of accumulation of the sort of industries that seek out similar relatively "backward" locations, such as the electrical/electronics industries are prone to do. Finally, it is also happening for universal reasons that are located within the global value regime in general. An effective analysis tries to bring all three of these perspectives into play.

Jonathan Friedman (1998), with a nod towards Ingmar Bergman, once aptly quipped that instead of searching for Geertzian "webs of meaning" anthropologists should look for the "tissue of lies" by which societies both get by and do not get by. The two narratives of worthlessness that we have discussed here do reveal one exact origin of alienation in these two cases: respectively, parents who embody a collusion of intimacy and intimidation, solidarity and exploitation, in the Eindhoven case, and liberal comprador elites that sell "the people" out in the Wroclaw and Polish case. But the narratives only reveal the most observable actors within their specific critical junctions of value production. They are therefore necessarily partial and inevitably obscuring and confused. Both expose the reigning local myths of enlightened liberal progress as a tissue of lies, the former doing so privately and uncertainly, the other publicly and assertively. But both also fail to understand their perpetrators, not as sovereign moral forces, but as dependent actors within a wider relational field that exerts pressures and sets limits. The same phenomenal property of capitalism that forced Marx to penetrate a concrete abstraction through a theory that makes use of the notion of abstract concreteness prevented Maria van de Velde and Krysztof Zadrozny, symptomatically, from revealing the further reaches behind their alienation.

References

Barber, P., Leach, B., and Lem, B. (eds) (2013). *Confronting Capital: Critique and Engagement in Anthropology*. London: Routledge.

Buchowski, M. (2006). 'The Specter of Orientalism in Europe: From Exotic Other to Stigmatized Brother'. *Anthropological Quarterly* 79(3): 463–482.

Burawoy, M. (1985). *The Politics of Production*. London: Verso.

Carbonella, A., and Kasmir, S. (eds) (2014). *Blood and Fire: Towards a Global Anthropology of Labor*. New York and Oxford: Berghahn Books.

Carrier, J., and Kalb, D. (eds) (2015). *Anthropologies of Class: Power, Practice, and Inequality*. Cambridge: Cambridge University Press.

Friedman, J. (1998). *System, Structure, and Contradiction: The Evolution of Asiatic Social Formations*. Walnut Creek/London: Rowman and Littlefield.

Gramsci, A. (1971). *Selections from the Prison Notebooks* (ed and trans. Hoare and Smith). New York: International Publishers.

Kalb, D. (1997). *Expanding Class: Power and Everyday Politics in Industrial Communities, the Netherlands 1850–1950*. Durham and London: Duke University Press.

Kalb, D. (2005). 'Bare Legs like Ice: Recasting Class for Local/Global Inquiry', in D. Kalb and H. Tak (eds) *Critical Junctions: Anthropology and History beyond the Cultural Turn*. New York and Oxford: Berghahn Books, pp. 109–136.

Kalb, D. (2009). 'Conversations with a Polish populist: Tracing hidden histories of globalization, class, and dispossession in postsocialism (and beyond)'. *American Ethnologist* 36(2): 207–223.

Kalb, D. (2011). 'Introduction: Headlines of nation, subtexts of class: Working class populism and the return of the repressed in neoliberal Europe', in D. Kalb and

G. Halmai (eds) *Headlines of Nation, Subtexts of Class: Working Class Populism and the Return of the Repressed in Neoliberal Europe.* Oxford and New York: Berghahn Books, pp. 1–36.

Kalb, D. (2014). 'Worthless Poles and Other Dispossessions: Toward an Anthropology of Labor in Postcommunist Central and Eastern Europe'. In S. Kasmir and A. Carbonella (eds) *Blood and Fire: Towards a Global Anthropology of Labor.* New York/Oxford: Berghahn Books.

Kalb, D. and Halmai, G. (eds) (2011). *Headlines of Nation, Subtexts of Class: Working Class Populism and the Return of the Repressed in Neoliberal Europe.* Oxford and New York: Berghahn Books.

Kalb, D., and Tak, H. (2005). 'Introduction: Critical Junctions – Recapturing Anthropology and History'. In D. Kalb and H. Tak (eds) *Critical Junctions: Anthropology and History beyond the Cultural Turn.* New York and Oxford: Berghahn Books, pp. 1–27.

Kideckel, D. (2009). *Getting by in Postsocialist Romania: Labor, the Body and Working Class Culture.* Indiana: Indiana University Press.

Marx, K. (1976). *Capital* (vol. 1). London: Penguin.

Narotzky, S., and Smith, G. (2006). *Immediate Struggles: People, Power, Place in Rural Spain.* Berkeley: University of California Press.

Ost, D. (2005). *The Defeat of Solidarity: Anger and Politics in Postcommunist Europe.* Ithaca: Cornell University Press.

Sider, G. (1986). *Culture and Class in Anthropology and History: A Newfoundland Illustration.* Cambridge: Cambridge University Press.

Turner, T. (2005). 'Marxian value theory: An anthropological perspective'. *Anthropological Theory* 8(1): 43–56.

Verdery, K. (1996). *What Was Socialism and What Comes Next?* Princeton: Princeton University Press.

Wolf, E. (1982). *Europe and the People Without History.* Berkeley: University of California Press.

9 Post-industrial Landscape: Space and Place in the Personal Experiences of Residents of the Former Working-class Estate of Ksawera in Będzin

Kazimiera Wódz and Monika Gnieciak

Introduction

Over the course of several decades the global capitalist economy has been reshaped by restructuring processes that have been described as a transition from an economy based on a factory system and mass production to an economy based on knowledge/information and signs (Castells 1996; Lash and Urry 1994), or from Fordism to post-Fordism (Scott 1988; Amin 1995 et al.). The effects of these worldwide transformations are particularly clear in the regions and towns whose origin and development were connected with mass production. Currently, the old industrial regions of Europe and the US are grappling with serious economic problems, subjected as they are to the pressures of global competition and post-Fordism's focus on flexible specialization, just-in-time production and the popularization of various forms of subcontracting that have scattered worldwide in accordance with the logic of minimization of transaction costs (Scott 1988).

The problems are becoming increasingly pressing, especially in those areas where declining industries are not being replaced through any major investments, where new jobs in the sector of services, especially specialist services requiring high levels of qualification (such as financial, legal, consulting, educational, public-relations services, etc.) are unable to make up for losses related to the liquidation of plants that once provided employment for hundreds or thousands of employees, including those with limited qualifications. Forced by external economic conditions, the processes of deindustrialization exert a negative influence across the lives of residents of former workers' estates that had been located near a place of work such as a factory, a steelworks or a mine. The decline of a plant is often seen by those affected as the beginning of a personal and a family drama, a struggle for survival and the emergence of identity dilemmas connected with attempts to cope with a new reality. This new reality, ushered in by the crisis of Keynesianism and the welfare state, is determined by a new, emerging symbolic order based on the doctrine of neoclassical economics and the economic practice of deregulation (Harvey 1989).

This chapter draws on research in Ksawera estate in the town of Będzin[1] (Silesian Voivodship) in southern Poland and formerly strongly associated with the "Paryż" coal mine until its closure in 1995[2]. The aim of this study was to reconstruct residents' memories and emotions related to changes linked to the industrial decline of the region. The research was based on individual interviews with residents on a workers' estate and group interviews conducted with former workers of the "Paryż" mine. The analysis highlights the dynamics of memories, visions of space and the changes that have taken place over the last 16 or so years since the mine was closed in 1995. The main aim of the chapter is to reconstruct the representations of places connected with the respondents' biographies, locating the analysis of transformations of the space of the post-industrial estate within the context of an *emotional geography*. This constitutes an interdisciplinary field linking the sociological perspective with an emphasis on the emotions associated with a sense of a certain space, with the subjective shape of feelings and mental reconstructions of places and landscapes (Davidson and Milligan 2004). The process of liquidation of the "Paryż" mine has resulted in deep transformations in everyday life, its rhythm and qualities. Many places have changed their spatial status, their functions and, often, their owners. Structural and spatial changes have affected the way residents used to perceive, value and describe their close surroundings. The importance of place is always connected with its emotional associations, whether of anxiety, distress, a sense of loss or love.

Place and Memory

In the classic representation of space and place made by Yi-Fu Tuan, space symbolized freedom, a multitude of possibilities as well as alienation and loneliness; place, however, referred to something intimate, known, safe and constant (Tuan 1987). This approach was slightly modified by the influences of the critical school in geography. While for Yi-Fu Tuan place is a profoundly positive term, in the writings of David Harvey (1993) or Tim Cresswell (1996) it is both a product of, and a tool for, establishing social hierarchies of power, exclusion and constraint. The importance of place is established by virtue of a social contract in which the voice of the stronger and the more privileged drowns the voices of minor groups and communities who are therefore excluded from the processes of making sense. The social importance of place is thus a product of uneven negotiations, which are never complete and never free from dispute or controversy. Moreover, unlike space or landscape, place must be experienced and "lived". Owing to the practices through which place is experienced, it is significant as a never-ending process rather than a constant state, part of the ongoing social production of sense.

Researchers dealing with topographies of memory indicate that many features of place share common ground with the concept of collective memory (cf. Halbwachs 2008; Nora 1997). Place brings back memories and serves as a symbolic and material implementation of the past, since "The preservation of recollections rests on their anchorage in space" (Wachtel 1986:216 after: Alderman and Hoelscher 2004: 348), although the durability of history it entails is relative and unstable. Obviously, many material objects are capable of evoking memories but the power of place is unique. It affects our senses in many different ways (through sight, sound, smell, touch and, sometimes, taste), becoming a convenient source of memory (Cresswell and Hoskins 2008). The experiential character of place links it to social remembering and is connected with practice; this way places are linked with individual and/or social dimensions of memory. In fact, as Casey points out "We might even say that memory is naturally place-oriented or at least place-supported" (1987: 186–87). Reading about certain events or viewing their representations in a museum is one thing—actually being in a place of historical interest is quite another matter.

Places of memory are more than monumental representations of important national events. Many of our evocations of the past are part of "collective memory", which is constructed and transmitted through a number of diverse cultural practices. What is thus commemorated is not synonymous with events in the past. Instead, the very process of commemoration defines what is significant and worthy of being remembered. There is thus a complex process whereby: "Memorials are important symbolic conduits not only for expressing a version of history but casting legitimacy upon it as well. They give the past a tangibility and familiarity—making the history they commemorate appear to be part of the natural and taken for granted order of things" (Dwyer and Alderman 2008: 167).

Places of memory are very distant from the clarity and durability associated with the senses, as variable as everyday pressures, ideologies and governments, and are far from being stable and anchored in the axiological order. Although they may represent history, they are not a natural expression of the past. Rather, they also reflect contemporary events, problems and social tensions. (Dwyer and Alderman 2008: 168). The creation of places of memory is a central process in the development of social memory and integral to formation of cultural identities as well as political communities (Agnew and Duncan 1989). Regardless of the range of struggles with the sense, form and location of places of memory—local, regional or national, they are often connected with more general disputes over who has the right to represent the past.

In the last decade or so, there has been a remarkable increase in the number of studies on the connections between place and memory. The most important reasons for the revival of interest in collective memory include the process of de-totalitarianization of Central and Eastern European countries that involves a profound process of de-semiotization and re-ideologization of public space, expressed in the destruction and erection of statues, the re-compositions of museum exhibitions, and changing the names of streets and squares. This revival has been accompanied by a multitude of studies on heritage, museums and places of memory reflecting the political character of actions on a living organism of the national/state/local past (Edensor 2005a, 2005b, 2008; Till 2005, 2006, 2007; Dwyer and Alderman 2008; Rose-Redwood et al 2008; Alderman and Hoescher 2004). Underlying the intense interest in social memory there have been in-depth reflections on the character of modernity and on the pace of social (and spatial) changes that don't entirely erase the traces of other visions, practices, and experiences:

> Modern imperatives to swiftly bury the past produce cities that are haunted by that which has been consigned to irrelevance. Accordingly, the contemporary city is a palimpsest composed of different temporal elements, featuring signs, objects and vaguer traces that rebuke the tendencies to move on and forget. The urban fabric retains traces of failed plans, visionary projects, and sites of collective endeavour and pleasure that have been superseded by more modish projects.
> (Edensor 2008: 313)

The political and economic transformations which took place in the years after the Second World War had an impact on the area under research: successive governments—communist between 1945–89, and liberal since the 1990s—had their own vision of how to administer big industry. For the communists, the Zaglebie area, with its industrial base, was the symbol of the socialist (meaning working-class) homeland. The advent of capitalism denoted the introduction of deindustrialization, dismantling large-scale places of work to be replaced by banks, call centers and supermarkets.

Paryż/Zawadzki/Paryż Mine

The Ksawera estate was formed as a company-owned worker's settlement[3] closely connected to the neighboring industrial plant. The "Paryż" coal mine was established between 1876 and 1890 as a modern mining and processing plant set up by the public limited company of the French Italian Association of Dąbrowa Coal Mines. After the Second World War the mine was nationalized and as indicated in the mine's monograph in response to the social and political activity of the pit and strong leadership there, the authorities requested that staff rename the plant to better reflect its place in Polish landscape and renounce the identification of the plant with the French capitalists that had exploited it. So, the plant was renamed, from Paryż to Generał Zawadzki (Rechowicz 1974: 121–122). Aleksander Zawadzki was born at Ksawera, and the story of his house will recur in this analysis. The change of names was a political measure that was part of much more extensive actions aimed at legitimizing the new authorities, both those of the mine and those of the country. Having the "Paryż" Mine renamed as the "General Zawadzki" mine anchored capital, assets and property within the boundaries of the Polish People's Republic. As Connerton has argued, the naming of place is highly symbolic not only as markers of place but also because "when names are assigned to places, those who do the naming are often particularly aware of the memories they wish to impose" (Connerton 2009: 10–11). Renaming of public places is strictly correlated with the decline of governments, revolutions, conquests or rapid processes of forming new collective identities built under the pressure of current events.

Several decades on, following the downfall of communism in Poland in 1989, we see that "history" has come full circle. As the residents of Ksawera reminisce, this time the return to the earlier name of KWK "Paryż", was defensive, as one of the steps taken in order to save the plant from liquidation. This second change of name was meant to restore the memory of the history of the mine, capture its origins before the Polish People's Republic. The changed name, evidence of the new and, in the view of residents of the post-mining estate, frankly worse times, gave rise to some complications, evident in generational differences. For example, the respondents in our study who would have spent all their adult life working in the "General Zawadzki" Mine still use this as the "true", and post-war, name. The younger residents, often former miners' children, tend to use the name of KWK "Paryż". A woman teacher, resident in Ksawera explained:

> They renamed it to "Paryż" later (. . .) but the younger generation of twenty-five year olds, who no longer remember this "General Zawadzki" Mine, tend to remember the "Paryż" Mine and they won't know [where this name came from—authors' note].

The actions taken to "defend" the mine were not successful; the plant has not been in operation for 16 years. But the mine is still present in the respondents' memory. A job in the pit provided the basis for family life; it structured the social relations within the estate, legitimized the divisions across the estate's class structure and shaped the community and everyday life. The mine remained at the center of everyday life after work, dictating the rhythm of everyday activities, organizing the spaces of leisure, funding holidays and trips and cementing friendships and neighborhood relationships. Unsurprisingly, therefore, the residents' memories, or the stories of the past, refer directly or indirectly to the place of work. Despite the fact that there are now shops and non-mining businesses on the premises of the former mine and a new housing estate, built to a higher standard, was erected nearby, in the stories told by older people the mine is still present although it no longer exists in physical form. A former mine worker who lost her employment when the mine went into liquidation said:

> I would rather prefer it was still in operation [the mine—the researcher's note]. Life on the estate used to be different then. You would see people (. . .). Everybody used to start at 7 am, loads of people, it was bustling

then. So very different! Everybody used to know each other, they would wait for one another and walk together to work in groups or bunches. And now it's so quiet.

Ruins and "Ghosts of the Past"

A recurring theme in our respondents' statements is loss, what they were deprived of in the process of transformation, and, incidentally, of what the surrounding space keeps reminding them. The ruins of the infrastructure of the former mine, such as the crèche (Figure 9.1) nursery school, canteen and restaurant (Figure 9.2), the shabby and derelict "Zagłębianka" sports complex (Figure 9.3), the desolate platform of the "Będzin Ksawera" railway station (Figure 9.4) with no station building and no ticket office, Aleksander Zawadzki's birthplace, regularly visited by schoolchildren during the Polish People's Republic period, and now in the process of being demolished. These are the places the residents of Ksawera would privilege in their stories, as evidence of their recent prosperity and a sad marker of the estate's decline.

In the descriptions of the space of the estate, various temporal orders mingle as former functions overlap with current uses of places. Time has lost its linear character, and the past interweaves with the present such that memories can oust reality. Ruins play with the mechanisms of memory, enhancing multiplications and intertwining the senses, reflecting complex landscapes of space place and affect: "[T]rauma and discontinuity are fundamental for memory and history, ruins have come to be necessary for linking creativity

Figure 9.1 The ruins of the crèche facilities, Ksawera Estate.

Figure 9.2 The former mine infrastructure: the canteen and restaurant buildings, Ksawera Estate.

Figure 9.3 The derelict swimming pool of the "Zagłębianka" sports complex.

Figure 9.4 Będzin Ksawera railway station.

to the experience of loss at the individual and collective level. Ruins operate as powerful metaphors for absence or rejection and hence, as incentives for reflection or restoration" (Settis 1997, after Edensor 2005a: 139).

Ruins are not "living pasts" as much as "allegoric re-presentation of remembered loss itself" (Stewart 1996: 90). For Tim Edensor ruins, or even places left behind by ruins, the "spaces between buildings" (2005b: 829) are places from which counter-memories of the society can be articulated. While developing official topographies of memories is part of the strategy which determines where and how things, activities and people should be placed (Berman 1982), there also appear places in the city where memory becomes revived, practiced and articulated in another way. Learning these memories is essential to see what has been made invisible, banished from social recognition (Gordon 1997). The city goes on endlessly, but throughout its constant changes it "leaves behind traces of previous material forms, cultural practices, inhabitants, politics, ways of thinking and being, and modes of experience" (Edensor 2008: 315). Traces of the past are clearly seen on the outskirts of towns where displaced memories have not been erased completely. Marginal urban spaces and their derelict streets "invoke Bataille's idea that production always generates its negative, a formless spatial and material excess which rebukes dreams of unity" (Edensor 2005b: 833). Ksawera, an estate which used to be a node of communication, a destination for hundreds of employees crowding its streets every day, has now become a forgotten, desolate place excluded from the rhythm of city life. In the words of a former employee: "it's just a 'dormitory town' nowadays".

Another woman, the wife of an ex-worker who was forced to seek an income after the closure of the mine in 1995 pointed out:

> When the mine was still in operation and the train went in between 5 and 6 am, masses of people would get off, everything was thriving, there was a canteen, they used to buy in a baker's, then the canteen was converted into a processing plant by a private proprietor, then he wound it up for some reason, I don't know why, dismissed the staff and closed down the business, and the rest was demolished by some youths (. . .) Over there where you can see that run-down building there used to be a nursery school, and also a crèche. They belonged to the mine. That shabby part that is still used is the nursery school, and the part that is renovated is now a waterworks, that is where the crèche used to be. When the mine was in operation women could enjoy good working conditions. The woman could leave her child in the nursery school or the crèche. They were run by the plant. It's all gone now. There is only one nursery school left.

For over a decade the "Zagłębianka" stadiums and swimming pool had been the pride and joy of the residents, their meeting place and an important space within their collective world. Now, the derelict "Zagłębianka" sports center is another focus of Ksawera residents' memories. It is for them a symbol of transformation, trauma, being abandoned and neglected, at the same time that encapsulates the complications of property and the instability of the real estate market and the incomprehensible laws of the capitalist market. The period of transformation is remembered by our respondents as a time of confusion, during which the facilities they used and needed lost their legitimate owner—the mine—and acquired a new one—municipal or local authorities or a private company administering the acquired facility, which were, according to our respondents, led by not always clear logic. The following exchange, which took place in a group interview with former miners from the Ksawera estate, expresses the depth of sentiment regarding what has been lost:

Respondent 1: this is what hurts the most—Zagłębianka and the whole sports center, which is . . .
Respondent 2: Yes it's over there behind the railway tracks.
Respondent 1: It's not only you that it hurts, because it's a huge area . . .
Respondent 3: This is tragedy. Three full size football pitches, tennis courts, swimming pool, volleyball, the area is fenced and is falling into ruin. When the mine fell down, it was over.
Respondent 2: There was a football team . . .
Respondent 1: I remember . . . there was Zagłębianka. It was called—the so-called "Sahara". It was just sand. And then when

	the mine was set up, it was fixed. It was one of the better stadiums in the region. The pitch was so good that the first league teams would come here. And then it was falling down slowly . . .
Respondent 1:	We were ready to—we wanted to share the costs ourselves. They were taking care of the stadium too, they mowed the lawn themselves, trained. Practically all residents would go to see a match. And now it's over.
Respondent 4:	But it was first league . . .
Respondent 1:	Women's team won the national championship.
Respondent 3:	Not only a match, there was a swimming pool; they would go to the swimming pool too. *When the stadium was alive*, and when there was a match, everybody would go with their families, kids, wives . . .
Respondent 4:	Yeah, it was just nice to spend time relaxing there.
Respondent 2:	In summer whole families used to relax by the pool (. . .).
Respondent 3:	Nice area, it was destroyed completely.
Respondent 4:	Just like the mine.

Another testament is provided by the wife of a former employee of the mine:

> It is easy to forget. I remember us going out to the Zagłębianka stadium for a match, enter the stadium, the neighboring pitches, I mean the side pitches at the Zagłębianka stadium center, where we used to play football or go to the swimming pool, this open air swimming pool in summer, well it is all gone now. Why is that? Was it because of the mine? I remember the time when they privatized it, a businessman invested some money in it—he must have had good intentions—unfortunately it failed and it is like that now.

According to the respondents, the sports complex fell prey to an incompetent policy, the financial degradation of the mine area and utter lack of ideas about how to develop the extensive leisure infrastructure. In the interviews respondents pointed out that there was a new way of dealing with land, there was a commercialization of what had once been communal spaces, and which became a commodity aimed at bringing profits as a result of transformations. A woman teacher resident in Ksawera said:

> They built a nice sports hall by the primary school. So what? The hall has been built and took this pitch where the kids used to play and there's no pitch at Ksawera now, no place for the kids to play football, just like at Zagłębianka. And this hall is not for the kids from the estate, the hall is earning money out of rent from various institutions that use it under lease.

After the time of "our" steelworks and mine came the time of "them", some unidentified administrators who are driven only by their own financial interest, and they did not take care of the residents' needs. The space ceased to be "ours" and instead became distant, "belonging to someone else". A strong emotional content is present in the vocabulary used by the respondents: the mine was not "restructured" or "put into liquidation", but it "died" just as the once "living" stadium did, as victims and witnesses of the decline of an era.

A particularly poignant marker of past prosperity and current deprivation of the working class and its loss of social prestige is a place that was the home of Aleksander Zawadzki. All that remains is a strip of grass with what used to be a shed, now converted into a private residence. In the 1990s some unknown delinquents set fire to the house, and the plaque marking the importance of the site was stolen. As was the case with the mine, for some of the residents this house still "exists" and functions within the mind map of the estate, living the life of a phantom. A former miner, who retired in 1987, explained that:

> This is where General Zawadzki came from. Soon after the war he became Voivode for the whole region of Silesia and Zagłębie. As he came from this region the mine was renamed to include his name. *There is still the house where he grew up.* Just at the end of Ksawera. It was located behind the school, in Ściślicki Street. Now it is ruined, just ruins. There used to be a plaque, recently removed . . .

The difference between the official history included in the consciously built places of memory and the history told through stories and ruins consists in the fact that the latter does not mystify the past, does not present a smooth course of events, changes without losses and costs, ideologically seamless narrative in the sequences of events and causal relations. Instead they evoke unfulfilled fantasies, former desires and unrealized plans of the past. Cherishing the memory[4] of the place where the home of Aleksander Zawadzki was located supports a history understood in terms of human life without big politics. This contrasts with what we see as black-and-white history, to produce a history that is boiled down to ordinary life in the framework of a different social order, which does not mean flawed, immoral or unimportant. "Although elites have had more control over the establishment of places of memory in public settings, they cannot control how they are perceived, understood, and interpreted by individuals or various social groups (. . .). Places of memory in a national capital, for example, are probably experienced differently by international visitors, by national citizens from various regions and social groups, and by the residents living in that city" (Till 2007: 297). According to a woman teacher who lives in Ksawera:

> [And] I am always wondering, because every period, every history, every epoch has its own people. Some people did a lot for their times. Nobody's perfect, it's obvious that they might have gone astray, or did something wrong. I look at it in a bit of a different way, this man general Zawadzki, did a lot for Ksawera. So I was surprised that so soon

they made him ... (...) These older people do owe a lot to communism. Although you couldn't buy much in the shops then and there were a lot of worries, but I remember those days as a child, that it used to be merrier at Ksawera, families used to be tied more closely, they would meet up outdoors, homes were left, so to say, wide open. As a child I remember me and other children eating dinner, six plates, everybody eating this soup together. Now it's gone.

Spatial Symbolic Representation of Capitalism

Residents of Ksawera cherish memories of the past removing whatever is unimportant or sometimes uncomfortable; it is part of the processes of social remembering, in which forgetting is the inseparable and constant reverse of memory. The capacity and power of memory have their limits and the turbulent times of the 1990s have left a lot to remember. The period of transformation is marked by chaotic ups and downs of businesses, new projects which were given up sooner than they were formed, and the instability of spatial elements, the functions of places, and generalized ongoing change of the map of the social world. A woman teacher explained

> There used to be a cash machine in the building which houses the residents' association; there was a cash machine for one year, and it was used mostly by older people, they had to open their accounts, a lot of them used it. They could withdraw money easily. It's gone now. They removed it. Now we have this Netto store, a fantastic square next to the association [irony—author's note], there used to be a fish processing plant which was liquidated it could have made a perfect site for a shop, but because of, as far as I have heard, the man who own the "Pszczółka" store and another one in the building, he is "well-connected", and took pains not to let that shop be set up, as it would be a competition for him. So apart from groceries, a butcher's, a green-grocers, a market square with some stalls, there is a hairdresser, three salons I think, there is nothing at Ksawera.

For the residents in our research banks, hypermarkets, concrete car parks (Figure 9.5) are the spatial symbols of post-transformational reality, as aggressive marks of the new space, in which they cannot see room for themselves. The crèche facilities, canteens, nursery schools and shops with a wide assortment and prices adjusted to working-class customers are replaced by facilities that alienate residents from their own space. A woman who had worked at the Paryż Mine and changed jobs several times after the mine was closed down described this process and reflects on the implications of the changes:

> And you see, everything closed down here, all businesses, mines, steelworks. And they opened supermarkets, but to go there you must have loads of money. How do you think you will make your living? Nothing's

Figure 9.5 The new urban landscape: the "Pogoria" hypermarket.

free. And everywhere these beautiful big supermarkets around. Pogoria, have you been to Dąbrowa Górnicza? Have you seen how much a pair of shoes is? I keep searching. I wouldn't buy such expensive shoes. Who is it for? For some elites, I guess. An average, ordinary person won't buy any because he can't afford this jacket or something. They opened them, and there's no manufacturing plant. If only there was one. Once it paid off to run some knitting business, they used to make some sweaters, knitwear and stuff, I don't know. Today they will import everything and on top of that . . . And how is it made there when they export stuff to us here. Plus a margin. And here in Poland nothing happens. And there are lots of banks everywhere. We have so many banks here in Będzin that you won't see anywhere else. There used to be just one. Just look over there, in Modrzejowska Street a new beautiful bank has opened. And over there where the bank is—I've forgotten the name- they have changed street names . . . You have two banks there. There's one on the corner and another one just behind it over there. One bank next to another. When you go down up there where the Biedronka store is located you will pass a bank after another, everywhere banks.

Conclusions

Since the beginning of the 18th century, when industry was developing in the territory of the present-day Upper Silesian Industrial Area, the pit and the steelworks were the symbols of the region. The miner's ethos and pride in working in the harsh conditions of the pit shaped the identity of the inhabitants of working-class settlements long before the Polish People's Republic was established. With the transition to the capitalist market, the biggest loser of the transformation proved to be the working class (Gardawski 2009: 74). According to David Ost, it is paradoxical that the decline of the working class and the degradation of their social world have their roots in the time of Communism, which presented workers with very particular conception of class. This conception—Ost says—although attractive for the working class had the effect of diminishing their position, and as a result the working-class movement became an exceptional power, but it did not simultaneously show concern for specific interests of workers. But it was this fascinating conception of class that caused the position of the working class to prove so weak and highly unfit to the post-communist conditions of market economy. Since the workers' movement represented universal interests, it did not represent the interests of workers as such (Ost 2007:257). Workers, and especially miners, so privileged during the period of Gomułka's rule, had an ideologically reinforced sense of the unique character of their work and enjoyed a certain resource of political and symbolic capital (at the same time that they suffered from the absence of economic or cultural capital). After the system changed, the political capital of the working class was exhausted, and the only capital workers possessed was the only one to be fully disavowed (Ost 2007:56).

Visiting desolate factories and penetrating the remains of steel plants in search of the residues of the industrial past, Tim Edensor admitted being "haunted by the ghosts of a working class". He cited Roger Bromley, who argued that this class has become a "ghost in the machine of contemporary British politics, the great 'unspoken' (Edensor 2008: 328). The experience gained in discussions based on international studies points to the parallel fate of Polish and British working class subjects as a result of rapid transformation. Working-class communities share a sense of alienation, helplessness, and nostalgia for bygone times, a mixture of pride and bitterness connected with the loss of a former valued position. Our respondents' statements lack a clearly formulated critique of social transformations from a broader political or economic perspective. They distinguish, more or less clearly, between the macro- and micro-political issues at the level of personal experiences and lived disillusions. These can be linked with the specific conditions of systemic transformations in Poland, which originated in the postulates put forward by the working class and the intelligentsia.[5] The market transformations were, after all, implemented with widespread support across the social spectrum. Revolt against the official policy and hypocrisy of public life under state socialism was common. However, tensions appeared between a rejection of an abstract vision of public order and the sense of attachment to some of the familiar and safe conditions of living in a concrete, everyday and intimate space. What is left is "discomfort with the reifications of old working-class culture and the disappointment over failed collective dreams" (Edensor 2008: 328). The transformation did not result in the disappearance of the working class, but it did accelerate the process of its fragmentation, marginalization and social isolation. This "decline of collective dreams" may be interpreted from the chaos of estate spaces, ruins that contrast with trim apartment blocks or a modern sports hall next to the derelict swimming pool of the "Zagłębianka" complex.

Notes

1 There were over 30,000 Jewish people in Będzin before the Second World War, that is, about 80 percent of town population. Almost the entire Jewish community was exterminated by the German Nazis at Holocaust. However, this tragic episode in a history of Będzin was not the part of scope of SPHERE research concerning analysis of post-industrial changes, which have occurred since the half of the 1990s of the 20th century (when the mine has been closed). Hence, social memory of inhabitants of Ksawery has been examined only in terms of memory about a mine "Paryż".
2 This article describes and discusses part of the results gathered within the SPHERE project: space, place and the historical and contemporary articulations of regional, national and European identities through work and community in areas undergoing economic restructuring and regeneration, 7th FP EU, theme 8.5.21 Coordinator: Middle Eastern Technical University, Turkey, partners: London Metropolitan University, UK and France, Institut fur Arbeitsmarkt—und Berufsforschung, Germany, Universidad Complutense de Madrid, Spain, University of Silesia-Poland.
3 Factory housing estates were created in close proximity to industrial works as a place of residence of workers employed in a mine or steelworks. Built by the owners of the works, the housing estates bound the life of employees and their families to the place of work. Successive generations inherited flats and the works enjoyed the stability of employment of skilled workers.
4 In their stories of the industrial past former workers, miners, steelworkers idealize history, smoothing over local conflicts and heroizing the hardships of working class life. This *smokestack nostalgia* (High and Lewis 2007) constitutes the common feature of the interviews collected in six post-industrial regions during the SPHERE research.
5 Workers and representatives of intelligentsia are the two social strata which actively contributed to the overthrow of communism in Poland. Within the ranks of the established in 1980, first, independent of the Communist Party, Solidarity Trade Union there were rank and file as well as management members who were representatives of these two classes. The postulates raised by Solidarity throughout the 1980s aiming at democratization of the state, underlay the bloodless system shift triggered off by the first free elections since the Second World War, which were held on 4 June 1989. This date marks the beginning of the social and political transformation in Poland.

References

Agnew, J., and Duncan J. (1989). 'Introduction', in J. Agnew, J. Duncan (ed) *The power of place: bring together geographical and sociological imaginations*. Boston: Unwin Hyman, pp.1–8.
Alderman, D.H. and Hoelscher, S. (2004). 'Memory and Place: Geographies of a Critical Relationship'. Social & Cultural Geography 5(3): 347–355.
Amin, A. (ed) (1995). *Post- Fordism: A Reader*. Oxford: Blackwell.
Berman, M. (1982). *All That Is Solid Melts into Air*. London: Verso.

Bondi, L., Davidson J. and Smith, M. (2005). 'Introduction. Geography's emotional turn', in L. Bondi, J. Davidson, M. Smith (ed) *Emotional Geographies*. Aldershot: Ashgate, pp. 1–16.

Casey, E.S. (1987). *Remembering: A Phenomenological Study, Studies in Phenomenology and Existential Philosophy*. Bloomington: Indiana University Press.

Castells, M. (1996). *The Information Age: Economy Society and Culture*, vol. I: *The Rise of Network Society*, Oxford: Blackwell.

Connerton, P. (2009). *How Modernity Forgets*. Cambridge and New York: Cambridge University Press.

Cresswell, T. (1996). *In Place/Out of Place: Geography, Ideology and Transgression*. Minneapolis: University of Minnesota Press.

Cresswell, T., and Hoskins, G. (2008). 'Place, persistence, and practice: evaluating historical significance at Angel Island, San Francisco and Maxwell Street Chicago'. *Annals of the Association of American Geographers* 98(2): 392–413.

Davidson, J., and Milligan, C. (2004). 'Embodying emotion, sensing place—Introducing emotional geographies'. *Social and Cultural Geography* 5: 876–899.

Dwyer, O.J., and Alderman, D. (2008). 'Memorial landscapes: analytic questions and metaphors'. *GeoJournal* 73: 165–178.

Edensor, T. (2005a). *Industrial Ruins Spaces, Aesthetics and Materiality*. Oxford, New York: Berg.

Edensor, T. (2005b). 'The ghosts of industrial ruins: Ordering and disordering memory in excessive space'. *Environment and Planning D: Society and Space* 23: 829–849.

Edensor, T. (2008). 'Mundane hauntings: commuting through the phantasmagoric working-class spaces of Manchester, England'. *Cultural Geographies* 15: 313–333.

Gardawski, J. (2009). 'Teorie struktury społecznej a świat pracy', in J. Gardawski (ed) *Polacy pracujący a kryzys fordyzmu*. Warszawa: Wydawnictwo Naukowe Scholar, pp. 65–85.

Gordon, A. (1997). *Ghostly Matters*. Minneapolis: Minnesota University Press.

Halbwachs, M. (2008). *Społeczne ramy pamięci*. Warszawa: Wydawnictwo Naukowe PWN.

Harvey, D. (1989). *The Condition of Postmodernity. An Enquiry into the Origins of Cultural Change*. Oxford: Blackwell.

Harvey, D. (1993). 'From space to place and back again', in J. Bird, B. Curtis, T. Putnam, G. Robertson, and L. Tickner (eds) *Mapping the Futures*. London: Routledge, pp. 3–29.

High, S. and Lewis, D. (2007). *Corporate Wasteland. The Landscape and Memory of Deindustralization*. Ontario: Cornell University Press.

Hoelscher, S., and Alderman, D.H. (2004). 'Memory and place: geographies of a critical relationship'. *Social and Cultural Geography* 5(3): 347–355.

Lash, S., and Urry, J. (1994). *Economies of Signs and Space*. London: Sage.

Nora, P. (1997). *Realms of Memory*. New York: Columbia University Press.

Ost, D. (2007). *Klęska Solidarności". Gniew i polityka w postkomunistycznej Europie*. Warszawa: Muza.

Rechowicz, A. (1974). *Kopalnia Generał Zawadzki. Dzieje zakładu i załogi*. Katowice: Śląski Instytut Naukowy.

Rose-Redwood, R., Alderman, D., and Azaryahu, M. (2008). 'Collective memory and the politics of urban space: an introduction'. *GeoJournal* 73: 161–164.

Settis, S. (1997), 'Foreword', in M. Roth, C. Lyons and C. Merewether (eds) *Irresistible Decay: Ruins Reclaimed*. Los Angeles: Getty Research Institute, p. vii.

Scott, A.J. (1988). 'Flexible production systems in regional development: the rise of new industrial spaces in North America and Western Europe'. *International Journal of Urban and Regional Research* 12: 171–186.

Stewart, K. (1996). *A Space on the Side of the Road: Cultural Poetics in an "Other" America*. Princeton: Princeton University Press.

Till, K. (2007).'Places of memory', in J. Agnew, K. Mitchell, and G. Toal (eds) *A Companion to Political Geography*. Malden: Blackwell Publishing Ltd, pp. 289–301.

Till, K. (2005). *The New Berlin: Memory, Politics, Place*. Minneapolis: University of Minnesota Press.

Till, K. (2006). 'Memory studies'. *History Workshop Journal* 62: 325–341.

Tuan, Y. (1987). *Przestrzeń i miejsce*. Warszawa: Państwowy Instytut Wydawniczy.

Wachtel, N. (1986). 'Memory and History: Introduction'. *History and Anthropology* 12(2): 207–224.

Section IV
The Politics of Resistance

10 Workers and Populism in Slovakia[1]

Juraj Buzalka and Michaela Ferencová

"There are three useless things in the world: male tits, women's hanky-panky and a trade union."

(Péter Hunčík 2011)

The heroes of Péter Hunčík's novel, *The Border Case*, live in a small town, the dominant type of settlement in Slovakia and most of Central and Eastern Europe. These towns are the seats of state offices, regional markets and shopping malls. The inhabitants do not trust the formal institutions of the state. Indeed, the frequency of top-down transformations experienced in Eastern Europe has encouraged a heavy reliance on family networks and friends. Furthermore, with few exceptions, which are more likely to relate to sports or entertainment rather than recognizably political events, there is little interest in mobilizing or organizing around particular causes. Even workers living in larger cities share patterns of behavior with these townfolk that could be described as politically passive. In this chapter we argue that this set of attitudes and behaviors is associated with what we call a "post-peasant" social setting.[2]

One of the origins as well as the outcomes of these attitudes of what looks like resignation lies in the fact that many workers in Slovakia and elsewhere in Eastern Europe have opted for casting protest votes in favor of the populist right, which mobilizes and is mobilized by feelings of anger through a process that is well described by David Ost (2005) in the case of Poland. We nevertheless believe that the wide support for the right—which we characterize as right wing despite claims of leftist orientations by some of the parties we are concerned with—can only partially be explained as effects of global neoliberal policies. We argue that wider 20th century developments under state socialism as well as the effects of the expansion of the market into everyday life after state socialism are critical in explaining the apparent passivity of workers and the ongoing success of populism. We argue that most of Central and Eastern Europe (CEE) broke from an agrarian structure relatively recently with the advent of modernization under state socialism, which had the unexpected effect of reproducing and even strengthening many elements of rural life, including the central importance of kinship, the cohesion of small-scale communities and the importance of national and religious conservatism. These elements became crucial in post-socialist development, including the recent "cascading" of market reasoning (cf. Gudeman 2008) into areas of life where the market had not been present before.

Post-socialist transformations relied upon, and have enhanced, what we call the post-peasant social setting. The specific outcomes of market expansion and of the current neoliberal stage have to be re-evaluated in the light of careful examination of what has taken place in the everyday lives of East Europeans in the process of modernization. What we describe as a "post-peasant" political culture that has remained relatively isolated from the world of capitalism, was to large extent formed across the region during socialism. We argue that market transformations after socialism drew on the small-holders' nostalgia, observable in the popularity of pre-socialist ideologies of property and self-sufficiency. These ideologies and practices were reproduced or invented in the context of the scarcity economy under socialism, and was then rejuvenated after socialism collapsed. State socialism also created its own "populist culture" evident in the ideologies of peasant-worker unity, in support for folkloric representations of the nation and the production of both "urban peasant" and rural urbanites.[3] We believe that this ambivalent state socialist modernization project played the key role in creating post-peasants.[4] With the neoliberal market the post-peasant setting served as a shelter from the effects of the post-socialist withdrawal of the state as the key provider of social security.

Our approach to post-peasant populism moves away from the peasant family as an economic and structural unit towards emphasizing a "rural" morality, imagery and ideology that is ingrained in memories and expressed in narratives, rituals and symbols that are found in large cities as well as in towns, villages and hamlets. All socialist countries saw massive influxes of rural people into urban centers that did not become urbanites in any straightforward sense. The economy of scarcity under state socialism also contributed to shaping the post-peasant world, in terms of actual practices and relations based on kinship and moneyless exchanges, as well as narratives about the essential nature of these practices and relations.

This romantic *Gemeinschaft* has been for long inspired by Herderian nationalism. Already at the beginning of the 20th century populism in much of East Central Europe came to be embodied in ideologies of peasantism, which emerged intellectually as reactions to both Russian populism and Western socialism (Kitching 1989). Peasantism, according to Ghita Ionescu, took peasants explicitly as the key social prototype and proposed molding the society and the state according to peasants' conceptions of work, property and administration. Peasantism blended these social-economic doctrines with a nationalist concern for the emancipation of the "people" from foreign domination. Finally, it claimed that the peasantry was entitled to take a position of leadership within political society, "not only on account of its electoral preponderance but also because of its innate spiritual and national values" (Ionescu 1969: 99). In his analysis of the interplay of religion and politics in South-East Poland Buzalka argued (2007) that post-peasant populism aimed to defend those who found themselves "the losers of transformations" but based its legitimacy on the established repertoire of state socialism while drawing on earlier well-established institutions, such as the Catholic Church. As a significant political force, post-peasant populism developed after the decline of socialism and in direct reaction to the expansion of the market.

By presenting the history of post-socialist workers at the largest steel plant in Slovakia, located in the second largest Slovak city, we aim to illustrate the development of this model of post-socialist politics. In Košice, with a population of 240,000 in 2010, large-scale steel production started in the 1960s as an element of socialist state industrialization. We also discuss the local history of workers at the steel plant in Podbrezová, a town of 4,000 inhabitants in Central Slovakia. This steel plant has a long history, going back to the middle of the 19th century. In contrast to the socialist city of Košice that is re-inventing its equally powerful pre-socialist urban tradition along with nurturing its socialist, industrial working class legacy, the majority of workers in Podbrezová have never left the mixed peasant-worker way of life inherited from their parents and grandparents.

Slovakia experienced its most dynamic industrial development in the period of "actually existing socialism" in the 1970s and 1980s. As a consequence of the mass recruitment of workers seeking employment in the new plant, the predominantly peasant inhabitants of the region experienced profound transformations, not least in terms of shifting to an urban environment. Košice grew in three decades from being a city of 70,000 to a regional center of 240,000 inhabitants, primarily steelworkers and their families who maintained contact with relatives in their village of origin and reproduced the patterns of solidarity learned in their place of birth in the city.

The Podbrezová plant was built in the 1840s and within the next few decades the region developed into one of the industrial centers of the Hungarian Kingdom. Nevertheless, industrialization was not reflected in a parallel process of urbanization, so that factories are located within small industrial towns or villages. Several generations have continued to live in villages surrounded by mountains and in close contact with the natural environment. An agrarian way of life helped sustain enduring kinship and friendship networks. Even those who left their region because of marriage or work generally remained in close contact with their relatives. Interestingly, the inhabitants of Čierny Balog near Podbrezová, where the major part of fieldwork in Central Slovakia took place, appear to identify very strongly with foresters' traditions associated with their environment—now understood in terms of cultural heritage—rather than with the industry that they see as complementing the foresters' way of life.

The legacy of the rural past has played an important role in post-socialist Slovakia. The representation of Slovaks as a rural nation began with 19th century nationalism and became incorporated within communist ideology through the notion of "the people". The Slovak term *ľud* ("the people" differs from *"občania"*—the citizens) denotes both a sense of ethnicity and of the cultures of lower classes, as opposed to the lords and elites. The sustainability of extended families and understandings of their important role in society formed the structural basis of both socialist and post-socialist politics. Backed by the strong position of the Catholic Church, broad family relations supplemented the collapsing state welfare system and, thus, softened the negative consequences of post-socialist transformation and the recent economic crisis. As Frances Pine (this volume) argues, socialist ideology and state practice devalued the private sphere as antisocial, bourgeois and individualistic, but for most people it became the sphere of trust and morality, and the center for practical kinship and social relatedness. The importance of the family as a source of emotional and economic support is reflected in housing patterns; nearly all the respondents from Čierny Balog near Podbrezová live in family houses divided into two or three sections (floors or attachments), providing space for separate households that are connected through kinship ties. Households are widely characterized by the circulation of goods, services (mutual help; e.g., shopping, care work), and common or shared domestic work (e.g., in the garden). Nevertheless, the circulation of goods and services is not limited to family members inhabiting the same house but is rather a matter that involves broader family and friendship networks. For example, it is still not uncommon to build a family house with the help of relatives and friends. Close distances enable frequent visits to elderly parents and/or grandparents, to help them in the household or with gardening and to get a supply of fresh home-made food. Even today, all the respondents from Čierny Balog reported food growing and/or animal breeding as a supplementary source of livelihood, a statement that corresponds with our own observation of small plots or gardens at almost every house in the village. These provisioning practices (Narotzky 2005) reduce dependence on wages and monetary income more generally, cushioning individuals and families from the fluctuations in the market for jobs and commodities and protecting them from the effects of the incursion of the market into everyday life. It also has implications for action and reaction to economic and political conditions.[5]

Post-Socialist Transformations

Despite the optimism prompted by the Czechoslovak Velvet Revolution of 1989, the pro-market transformations first introduced in 1991 posed new dangers to the country's development towards a tolerant, market-based society. The decisive intellectual leaders of the revolution conceived of the market as an economic expression of a genuinely free (civil) society. At the same time, other intellectuals who lost prominent positions they had enjoyed under state socialism shifted towards nationalist positions that included a "populist" critique of pro-market transformation. In the 1992 Czechoslovakian elections voters supported secessionist movements and populist economic ideologies. Combining autocratic methods with the mobilization of voters through nationalist ideologies, Vladimír Mečiar became the key figure in disqualifying socially sensitive alternatives to market liberalism in Slovakia. Supporting the emergence of a "domestic capitalist class" through privatization, Mečiar's rule came to symbolize the peak of cronyism and corruption after the fall of state socialism, which had itself been identified with the informal economy, familism and corruption. The success of foreign privatization that followed the end of Mečiar's rule in 1998, including the privatization of banks, healthcare and pensions, some of which were transferred to international corporations, would not have been easily accepted by the population if "national privatization", which drew primarily on surviving socialist power networks, had not allowed this previous extensive 'state capture' under the national populism of Vladimír Mečiar.

When it came to joining the EU, membership required the restructuring of heavy industry, privatization and internationalization (Trappmann 2013). The popular notion of a "return to Europe" was perceived as integral to economic liberalization. In the 1990s Slovakia produced and exported mostly low value-added products, with steel products representing the exception to the rule. Since the early 2000s, manufacturing benefited from direct foreign investment that introduced higher levels of technological and managerial sophistication, especially in the automotive industry, in electronics and in steel production. The Slovak economy experienced stable and continuous growth until late 2008, when the economic crisis began to weaken demand for exports, especially automobiles and electronics. Economic growth and increased production were associated with higher levels of employment. As the economy gradually recovered from the crisis after 2011 wages increased. The growth of the automotive industry encouraged the development of subcontracting supply chains of firms, including the steel and metal sectors. The introduction of a flat tax rate in 2004, in place until 2013, increased the attractiveness of the Slovak Republic as a business location for domestic and foreign capital and, together with cuts in welfare benefits, initially had the effect of incentivizing employment. In fact, the benefits of high levels of growth in the 2000s remained largely concentrated in areas with the highest levels of foreign direct investment, especially Western Slovakia, resulting in regional disparities. Historically underdeveloped Eastern Slovakia suffers from a lack of domestic and foreign investment as well as state investment in infrastructure. As a result of uneven development, economic emigration to more developed parts of Europe has increased rapidly. Additionally, the social exclusion of the poor has increased, especially for the Roma population who are mainly concentrated in Eastern Slovakia. This, along with long-term unemployment, continued to challenge state policies. Given the loss of trust in the state and the law, elites have either tended to concentrate on the market as the basis of a legitimate modernizing project or remained 'populist' with no feasible alternative development program. Because the state was discredited both in relation to socialism and post-socialism, pro-market policies offered seemingly fair and democratic options in a society described by its members as corrupt and nepotistic. These developments are explored in the following sections in relation to two research sites.

Steel Making in Košice and Podbrezová[6]

As one of our informants, a 39-year-old worker in Košice remembers, "socialism was falling apart slowly. Comrades were still enjoying their positions and if not comrades then their children were!" One of the major instruments—and effects—of post-socialist transformation in Slovakia has been the privatization of state-owned industry. The process has been generally perceived as based on corruption, nepotism and cronyism. The most important Slovak steel plant, *Východoslovenské železiarne* (VSŽ) in Košice, was privatized in 1995, becoming the property of factory managers and trade union bosses through clientelistic relationships. In 1998 the firm was almost bankrupted as a result of incompetent management and after it was rescued by the state, it was finally purchased by the US Steel Corporation in 2000.[7] The plant in Podbrezová followed a similar privatization path but remained in the hands of local managers who gained full control over the firm in the middle of the 1990s and have enjoyed a reputation for responsible ownership. Since privatization both companies have continued to be the major source of income in their region.

The major difficulty for the workers has been the fact that the country experienced massive deindustrialization in the decade following 1989. The re-industrialization that took place in the 2000s, based on automobile and electronics manufacturing in Western Slovakia, could not offer enough well-paid jobs for the tens of thousands across the country who had worked in factories under the socialist system. In effect, the number of workers employed in the Košice steel plant has fallen by more than 50 percent, to the current level of 12,000, and in Podbrezová, employment levels have declined from 5,000 to 3,000 workers. The US Steel workers have continued to enjoy living standards well above the regional standard; however, the lack of employment opportunities—the unemployment rate in Eastern Slovakia was above 17 percent in 2014 after the deeper decline above 20 percent in 2011—and flexibility requirements at work have prompted anxieties about job loss. In Podbrezová, a position in the steel plant has remained even more desirable among the inhabitants of the Horehronie region, where unemployment has been higher than in Košice.

In 2011 the Podbrezová workers reported monthly salaries of about 600 Euros net. In Košice the average wage of skilled workers with a permanent contract was about 750 Euro in 2010 (roughly the nominal average wage in Slovakia by 2011). In 2013, official statistics from the factory suggested that the average worker's wage rose to 1400 Euro in Košice. In Podbrezová wages increased more modestly since the crisis. Our informants say wages have probably reached 900 Euro net in 2014. According to workers from Podbrezová, the managers employ rhetorical devices, such as the claim that there are "thousands of unemployed waiting for a job in front of the factory gates", and this image is in accordance with the widespread opinion that "Soták [the director] is feeding the region." This representation of the factory director as a benign feudal lord overseeing his domain explains some patterns of local political culture, built on agrarian hierarchies but bolstered by conspiracy theories about Podbrezová managers making deals with local politicians to prevent competitors for local labor from emerging.[8] As an economic and social center for Eastern Slovakia, Košice differed from Podbrezová, with a wider range of jobs available, including those in the public sector and services, as well as in the IT sector, education and culture.[9] The Socialist era's investment in metal production offered advantages regarding the availability of skilled labor to support development in other sectors, such as IT (Hudec and Šebová 2012). New jobs for young educated employees were created, with further investments arising when Košice was nominated European Capital of Culture 2013. Although unemployment has remained high—and extremely high among Roma—in recent years, with a national average of 14 percent in 2014 but almost 20 percent in some parts of Eastern Slovakia, the lack of skills and education of the workforce has created a demand for skilled workers across the country. By 2015, Slovak work agencies were stating that there was a need to import workers from abroad, especially for automotive and its auxiliary industries.

Despite the overall changes, most steelworkers interviewed in Košice and Podbrezová in 2010 and 2011 claimed that recruitment and promotion are still heavily based on personal connections and family ties, much in the same way as obtained under socialism. Sometimes this patronage system is presented as the firm's strategy for supporting "the families of ironworkers" or aimed at employing people who are loyal to the "steelworker's destiny". In this instance the job is "inherited" by sons from their fathers or other close relatives. In Podbrezová this principle has been officially incorporated within the enrollment practices for holiday jobs and internships for secondary school and university students. Holiday jobs are provided on condition that at least one of the applicant's parents is employed in the firm. In the case of internships, applicants are required to inform the firm whether they have—or have had—relatives working in the firm. A positive response enhances the chances of success. Generally speaking, but especially in worker-peasant Podbrezová, patronage contributes to uphold the position of employers as an influential regional elite.

While family networks are important, workers in both plants describe the effects of new forms of work organization, especially in relation to pressures in favor of efficiency and discipline, including the introduction of strict anti-alcohol measures, which erodes contact between workers and reduces the opportunities for socializing. Investment in new technologies, the flexibilization of work, including subcontracting and temporary contracts, contributes to these effects as workers with similar experience are divided by the differences in their contracts. New models of individual advancement based on certification and continual individual evaluation, target-based individual systems of payment contribute to higher levels of workplace competition, gossip and envy. The recruitment of workers hired from outside the steel sector has increased competition for jobs and split the workforce between new and older employees. In response, older workers exclude newcomers from strategically important information circuits, signaling job insecurity across both groups and confirming the central role of patron-client relations. This contradiction—on the one hand the continuing effects of patronage and on the other, recruitment on the basis of 'individual achievement'—does not eliminate the patron-client system. The individualized system is carried out by managers who are themselves involved in the informal power bargaining at the workplace, making decisions about the individual worker's fate. A 51-year-old informant reported: "If you are honest, they tell you that you are stupid. Those who are slim, they live best, whisperers and the like . . . Someone who works does not get the benefits, nothing . . . The one who sneaks gets the bonuses".

The steelworkers have remained as removed from protest as they were during the massive deindustrialization of the 1990s and the lay-offs of the post-2008 crisis, despite these unfavorable changes. Considering the prestigious position workers enjoyed under state socialism, it is important to ask what factors contribute to this passivity and how, instead, foreign investors praise the disciplined labor of Slovakia. The absence of mobilization or of alternative political proposals from the left must be understood not only as effects of neoliberal policies. Rather, explanations must reach beyond the factory and the ideologies and practices of contemporary capitalism to consider the autochthonous traditions of post-peasant populism with roots in pre-socialism and how it developed under state socialism.

Mobilization and Populism

Some elements of the explanation for the lack of mobilization over changing conditions of work—and the turn towards right wing populism—can be identified in the local histories of the trade unions. Under socialism there was a single trade union organization with workplace branches, based on compulsory membership. This contributed to worker apathy, aggravated by the fact that the unions did not depend on their members and had little incentive to fight on their behalf. Workers' main recollections of that period revolve around trips and holidays organized by the union; furthermore, in late socialism several advances were made, especially for industrial workers, without the intervention of the trade union.

More recently, a significant decline in trade union membership is attributed to the domination of leadership positions by older men, a failure to address workers' concerns and organizational weaknesses (Uhlerová 2009). Rather than being the champions of workers' rights, trade union leaders were for long identified with the dominant interests of the communist state, and later, of the employers. On the other hand, as working conditions and salaries in the steel plants remained at levels that were above regional averages, there was little pressure on union bosses or on their patronage networks; workers in Košice and Podbrezová saw the trade unions as powerless and largely obsolete.[10] While union leaders claim that their pressure on management is responsible for the social peace that has prevailed in the factory since privatization, workers suggest that the peace is based on the complicity between union leaders and the factory owners.

In Podbrezová workers' relationships with their patrons are characterized by ambivalence, as anger mixes with gratitude. As we have seen, the director of the plant is seen as a powerful man with a tough character who is in control of the situation, and whose qualities account for the success of the firm. Some workers believe that he is directly responsible for each worker's fate; others think of him as a good patron who understands their needs but is led astray and is misinformed by his subordinates. Among his virtues is his ability to secure better access to healthcare for his workers, his support of employees studying at university, and his invitation to specialists to give lectures in local towns to reduce students' need for travel.

Beyond the specific patterns of power relations in the factory, there is the widespread devaluation of the notion of class since the end of the socialist regime (Ost 2005). The decline in the efficacy of class symbolism in the public sphere accounts for a deeper decline of working class identities than we see in parallel cases of transformation towards post-industrial reconfigurations in Western Europe. As we argue, this "weak working class identity" has strong autochthonous origins in Slovakia and other parts of Eastern Europe. A more nuanced approach to populism in the post-peasant setting is needed, recognizing the meaning and significance of "the people" as opposed to the elites, rather than the weak proletariat facing the mighty interests of global capital. This argument points to the longer-term transformations of class and of the agrarian sector that preceded socialism, further developed under state socialism and deepened under the impact of global neoliberalism.

In 2015 one of Buzalka's key informants (a 45-year-old manufacturing worker) posted a joke on his social media page. The joke, entitled the "seven wonders of socialism", claimed that under socialism: (1) everybody had a job; (2) even if everybody had a job, nobody worked; (3) even if nobody worked, the plan was 100 percent fulfilled; (4) even if the plan was followed, there was nothing available; (5) even if there was nothing available, everybody had everything; (6) even if everybody had everything, everybody was stealing; (7) even if everybody was stealing, nothing was missing. The joke illustrates the mixture of rational calculation of conditions (shortage economy and corrupt state) and deep nostalgia for relaxed work conditions, relative affluence and a "good life" among workers under state socialism. The vast majority of workers in Slovakia do not want a return to the old communist system. Their nostalgia for a socialist past reflects a much wider set of issues that we have characterized as relating to the social and economic relations of a post-peasant setting. This explains why workers today are receptive to those politicians who do not promise a return to a socialist past but who do offer them a promise of security, encapsulated in the protection of family values, and support of a way of life they once supposedly enjoyed and that includes both the importance of conservative values, including religion, and the relative social peace that characterized the countryside during late socialism socialism, as well as defense of the nation, its cultural uniqueness and need for self-sufficiency. East European liberals and the left—writes David Ost (2005)—abandoned a concern with class, leaving open a space for the right and populist movements to mobilize the "people" instead. Although the case for a de-legitimation of class can be made, we would argue that in countries like Slovakia "class" has always been subordinated to the concept of "the people". These were represented as rural folk with distinctive cultural features and traditions that distinguished them from agrarian, communist, and later cosmopolitan elites. In other words, in contrast with the workers of major Polish cities that gave rise to strong workers' movements, in the small industrial towns of other Eastern European countries as well as Poland, what emerged under socialism was not an industrial working class, but a widely conceived non-elite class of worker-peasants that embraced conservative values.

The relatively recent departure from agrarian social structures in Central and Eastern Europe (CEE) achieved through the modernization processes brought about by state socialism, failed to produce a break with many aspects of rural life that remained important during socialism and following its demise. Ost recently argued that nationalism and other culturally grounded discourses are not an escape from class, "but a path of workers from the dominant culture to realize their class aspirations" (Ost 2015: 69). Following Tomasz Zarycki (2015) who argued in favor of the analyses of class and rank as 'dually stratified' processes in a tension that is far more significant in Eastern and Central Europe than in West European society, we would extend his observation to argue that class politics in countries like Slovakia has always had a stronger base in peasant values and social structures than in those we might associate with an industrial economy.

Final Remarks: Post-peasant Proletariat

In relation to the recent rise of populism in Europe, Don Kalb (2011) argues that nationalist populism is "in fact a displacement of experiences of dispossession and disenfranchisement onto the imagined nation as a community of fate, crafted by new political entrepreneurs generating protest votes against neoliberal rule" (Kalb 2011: 1). According to Kalb (2011: 3–4) "cultural" dependency based on a nation's narratives needs to be replaced by more dynamic, class-centered, world-systemic multi-level view on populism as "critical junctions" of local and global processes (Kalb 2011: 11–12). We agree with Kalb that the focus should be "on social relations first and only secondly on cultural symbols" (Kalb 2011: 11–12). However, local processes and the specific sets of relations that strengthen the appeal of populist discourse do not always clearly reflect junctures with the "structural power" embodied amongst other things in the global market. We argue that the case studies we carried out in Slovakia reveal the continuing significance of (post)agrarian rather than (post)industrial parameters. It is the post-peasant condition rather than the circumstances of a post-industrial proletariat that, drawing on religious, rural and ethnic representations, were mobilized long before the wave of neoliberal transformations reached the shores of postsocialism. The history of the state in Slovakia renders the forms of populism we encounter here very different from those we observe historically in Western and Southern European and Latin American forms of populism. A fundamental difference is to do with the experience of the ambivalent modernizing interventions carried out in the socialist era. There have never been feasible liberal programs preceding the rise of populism, criticizing (market) liberalism in Eastern Europe, as Kalb argues in his theory of junctions (see Kalb 2011; see also Kalb in this volume). We argue that patterns of post-peasant populism had already existed for decisive parts of populations before, under—and due to—the impact of autocratic communism, and in case of Slovakia and several other East European countries, due to earlier legacies of fascist autocracies under Nazi tutelage with deep roots in the Herderian concept of *Volkgeist*. As has been pointed out by many authors in the field, these histories are decisive in defining and understanding the current advance of populist politics in Eastern Europe (Hann 1985; Eyal et al.1998; Nagengast 1991; Pine 1987; Dunn 2004; Kalb 2011).[11]

Nevertheless, the entanglement of deeply rooted local values and structural domains is perhaps best illustrated in what is apparently the most significant evidence of the importance of the deep cultural patterns of contemporary populism: the historical animosities towards Roma. Michael Stewart's edited volume (2012) approaches anti-Gypsy attitudes within broader shifts in European politics and culture, especially as a by-product of the European project. Drawing inspiration from Douglas Holmes' concept of "integralism" (2000) and Mabel Berezin's sociological perspective on social and political insecurity (Berezin 2009), Stewart argues that the EU project "creates the broad conditions of receptivity to xenophobic politics" (Stewart 2012: 3). This politics is based on a shift away from mid-20th century racism towards a cultural politics resembling Huntington's "clash of civilizations", which, "re-framed as incomparability and purportedly culturally distinct behaviors is being used to justify radical demands for 'root and branch' reform of educational, welfare, and, in extreme cases, citizenship regimes" (Stewart 2012: 9). This analysis highlights the social and historical depth of cultural frameworks and responses. We suggest that a framework that recognizes the importance of post-peasant values is more sensitive to these complexities than the conclusions afforded by the post-industrial paradigm favoring the decisive role of global neoliberalism.

In this chapter we wished to show that longer term, historical traditions of populism in Eastern Europe are important for understanding the success of contemporary populist positions prompted by Viktor Orbán in Hungary, Róbert Fico in Slovakia and Jarosław Kaczyński in Poland among others.[12] These historical legacies intersect with the pressures of global neoliberalism, which is increasingly the target of these skilled populist entrepreneurs. As we emphasized, the role of ambivalent socialist modernization in the creation of post-peasant settings has been the key internal factor in populism's success. This contributed to workers' passivity and sympathy for the message of populist leaders. The parallels between the rise of populism in Eastern and Western Europe may, in our view, be emphasizing their origins in a systemic reaction to the pressure of global capital at the expense of the crucial importance of recognizing their autochthonous origins and relatively independent operation as forms of post-peasant populism in most of Eastern Europe.

Notes

1 We would like to express very sincere gratitude for careful comments on the earlier version of the draft of this paper to Victoria Goddard. The research and this text were prepared thanks to the support of MEDEA—Models and their Effects on Development paths: an Ethnographic and comparative Approach to knowledge transmission and livelihood strategies; collaborative project no. 225670 of the EU 7th Framework Program. The final versions of the text were prepared thanks to WOGYMARKET—Workers, Gypsies, and the Market: The Anthropology of New Fascism in Eastern Europe; FP7-PEOPLE-2013 IOF contract No. 626128.
2 A more thorough elaboration of the issue of post-peasant settings, with a focus on Catholicism, can be found in Buzalka 2007.
3 For more details on how the socialist state reproduced populism in Slovakia, see Buzalka 2004.
4 For a discussion about ambivalent socialist modernization of Slovakia, see especially Podoba 1999; 2003; 2015.
5 The major part of fieldwork in Eastern Slovakia was carried out in Šaca, a distant suburb of Košice with five thousand inhabitants, located very near the steel plant. The suburb resembles a village more than an urban district, as it is built on what had been two pre-socialist agricultural settlements. This rural character of the suburb has provided appropriate conditions for agricultural activities even if only on a limited basis, of some gardening and/or animal breeding for one's own family needs. The lowland region south of Košice, the steel plant location, is surrounded by villages and small plots of vegetable gardens where urban inhabitants come to spend their weekends and holidays, contributing to the suburb's atmosphere of informality and conviviality.
6 The fieldwork was carried out over several periods in 2010 and 2011 in Košice and Podbrezová; in total more than 40 current and former workers in both sites were interviewed in greater depth in summer and autumn 2011.

7 US Steel is an integrated steel corporation with major production operations in the United States, Canada and Central Europe (see www.ussteel.com).
8 Under socialism, workers were trained in secondary schools attached to the factories and work trajectories were predictable from the moment of school enrolment. After privatization education was detached from production and high unemployment levels meant that the number of skilled workers available for employment in the declining industry was high. There was no need to employ inexperienced school alumni. In the case of Podbrezová, qualified workers were hired by the steel plant from the collapsing machine factories in the declining region and even from the bankrupt chemical factory (e.g., locomotive drivers and shunters). Former well-positioned employees had to take lower grade positions in the organization of steel production, if they wished to have a job at all.
9 The city was a hub for technical and technological innovation, at least in part because the Technical University in Košice, which cooperated closely with the steel plant, has remained one of the top higher education institutions in the country,
10 According to official sources, the president of US Steel Košice, George Babcoke, earned 4,85 million Euro in 2014 (as a matter of curiosity, in the same year the USS corporation base in Pittsburgh was releasing 10 percent of its workforce). As a local journalist noted, the average US Steel employee would need 275 years to earn as much as the president earned in one year. In a similarly telling comparison, the amount earned by the president annually equals the price of 60 three-bedroom apartments in Košice. See http://kosice.korzar.sme.sk/c/7707338/babcoke-minuly-rok-v-kosiciach-zarobil-485-miliona-eur.html, accessed on 21st March 2015.
11 Analyzing the failure of the Polish state to collectivize the peasantry, Chris Hann (1985: 169) registered a 'contradictory persistence of peasantry' and of a 'peasant ethos' in rural, socialist south-east Poland, as well as a 'late flowering of peasant populism'. He also noticed similarities between the rural Solidarity movement of the 1980s and populist protests from before the Second World War. Hann was unsure what sort of populism could be preserved by modernized family farmers, but he noticed in his "village without solidarity" that the only functioning community institution was the Roman Catholic Church. He wrote that "certainly the ethos has survived and peasants are united in their profound suspicion of the authorities", and "peasant religiosity remains at a high level, ensuring that the Catholic Church remains the major solidifying force in local communities and in the nation" (Hann 1985: 176). Nagengast's (1991) description of the reproduction of class relations in Poland during the socialist period offers perhaps a more direct view of the reproduction of some elements of pre-war populism. Focusing on elites, Eyal et al. (1998) called what happened in Central Europe after 1989, "making capitalism without capitalists". They characterized this process as a distinctive new strategy of transition adopted by an alliance of technocratic and intellectual elites in societies in which no class of private owners had existed before the introduction of the market. The most important mechanism for the installation of capitalism was the reproduction of various forms of capital based on status, prestige, skills and social ties that the elites held and reproduced despite regime changes. In Poland, Pine (1987) observed continuity in issues of land and inheritance, in social stratification and family structures and in cultural practices and ideologies, all of which took only slightly different forms under socialism. Dunn (2004) found that in a food processing plant in Poland the Catholic values of the family were reproduced in the workplace in post-socialist capitalism. The surviving peasantry, the role of the family and the existence of an independent Catholic Church are the most important examples of this kind of continuity from the agrarian era in Eastern Europe. Last but not least, Kalb

also acknowledges the "different surface" of East European populisms, even while predominantly focusing on the "big picture" of synchronized appearance of populisms East and West, driven by neoliberalism (Kalb 2011).

12 The leaders of the respective East Central European countries have been frequently known for, and accused of, populist demagogy and illiberal attitudes. After his victory in 2014, the Prime Minister of Hungary Viktor Orbán even introduced changes towards illiberal constituionalism and has been criticized for xenophobic nationalism, and openly anti-European attitudes. After the elections held in the autumn of 2005, the new Prime Minister and and, since the Autumn of 2015 the leader of the government party Jarosław Kaczyński, announced the Fourth Polish Republic with a program of reforms couched in moral terms, invoking patriotism and proclaiming the moral recovery of Polish society based on conservative Catholicism. Nominal social democrat and twice Prime Minister of Slovakia Róbert Fico, whose party won the parliamentary elections of 2016, has been known for expressing controversial xenophobic attitudes towards minorities, including Hungarians, Roma, sexual minorities and recently, also Muslims.

References

Berezin, M. (2009). *Illiberal Politics in Neoliberal Times: Cultures, Security, and Populism in a New Europe.* Cambridge: Cambridge University Press.

Buzalka, J. (2004). 'Is rural populism on the decline? Continuities and changes in twentieth century Central Europe: The case of Slovakia.' *SEI Working Paper No. 73*, University of Sussex, Brighton. Available at http://www.sussex.ac.uk/sei/documents/wp73.pdf. Accessed on 24th September 2016.

Buzalka, J. (2007). *Nation and Religion. The Politics of Commemoration in South-East Poland.* Berlin: Lit.

Dunn, E. (2004). *Privatizing Poland. Baby Food, Big Business, and the Remaking of Labor.* Ithaca and London: Cornell University Press.

Eyal, G., Szelenyi, I., and Townsley, E. (1998). *Making Capitalism without Capitalists: Class Formation and Elite Struggles in Post-Communist Central Europe.* London: Verso.

Gudeman, S. (2008). *Economy's Tensions, the Dialectics of Community and Market.* New York and Oxford: Berghahn.

Hann, C. (1985). *A Village without Solidarity: Polish Peasants in Years of Crisis.* New Haven: Yale University Press.

Holmes, D. (2000). *Integral Europe: Fast-Capitalism, Multiculturalism, Neofascism.* Princeton: Princeton University Press.

Hudec O. and Šebová, M. (2012). 'The ICT Sector Evolution in an Industrial Region of Slovakia'. *Ekonomický časopis* 60(1): 65–82.

Hunčík, P. (2011). *Hraničný prípad.* Bratislava: Kalligram.

Ionescu, G. (1969). 'Eastern Europe', in G. Ionescu and E. Gellner (eds) *Populism: Its Meanings and National Characteristics.* London: Weidenfeld and Nicholson, pp. 97–121.

Kalb, D. (2011). 'Introduction. Headlines of Nation, Subtexts of Class: Working Class Populism and the Return of the Repressed in Neoliberal Europe', in D. Kalb and G. Halmai, (eds). *Headlines of Nation, Subtexts of Class. Working*

Class Populism and the Return of the Repressed in Neoliberal Europe. London: Berghahn Books, pp. 1–36.
Kitching, G. (1989). *Development and Underdevelopment in Historical Perspective: Populism, Nationalism and Industrialization.* London: Routledge.
Nagengast, C. (1991). *Reluctant Socialists, Rural Entrepreneurs: Class, Culture, and the Polish State.* Boulder: Westview Press.
Narotzky, S. (2005). 'Provisioning', in J. Carrier (ed) *A Handbook of Economic Anthropology.* Cheltenham and Northampton: Edward Elgar Publishing, pp.78–93.
Ost, D. (2005). *The Defeat of Solidarity: Anger and Politics in Postcommunist Europe.* Ithaca: Cornell University Press.
Ost, D. (2015). 'Class and social order. Political consequences of the move from class to culture', in V. Goddard V. and S. Narotzky (eds). *Industry and Work in Contemporary Capitalism. Global models, local lives?* London and New York: Routledge, pp. 64–78.
Pine, F. (1987). *Kinship, Marriage and Social Change in a Polish Highland Village.* PhD thesis. London: University of London.
Podoba, J. (1999). "... they have always known to knock on the right door ..." Continuity, Modernisation and Transformation in one Sub-Tatras Community. *Geographia Slovenica* 31: 201–207.
Podoba, J. (2003). 'Cultural lag as a determinant of social conflicts of the transformation period', *Anthropological Journal on European Cultures*, 12: 157–185.
Podoba, J. (2015). '*Pragnienie nadmiernej konsumpcji. Realny socjalizm, neoliberalizm i wartości na słowackiej wsi*' (Desire for Excessive Consumption. Actually Existing Socialism, Neoliberalism and Values in the Slovak Village), in J. Burszta and A. Kisielewski (eds) *Kultura pragnień i horyzonty neoliberalizmu.* Poznań: Wzdawnictwo nauka i innowacje, pp. 277–307.
Stewart, M. (ed) (2012). *Gypsy 'Menace'. Populism and the new anti-Gypsy politics.* London: C. Hurst and Co.
Trappmann, V. (2013). *Fallen Heroes in Global Capitalism. Workers and the Restructuring of the Polish Steel Industry.* Basingstoke: Palgrave Macmillan.
Uhlerová, M. (2009). *Inštitucionalizácia sociálneho partnerstva* (Institutionalisation of Social Partnership). PhD thesis. Bratislava: Univerzita Komenského, Filozofická fakulta.
Zarycki, T. (2015). 'Class analysis in conditions of a dual-stratification order'. *East European Politics and Societies and Cultures* 29(3): 711–8.

11 'A Trojan Horse in Our Midst'
The Saturn Plant and the Disorganization of Autoworkers in the US[1]

Sharryn Kasmir

The Saturn automobile factory in Spring Hill, Tennessee was idled during GM's bankruptcy reorganization in 2009. The decision to temporarily shutter the plant was part of the restructuring plan presided over by the US government after it put up tens of billions of dollars in loans and cash and became the majority stakeholder in the company. By the time of the bankruptcy, fewer than 3,000 people worked at the Spring Hill facility. Most of the 7,200 union autoworkers employed there just a decade earlier had taken buyout packages or transferred to other GM plants in the intervening years, as Saturn sales dropped off, Spring Hill lost bids for new products and the plant bled jobs. In 2011, GM finally made public its plans to assemble a Chevrolet model and employ 1,800 people in Spring Hill; 400–500 in a first round of hiring, the rest later. But the majority of those who moved to Tennessee in the 1980s-90s to work at Saturn had already left the area. The facility would therefore reopen with new GM employees, in entry-level jobs. Significantly, the United Automobile Workers (UAW) contract signed in the wake of GM's bankruptcy permitted newly hired workers to be paid roughly half of what veteran workers earn (*New York Times*, July 12, 2011 and November 11, 2011, *The Tennessean*, Dec. 29, 2011).[2] Spring Hill would thus offer a compensation packet to union autoworkers equivalent to that paid to nonunion workers in Nissan, Honda, and Toyota plants in nearby, southern locations.

The fact that GM is now hiring in Tennessee and elsewhere in the US speaks to the significant savings it secured after the government bailout helped deliver UAW concessions and cheapen unionized labor. Despite concessions on entry-level wages in recent contracts, the UAW held out against a widespread, two-tier workforce, for the inequality among members and diminution of union power it would bring.[3] GM, Ford, and Chrysler—the US "big three"—won this give-back under threat of bankruptcy and the strong hand of the state. This situation replayed the government's bailout of Chrysler in 1979. Then, the UAW granted wage cuts to Chrysler and set into motion GM's own pursuit of concessions on wages, benefits and work rules. The combined power of state and capital won historic setbacks against US autoworkers in both 1979 and 2009.

At first appearance, Spring Hill's diminished current condition seems a stark reversal of the facility's origins as a highly touted *model* plant. Saturn was planned in the 1980s, when Japanese automakers were gaining an increasing share of the small-car market and their management innovations offered labor cost savings and flexibility that US firms could not match. Saturn was GM's response to Japanese competition. It was designed to have the most developed team concept and worker participation programs in the US, and its advertising and carefully crafted brand image claimed it was creating a new labor elite, using cooperation rather than labor conflict to remake the industrial workplace and class identity. Saturn's UAW Local 1853 collaborated with management in this project to make Saturn workers *better than* and *different from* other union autoworkers. It cast aside the national UAW contract and adopted a local Memorandum of Agreement that instituted the farthest reaching regime of labor-management cooperation in the industry and that served as its only labor accord. UAW autoworkers moved to Tennessee from Michigan, Ohio, California, and other states, where their GM plants were struggling or had closed. Some believed they would find more rewarding and fulfilling work lives; others hoped that Saturn would prove to be the "100-year company" that the company promised and that union involvement in planning, managing, sourcing and cost saving would provide the long-term security that eluded them in the places they left.

I argue in this chapter that Saturn instead contributed to widespread insecurity by facilitating the disorganization of autoworkers, one of the most powerful sectors of the US working class. I sketch the part Saturn played in this process by charting three moments in which distinct scales of working-class identification, alliance and struggle—local, national and international—were made and unmade. Following these political moments, we see autoworkers and their union sometimes expanding and other times constricting their political vision and aspiration; sometimes in a position of relative power *vis a vis* capital while at other times backed into defensive postures. Viewed in this way, the case of Saturn lends insight into the *long* unmaking of the US Fordist working class.

I reflect on these insights at the conclusion of the chapter by engaging David Harvey's (2001) essay on a campaign to save jobs at the Cowley auto plant in England. The case of Cowley offers important parallels with Saturn. Notably, both expose the shortcomings of "militant particularism" divorced from "abstract universalism", paired terms that Raymond Williams (1989) conceived to capture what he considered the central dialectic of working class power—the relationship between the immediate, particular feelings and loyalties at the plant or community level, and the universal sentiments and wider geography of struggle and solidarity made through organizational connections and ties (see also Narotzky 2011). Harvey used this framework to express his misgivings about Cowley and the fact this fight to keep one plant open and to save jobs in one location might foreclose a broader, anti-capitalist struggle. However, to stop analysis there and to cast labor struggles such as those in Cowley or Spring Hill as defensive actions with little political potential, as Harvey does (2003), is a mistake. If we are to fully confront the processes at the heart of working-class disorganization, we are better served by the vantage point of historical ethnography that brings into focus an understanding of how workers' visions came to be limited, how organized labor was dismantled in particular places and sectors and how wider alliances and aspirations were defeated in the course of these events. What follows is a (necessarily) brief account of the role of Saturn in these developments in the US auto industry.[4]

Localism and Difference

During contract negotiations in 1991, UAW Local 1853 President Mike Bennett led a brief job action in which Saturn workers wore black-and-orange armbands and staged a slowdown to protest quality problems in the plant; the display was meant to symbolize workers' commitment to the company and to their unique cooperative labor-management pact. It was also intended to delay the launch of Saturn's "risk-and-reward" pay structure, which tied 20 percent of wages to production and quality targets. The unusual stunt won the union praise from Saturn's corporate president who commended workers for refocusing "everyone to the sense of urgency to get the quality problems fixed" (*Business Week*, Dec. 2, 1991: 117). The job action vividly positioned the union as the defender of the brand, and it signaled that 1853 was "a different kind of union", a message that its leaders frequently sounded and that pointedly echoed Saturn's advertising slogan "a different kind of company".

Bennett demonstrated his devotion to Saturn's difference during a 1992 strike at a stamping plant in Lordstown, Ohio over GM's plan to outsource to a nonunion facility. Spring Hill and eight other assembly plants were stalled for lack of parts due to the walkout, and Bennett complained to the press that the International UAW should allow those workers making *Saturn* parts to cross the picket line. In his view, UAW solidarity was less important than protecting the maverick experiment at Saturn and keeping that facility open. Bennett did not support the strike; to the contrary, he believed that Lordstown strikers should support Saturn. He insisted that the role of a local union should be to help the company find ways to compete, including outsourcing. "I don't support the current process", he told the *Wall Street Journal*. "We can't continue to remove wages from competition in the international economy". Although it was hardly necessary, he clarified, "That's my position, not the UAW position", underscoring his distance from the International and what he deemed its adversarial approach to labor-management relations (*Wall Street Journal*, Sept. 4, 1992: A8). Bennett's public comments were all the more consequential since the strike was widely considered to be the UAW's "test of GM's toughness", as the corporation rolled out a three-year plan to shut 21 plants and eliminate 70,000 jobs.

Indeed, GM closed a plant in Van Nuys, California and laid off 2,500 workers on the very day that Lordstown workers went on strike (*Los Angeles Times*, Aug. 28, 1992; Parker and Slaughter 1997:18; *Wall Street Journal* Sept. 4, 1992:A8).

Bennett's disregard for solidarity is evident from his public comments, as is his conviction that 1853 was different from and superior to other UAW locals, but his position is also a manifesto on the geography of working-class identity, alliance and struggle. On this occasion and others, Bennett asserted, "if unions have a future . . . it's 'at the local level' where they can help companies 'explore opportunities to compete'" (*Wall Street Journal* Sept. 4, 1992:A8). He strongly "advocated that unions pursue their interests at the *local level*" (emphasis added, Parker and Slaughter 1997:218) rather than in a national or international field. I interviewed Bennett during my fieldwork at Saturn in 1998–99. He was a committed reformer who *believed* in the Saturn project. Along with hundreds of others who held union-side leadership positions in the plant and who were members of his Vision Team union caucus, he considered that he was playing an historic, transformative role in the US labor movement. He became a national spokesman for labor-management cooperation, authoring articles and persuading other unions to institute Saturn-like reforms. To Bennett labor-management cooperation was a local-level endeavor to collaborate with management to preserve the wage bargain in the US, *one plant at a time*. But this necessarily involved putting union locals into fierce competition with each other in ways that eroded union control of the shop floor and dismantled UAW power at the national and international scales. This development had important ramifications for disorganizing North American autoworkers.

Whipsawing and the Defeat of Internationalism

Fordist localism initiated a key dimension of monopoly capitalist control in the US beginning in the 1920s. It was reinforced in the ensuing decades by federal legislation that codified decentralized labor agreements and outlawed secondary boycotts, mass picketing and multi-employer actions, therein placing significant restriction on labor's sphere of action. This long legal and cultural project of capital and the state, "Americanism and Fordism" in Gramsci's phrasing, severely undermined the ability of labor unions to coordinate actions across space (Carbonella 2014). Localism was greatly extended and deepened in the US during the 1980s, as capital and the state put union chapters into competition, just as they pitted municipalities and states against each other, all vying for investment in an age when the threat of capital flight was ever-present and real. The devastating effect of deindustrialization in cities such as Youngstown, Ohio or Flint, Michigan became part of the national political and popular discourse and a central symbol for the emerging common sense that competition for investment was necessary and urgent. These counter moves narrowed workers' worldviews and disciplined a working class that had become restive, relatively well organized and increasingly radical in the late 1960s to early 1970s (Lembcke 1991).

In auto, this nascent working-class consciousness was manifested in the cross-fertilization of new social movements with political developments in the factories and unions. The important influence of the counter-cultural movements and the anti-authoritarian protests against the US War in Vietnam on workers' consciousness and subjectivity was apparent during the 1973 wildcat strike at GM Lordstown. This infamous strike was over work pace and quality of work life, rather than wages or benefits. The protest of Lordstown's largely young, male workforce signaled that they viewed masculinity, their own humanity and their class subjectivity differently than had their fathers, whose version of working-class manhood was grounded in how much they produced and how tough they were on the job. The sons, on the other hand, demanded more respect and more meaningful work than their rote and exhausting assembly tasks afforded (Rothschild 1973; Terkel 1972: 256–265). The UAW's tactic of staging unannounced, targeted wildcat strikes across the industry, such as the one in Lordstown, similarly evinced a changing political climate and workers' increasing willingness to be militant. Union locals pursued grievance after grievance in order to provoke strikes, and workers used this method to wrest a measure of control over the pace of work and their time, often walking out on a Friday to get a three-day weekend (Rubenstein 1992:237–238). For the UAW this cross-local, national strategy signaled a wider struggle beyond the local wage bargain.

The Civil Rights and Black Power movements likewise influenced organizing, activism and scale in auto. African-American workers formed the Revolutionary Union Movement and League of Revolutionary Black Workers, Marxist-Leninist groups that issued a trenchant critique of racism in the auto industry and the UAW. Their members ran for union office; published radical newsletters connecting exploitation in US car factories with that experienced by black and brown workers in the Third World and farm and service workers in the US; marched in solidarity with Palestinian-American autoworkers protesting the UAW'S investment in Israeli government bonds; and in other ways voiced socialist and internationalist visions that mapped a global geography of identity and struggle (Georgakas and Surkin 1998: 62–68, 132; Geschwender 1977: 92).

In reaction to these developments, GM moved production from the centers of militancy and set out to build plants in the US south, where a strong anti-union tradition and a legacy of racism had long thwarted labor organizing. In response, the UAW focused attention and resources on organizing in the south and successfully subverted this spatial assault by unionizing all of the new GM plants by 1979. GM then turned from its "southern strategy" to a decidedly global plan, and the company invested in technology, experimented with new managerial strategies and set union locals against each other to further undermine labor's power.

The strategy of provoking competition among locals had its seeds in the 1935 National Labor Relations Act's provision for decentralized labor agreements, but it was considerably furthered by GM in 1982, when the corporation demanded that the International UAW reopen its contract to negotiate a cut in hourly wages. Such a concession had been granted to Chrysler during its bankruptcy reorganization and government bailout three years earlier. GM now wanted to cheapen its labor costs to match Chrysler's. The union refused and GM immediately announced it would close four plants; within months it shut Southgate in California. With this heavy-handed maneuver, GM perfected the tactic of threatening plant closings to win national-level give-backs. The company then applied this policy to union locals, requiring them to submit bids in order to secure new product lines; the bids involved plant-specific concessions to make the local attractive enough to win investment and secure work for its members. This practice of pitting local against local is known as "whipsawing" (Mann 1987).

Whipsawing was quickly challenged in Van Nuys, California where Local 645 organized to save their threatened plant. The struggle began after several California factories were closed, including nearby Southgate. In strategizing the campaign, Local 645's political action committee asked the critical question: "[W]hy, except for the most narrow self-interest of its 5,000 workers, the plant *should* be kept open" (Mann 1987: 108). They envisioned their campaign as a fight for worker and community control over economic planning, and the organizers saw themselves as mavericks within the UAW, charting a more militant response to plant closings than had the International, which responded by offering give-backs and facilitating the transfer of workers from plant to plant. Local 645 leaders hoped to set a different course to be followed by other locals and that would push the International to a more radical stance. The campaign moved from the local to the general, developed alliances across ethnic and racial lines and geographic space, and had aspirations beyond saving jobs. In these ways, the Van Nuys fight productively engaged the dialectical relationship of militant particularism and abstract universalism.

Local 645 sent delegates to the 1983 UAW convention, where they raised questions about labor geography and class power: "Why isn't your International union doing more to stop these plant closings?" "Why isn't your local doing more to get other UAW locals to develop a national strategy against plant closings?" (Mann 1987:155). At this juncture, the UAW might have devised a challenge to global capital and made demands of the state, and the effort to protect jobs might have moved to an international stage and broader class politics. But the UAW instead sounded, "the constant theme [of] the battle against imports and calls for protectionist legislation. While delegates cheered wildly at every verbal assault against Japan, there was no strategy offered with which to confront the Big Three automakers on the issue of capital flight or the widespread problem of whipsawing" (Mann 1987:156). Activists again brought their agenda to the 1986

UAW convention, where they joined the dissident caucus New Directions Movement to fight concessions and build a more progressive, internationalist working-class organization. But their New Directions protest slate lost the union elections, and more conservative candidates prevailed. Van Nuys activists likewise lost their fight when their plant finally shut in 1992.

With their position sidelined, whipsawing and intense localism became an ordinary, daily fact of UAW micropolitics. The widespread and unrelenting competition it engendered narrowed the political visions of local unions and their members and pitted insecurity in one place against investment, employment and (temporary) job security in another. Competitive bidding weakened the International, turning it into what one New Directions leader called "a loose federation of locals competing among themselves" (quoted in Mann 1987: 82). Losing a bid for a product might mean that workers faced lay off or saw their factory permanently closed. Successful bids required locals to implement quality circles, worker participation programs and the team concept, a set of practices associated with labor-management cooperation: this managerial regime became the rule of the day. The New Directions Movement and the left labor journal *Labor Notes* considered these so-called cooperative work arrangements to be thinly disguised union-busting tactics. They maintained that the team concept turned workers into petty supervisors of each other's efforts and robbed the union of control over job classifications and seniority rules, two long-time sources of union power on the shop floor. Further, participation and quality programs facilitated the introduction of lean production and brought a speed-up throughout auto (see Parker and Slaughter 1985, 1988, 1994). The Canadian wing of the UAW so strongly opposed labor-management cooperation that it left the International in 1985 over the issue, thereby limiting the union's reach at a time when international connections were more important than ever.

Saturn was the standard bearer of labor-management cooperation, and as such it exerted considerable pressure on the rest of the UAW to adopt flexible, cooperative work rules. Saturn "team members" (as employees were called) worked in groups of 10 to 15 and rotated tasks, thus eliminating job classifications and seniority, and enabling them to replace fellow workers who were late or absent. Teams were "self-directed," operating like small businesses within the plant, responsible for their own budgets, schedules, quality and records. Workers traded hourly wages for a formula that held a portion of compensation "at risk" and paid "reward" based on factory-wide training, quality and production targets, something that looked to critics like a petty form of capitalist return on investment. Rather than a grievance procedure, errant workers went to "coach and counsel" sessions where they were asked to commit themselves to more self-regulating attitudes and behaviors. These techniques were meant to encourage an entrepreneurial ethos on the shop floor (Kasmir 2001) and to harness for corporate profit workers' own aspirations for more rewarding, less monotonous work that was demonstrated in the 1970s at Lordstown and throughout auto by workers who questioned the meaning and purpose of their labor.

Saturn's labor accord departed from the national contract in other important ways, as well. Significantly, it extended job security to 80 percent of the workforce "except in situations of . . . unforeseen or catastrophic events or severe economic conditions" (Memorandum of Agreement 2000:16). In this event, workers would be left without transfer rights or lay off assistance provided by the national contract. The 20 percent without job security had no protection at all, leaving them more vulnerable than were workers covered by the national contract (Rubinstein and Kochan 2001:16). In these many ways, Saturn afforded management a far greater degree of flexibility than any other division of GM, something the corporation wanted to achieve across its workforce.

Along with these contractual changes, corporate managers, counting on the active participation of the Vision Team union leaders, crafted a cultural and ideological campaign carried out in the factory and the public sphere. This campaign had much in common with the Fordist corporate programs of the 1920s that set out to remake class relations. Saturn workers were the objects of a dense public-relations effort that extolled their difference from other autoworkers, who they left behind in the "old-world" of Detroit, Flint, Lordstown, and other ailing industrial cities, where, as the narrative went, the "baggage" of labor-management conflict created a poor work ethic and jeopardized the future of auto manufacturing in the US (Kasmir 2001, 2014). The combined effect of Saturn's labor accord and cultural/ideological project was so great that the president of a Michigan local considered that "Saturn had become a Trojan horse in our midst. Armed with the threat of plant closing, the company is now playing local against local to see who will meet or exceed Saturn's give-backs" (quoted in Mann 1987: 82). Saturn thus marked a milestone in the dismantling of labor's power in auto, a process that began with capital flight in the 1970s and continued in the 1980s with labor-management cooperation, lean production, whipsawing and localism. It was a short step from the narrowed spatial scale of working-class identity and struggle that these developments brought about to Mike Bennett's fervent public defense of localism and difference.

The UAW Contract and a National Geography of Dissent

Given the divisive role 1853 played within the UAW, it is not surprising that when Saturn workers finally expressed their dissent, their opposition came as a refusal of 1853's extreme localism and their own difference from the rest of the union. Dissatisfaction mounted in 1998 amidst growing insecurity in the plant. Sales were off, reward payments and overtime were cut, and there was no sign of a much-needed new product. Saturn workers had already been displaced and their families uprooted (some two or three times before), and they sensed that Saturn would not be a 100-year company and they would face lay off yet again. In this context, union dissidents affiliated with New Directions and *Labor Notes* formed Concerned Brothers and Sisters and waged a months-long effort to return Saturn to the national contract. They sought to regain the security offered by layoff protections (guaranteed income stream, sub-benefits, and the job bank) and transfer rights provided the national UAW contract but not by their Memorandum of Agreement. They also meant to express solidarity with the International.

Concerned Brothers and Sisters held meetings, distributed leaflets, encouraged workers to send letters and emails to the International and they raised questions of identity and alliance. One member expressed his frustration at the destructive impact of Local 1853: "This membership is tired of being the *Experiment that is Tearing down the Foundation Our Great Union was Built Upon*" (Benavides, Feb. 6, 1998). Another assembly worker implored the International to come to Spring Hill and set the local straight: "Please, brothers and sisters of the International don't forget us down in 1853 for our local leadership has lost the way" (Dalton, n.d.). With a restive shop floor and pressure from the International, Concerned Brothers and Sisters forced a referendum on returning to the national contract. Although the referendum was defeated, activists were nonetheless emboldened by their stronger ties to the International and by their success in orchestrating dissent.

Months later, a GM-wide strike that began at two Flint parts plants over outsourcing to nonunion plants offered Concerned Brothers and Sisters a chance to act. With the supply chain interrupted and given widespread concern that GM intended to spin off the Delphi parts division and leave 53,000 workers outside of the GM system (a fear that was soon realized) strikes quickly spread throughout GM. The combined action of the locals had the distinct appearance of a solidarity strike in support of Delphi workers fighting for their jobs: 186,000 workers were out, and 27 of 29 North American assembly plants and scores of parts facilities shut down in the biggest labor stoppage in GM since the 1970s (see Collins 1999). It was an exhilarating time when localism was briefly overcome and the UAW demonstrated resistance that extended across the US and to Canada. Saturn workers, however, remained on the job.

This situation was a disturbing reminder of Mike Bennett's inflammatory position in 1992 during the Lordstown strike. It looked as if Saturn workers would once again stand against their fellow autoworkers, as their union worked with management to find alternate parts suppliers. The *New York Times* reported that 1853 leaders "set aside union solidarity by assembling cars using parts from Japan and at least one nonunion American company, instead of parts from Flint" (July 22, 1998). This was deeply shameful to men and women who came from union cities and UAW families, and whose brothers, sisters and former co-workers were on strike. Their difference had gone too far, and, as they told me, they felt like "scabs". Concerned Brothers and Sisters worked with the International to force their local leadership to hold a strike authorization vote. It was the first time Saturn workers took such a vote, and it was an exciting and emotional time when they rejected their localism in favor of solidarity and broader alliance. The strikes were a month-and-half old when the vote was taken; nevertheless, Saturn's decision to join them was momentous.

Concerned Brothers and Sisters rallied again in 1999 to support Members for a Democratic Union (MDU), a dissident caucus that ran candidates for chapter elections on a platform of bringing Saturn closer to the national contract. In a stunning defeat, all thirteen officers from the Vision Team, including Mike Bennett, were unseated by their opponents. After the elections, there was renewed discussion of returning to the national contract, and in 2004, 1853 voted by overwhelming majority to scrap its Memorandum of Agreement. This decision marked Local 1853's unity with the International, and it suggested an expanded geography of class identity and struggle. But the International was now much diminished: it had suffered decades of capital flight, whipsawing and localism, some of which was facilitated by 1853 itself. The disempowered International was unable to do much to protect jobs in Spring Hill, or anywhere else, and the plant steadily downsized. Workers retired or used the transfer rights they regained in the national contract to move to other GM plants.

Spring Hill no longer produced Saturn models by 2007. GM assigned a portion of the plant to a Chevrolet model, and the remainder went unused. During bankruptcy, GM terminated the Saturn brand altogether and put Spring Hill on hold, until it reopened in 2012 with a two-tier workforce and new hires paid half the wage of veteran workers. Production of a new Cadillac model to begin in 2016 will finally engage the whole facility but only one-third of the workforce. Rather than suffering a reversal of fortunes from its original promise, Saturn might be said to have done its job well. Its purpose was not to dole out privilege by shoring up livelihoods and better working conditions for workers in one location, as the lore of the Saturn model told, but to make a difference among workers and UAW chapters, to encourage localism and competition and to further the disorganization of a once powerful segment of the Fordist working class in the US.

Politics and the Disorganization of US Autoworkers

David Harvey makes a provocative interlocutor for reflecting on Saturn. Harvey joined activists in the late 1980s to help stop the closure of the Rover Group's car plant at Cowley, and he co-edited a volume (1993) with Teresa Hayter to document the campaign. Years later he revisited his political differences with Hayter, who had aligned herself with the militant shop stewards who led the fight (Harvey 2001). Harvey was concerned that the effort to save jobs at Cowley was backward looking, since it sought to protect the privileges of Rover workers and to preserve the social relations of capital rather than imagine a more universal struggle for human betterment. He even questioned whether he should have defended the auto jobs at all, since there was overcapacity in the industry, the plant was a notorious polluter, and Rover made luxury cars for the rich. His long list of misgivings indicates how carefully he weighed his responsibility to the campaign and for the published volume.

Most significantly, Harvey was torn between his support for the militant particularism born in and around the plant and his hope for a broader socialist movement. As he saw it, the campaign was a necessary battle against the company, but waging this local fight might at the same time thwart a larger struggle. Harvey had wanted the conclusions to the book to reflect the complicated nature of the struggle; however, his co-editor prevailed, and they published a more partisan chapter in favor of the shop stewards. After reading *Second Generation* and other works of Raymond Williams' fiction, in which the characters experienced the contradiction between their local loyalties and socialist aspiration, Harvey believed he should have held out for a Brechtian conclusion to expose the shortcomings of the campaign, while also leaving open the possibility that future struggles might emerge from this one. This thoughtful essay has long engaged and troubled me, and my analysis of Saturn developed in dialogue with it. The tensions Harvey pointed to for Cowley resound for Saturn as well. Taking his critique to heart, I similarly reserve endorsement of Saturn dissidents' campaign to return to the national UAW contract as a real advance for labor; at best it was a small victory that suggested that the expansion of political horizon was possible. But if Harvey imagined a rewritten, Brechtian conclusion in order to recuperate the future political possibilities that his initial pessimism might have precluded, I fear that his analysis shortchanged Cowley's past.

When he encountered them in 1988, and as some of the chapters in the co-edited volume detail, Cowley workers had already suffered protracted defeat. In brief, and parallel to the developments in US auto, in the late-1960s and early-1970s workers' frustration resulted in absenteeism, sabotage and constant strikes; in the main, the strikes were not for higher wages, but over conditions of work. This labor unrest together with a militant shop-steward movement coincided with a slowdown in the car market and a decline in the rate of profit. According to John Holloway (1987), workers' militancy was undermining the post-Second World War structure of control; capital was threatened, and British Leyland (BL), then-owner of the Cowley works, sought fixes in technology, but also in a concerted drive to discipline workers. The company declared bankruptcy in 1975, and the restructuring plan effectively nationalized the firm. BL then appointed a get-tough director who called for the full or partial closure of 13 factories, the loss of 25,000 jobs, and a defeat of the shop stewards' power. Management intended to strip stewards of their role in negotiating wages, bonuses and workloads. There was considerable opposition to this effort, but management prevailed. The effect was brutal. One Cowley worker described the impact,

> There's now a constant attack, and all the protective agreements that were established in the sixties are now all gone. Workers are herded

around like cattle [. . .] Workers [. . .] that have worked in off-track jobs for thirty or forty years are given five minutes' notice to get onto track. Often with medical conditions. Often working in a pit with overhead conditions that make it absolutely impossible for them to do the job. And they're just directed totally ruthlessly after forty years of working with the company. 'Get into that pit and do that job or find yourself another job outside.' And I'm not exaggerating at all—that is what is happening every day. Every day in those plants. And the difference between that and what existed when the trade unions had power a few years ago is absolute difference if chalk to cheese.

(quoted in Holloway" 1987: 150)

The iron-fist phase of management was temporary, meant "to destroy the obstacles to managerial control," and deliver a "resounding defeat for labor. What management need to do now is build on this defeat and mould the submissive worker into an enthusiastic worker, proud of his company" (Holloway 1987: 151). In the 1980s Cowley workers were summoned to be enthusiastic, enterprising, and cooperative, as were workers in Spring Hill.

By the time Harvey joined their struggle, Cowley workers had lived through bankruptcy, recovery plans, rounds of corporate merger and division, nationalization, privatization, authoritarian management and finally a cooperative managerial regime that cast them as privileged. This complicated chain of events, characterized by small and large defeats, but also by partial victories and promise, would surely have been difficult to navigate. It might therefore be useful ask the same historical ethnographic questions for Cowley as for Saturn: How were workers' political visions so narrowed that they did not build a struggle beyond attempting to save their own jobs? How were wider alliances and aspirations defeated over the long course of events?

Disorganization is often a protracted process, having the effect of dissipating struggle, rupturing alliance and narrowing fields of identification. Local 1853 leaders and those in other union locals throughout the US engaged in hyper-local politics, and the deleterious effects of their support for whipsawing and labor-management cooperation are an important part of the story of the disempowerment of the UAW and of US labor more broadly. But union members and locals, such as Concerned Brothers and Sisters, Van Nuys Local 645 and the New Directions Caucus, also pursued national and international solidarity. Indeed, the successes of these kinds of larger struggles in the 1960s–1970s triggered revanchist GM's strategy of capital flight, plant closure, whipsawing and a new managerial regime. To neglect this history is to do injustice to the past victories of working classes and to offer analyses that do little to envision a different future. If this short-sightedness with regard to organized labor were Harvey's alone, the point would be academic, but the tendency for Western scholars, even Marxian ones, to dismiss labor while they support what they deem to be more radical social movements is widespread (Collins 2012; Heroux and Palmer, n.d.; Kasmir 2009). Instead, we need to pay close attention to the lives of exploited people, such that we can reconstruct experiences of loss but also of organization and strength, even when those successes have been erased by political discourse, media and official history. We see this attempt in historical ethnographies that carefully trace the processes by which capital and the state unmake working classes—through violence and fear, the creation of difference, dismantling connections and alliances across space, destroying working-class publics—and that assess the manifold effects of these moves on politics and consciousness and the ways that possibilities and scales are closed off (e.g., Narotzky and Smith 2006; Kasmir and Carbonella 2014; Striffler 2002). More than a critique of the defensive struggles that workers in many places have backed into, this fuller perspective allows us to pose the "very radical question of whether or not another life had once been possible and could be again" (Carbonella 2014: 110).

Notes

1 My research was supported by Vanderbilt University's Robert Penn Warren Center for the Humanities, the National Endowment for the Humanities, and Hofstra University.
2 As this volume is being prepared for press in the fall of 2015, GM announced a new Cadillac model and 1,100 new jobs for Spring Hill. This will bring total employment to approximately 2,900 in 2016. Reports are that these will likely be entry-level, tier-two jobs, although the local union is still in negotiations over this issue (The Detroit News, Oct. 13, 2015).
3 There were earlier instances of two- and even three-tier concessions in individual plants, and the 2003 and 2007 national contracts with the Ford, GM and Chrysler contained temporary two-tier concessions. However, the post-bailout agreement more firmly entrenched this practice and facilitated the wider use of entry-level wages throughout the industry.

In fall 2015, contract negotiations were stalled on this issue, and tensions between UAW members and leadership were evidence of the damage done by these concessions. UAW finally bargained wage (but not full benefit) parity to be implemented over eight years. While the prolonged timeframe may mean that two-tier wages will have to be fought again in 2019, and while this provision is balanced against increased leeway in hiring temporary workers, it represents an important advance.
4 For a fuller discussion, see Kasmir 2012, 2014.

References

Benavides, R. (February 6, 1998). 'Letter to Richard Shoemaker. UAW. V.P.-GM Dept.' (xerox).
Business Week. (December 2, 1991). 'At Saturn, What Workers Want Is . . . Fewer Defects', pp. 117–118.
Carbonella, A. (2014). 'Labor in Place/Capitalism in Space: The Making and Unmaking of a Local Working Class in Maine's 'Paper Plantation", in S. Kasmir and A. Carbonella (ed) *Blood and Fire: Toward a Global Anthropology of Labor*. New York: Berghahn Books, pp. 77–122.

Collins, J. (1999). 'Industrial Innovation and Control of the Working Day: The 1998 General Motors Strike', *Social Politics* 6(1): 76–84.
Collins, J. (2012). 'Theorizing Wisconsin's 2011 Protests: Community-Based Unionism Confronts Accumulation by Dispossession'. *American Ethnologist* 39(1): 6–20.
Dalton, K. (n.d.). 'Get a Real Job Roland' (xerox).
The Detroit News. (October 13, 2015). 'GM to begin taking applications to work at Spring Hill.' Available at http://www.detroitnews.com/story/business/autos/general-motors/2015/10/13/gm-begin-taking-applications-work-spring-hill/73859852/. Accessed November 30, 2015.
Georgakas, D., and Surkin, M. (1998). *Detroit: I Do Mind Dying. A Study in Urban Revolution.* Cambridge, MA: South End Press.
Geschwender, J.A. (1977). *Class, Race and Worker Insurgency: The League of Revolutionary Black Workers.* London and New York: Cambridge University Press.
Harvey, D. (2001). 'Militant Particularism and Global Ambition: The Conceptual Politics of Place, Space and Environment in the Work of Raymond Willliams', in D. Harvey, *Spaces of Capital: Towards a Critical Geography.* New York: Routledge, pp. 158–188.
Harvey, D. (2003). *The New Imperialism.* Oxford and New York: Oxford University Press.
Hayter, T., and Harvey, D. (ed) (1993). *The Factory and the City: The Story of the Cowley Automobile Workers in Oxford.* London: Mansell Publishing Ltd.
Heroux, G., and Palmer, B.D. (n.d.). 'Cracking the Stone': The Long History of Capitalist Crisis and Toronto's Dispossessed (unpublished ms.).
Holloway, J. (1987). 'The Red Rose of Nissan'. *Capital & Class.* 11: 142–164.
Kasmir, S. (2001). 'Corporation, Self, and Enterprise at the Saturn Automobile Plant'. *Anthropology of Work Review* 22(4): 8–12.
Kasmir, S. (2009). "Toward an Anthropology of Labor". *City and Society* 2(1): 11–15.
Kasmir, S. (2014). 'The Saturn Automobile Plant and the Long Dispossession of US Autoworkers', in S. Kasmir and A. Carbonella (ed) *Blood and Fire: Toward a Global Anthropology of Labor.* New York: Berghahn Books, pp. 203–249.
Kasmir, S., and Carbonella, A. (ed) (2014). *Blood and Fire: Toward a Global Anthropology of Labor.* New York: Berghahn Books.
Lembcke, J. (1991). 'Why 50 Years? Working Class Formations and Long Cycles'. *Science and Society* 55(4): 417–446.
Los Angeles Times. (August 28, 1992). 'UAW Strike in Ohio Closes GM Saturn Plant'.
Mann, E. (1987). *Taking on General Motors: A Case Study of the UAW Campaign to Keep GM Van Nuys Open.* Los Angeles: Center for Labor Research and Education, Institute of Industrial Relations, University of California.
Memorandum of Agreement. (2000). Saturn Corporation and the UAW.
Narotzky, S. (2011). 'Structures Without Soul and Immediate Struggles: Rethinking Militant Particularism in Contemporary Spain'. *Identities: Global Studies in Culture and Power* 18(2): 92–116.
Narotzky, S., and Smith. G. 2006. *Immediate Struggles. People, Power and Place in Rural* Spain. University of California Press.
New York Times. (July 22, 1998). 'Labor's Peace with G.M. Unraveling at Saturn'. A1, D2.
New York Times. (July 12, 2011). 'With Sonic, G.M. Stands Automaking on Its Head'. Available at http://www.nytimes.com/2011/07/13/business/with-chevrolet-sonic-gm-and-uaw-reinvent-automaking.html. Accessed February 1, 2011.

New York Times. (November 11, 2011). 'Ex-Saturn Plant to Reopen, And G.M. to Add 700 Jobs'http://www.nytimes.com/2011/11/22/business/saturn-plant-to-reopen-with-700-jobs.html?_r=0. *Accessed November 30, 2015.*

Parker, M., and Slaughter, J. (1985). *Inside the Circle: A Union Guide to QWL.* Detroit: Labor Notes.

Parker, M., and Slaughter, J. (1988). *Choosing Sides: Unions and the Team Concept.* Detroit: Labor Notes.

Parker, M., and Slaughter, J. (1994). *Working Smart: A Union Guide to Participation Programs and Reengineering.* Detroit: Labor Notes.

Parker, M., and Slaughter, J. (1997). 'Advancing Unionism on the New Terrain', in B. Nissen (ed) *Unions and Workplace Reorganization.* Detroit: Wayne State University Press, pp. 208–227.

Rothschild, E. (1973). *Paradise Lost: The Decline of the Auto-Industrial Age.* New York: Vintage.

Rubenstein, J.M. (1992). *The Changing Auto Industry. A geographical Analysis.* London and New York: Routledge.

Rubinstein, S., and Kochan, T. (2001). *Learning from Saturn: A Look at the Boldest Experiment in Corporate Governance and Employee Relations.* Ithaca, NY: ILR, Cornell University Press.

Striffler, S. (2002). *In the Shadows of State and Capital: The United Fruit Company, Popular Struggle, and Agrarian Restructuring in Ecuador, 1900–1995.* Durham: Duke University Press.

The Tennessean. (December 29, 2011). 'Middle class hit hard by factories' wages latest hires of autoworkers appreciate pay, even at half the previous amount.' Available at http://www.tennessean.com/article/20111229/BUSINESS03/312290032. Accessed January 3, 2012.

Terkel, S. (1972). *Working: People Talk About What They Do All Day and How They Feel About What They Do.* New York: Ballantine Books.

Wall Street Journal. (September 4, 1992). "Labor's Days at GM', A8.

Williams, R. (1989). *Resources of Hope: Culture, Democrary, Socialism.* London: Verso.

12 Getting by Beyond Work, or the Intertwining of Production and Reproduction among Heavy Industry Workers and Their Families in Ferrol, Spain

Irene Sabaté Muriel

Introduction

This chapter is based on an ethnography[1] of heavy industry workers in Ferrol, Galicia. The region's economy is largely dependent on the state-owned shipyards of Navantia, formerly Bazán, which have undergone a restructuring process since the 1990s that threatens the continuity of the local industrial fabric. In contrast with this general situation, a family-owned steel plant founded in the 1950s continues to thrive, even during the first years of the present economic crisis. Its success can be attributed to the profitability of the plant, to the tight discipline imposed on workers by an authoritarian employer and to the flexible adaptation of production to changes in demand. The support of local authorities, who value the company as one of the few remaining sources of employment in the region, and the company's close connections with national and international distribution networks, may also account for its success.

Aside from two major strikes in the early and late 1970s, the workers in this company have been docile relative to the lively and prominent labor movement that developed around the shipyards. The rural origins and the middle age of the first generation of workers, who were bound to the company's owners by patron-client relationships, contributed, along with their weak identification with the industrial working class, to a lack of mobilization. In the last decade, however, the workers' committee has called for strikes and protests, with considerable success. Furthermore, the cohesion among blue-collar workers during mobilizations is outstanding, as they feel well represented by their leaders. Their claims, made in the framework of particularly harsh collective bargaining processes[2], include a wide range of demands. The most veteran members of the union identify an evolution of earlier demands, namely the so-called "social" demands that seem to be replacing the "economic" aspirations of previous generations of workers, focused primarily on wages and health and safety measures:

> We started off with economic claims, because that was the most urgent issue. [...] When we started to have economic results, we started aiming

for social issues. And the company wasn't used to that. It was hard to negotiate social issues with them... Now, with this new agreement, we have another personal day, the second [per year]. We're slowly moving ahead. Young people now value social aspects more than money. And we have to take advantage of that in order to make things better.[3]

But what do workers and trade union members mean by the adjective "social"? I argue that the "social" aspect of working conditions provides the clearest indication as to how steelworkers are embedded in their households and communities. In past decades, while most of men's domestic responsibilities revolved around their role as breadwinners, their claims were articulated in relation to a "family wage" (Borderías 2001), with little attention paid to time issues, such as shift work. But now a new generation of industrial workers who find themselves in traditionally male jobs (Strazdins et al. 2004) seems to be facing domestic requirements in a more acute manner. As the need for a double source of income leads wives to participate in wage work, industrial workers are increasingly required to perform tasks at home that make considerable demands on their time.[4]

Diverse social agents, including policy makers, trade unions and other civil society associations, as well as researchers, have discussed the reconciliation of work and family life. This debate has had an impact on labor law and social policy, for example, with the implementation of parental leave and career breaks, more flexible work schedules and improved childcare facilities (Eurofound 2006). Such measures are critiqued by feminists because they are solely aimed at women, and because gender-specific protective regulations (Humphries 1981) fail to question the gender division of care and domestic work at home (Torns et al. 2007). Critical voices suggest instead that there is a need for a broader and more ambitious analysis and transformations of the "politics of time" to generate more egalitarian distributions of productive and reproductive work between genders (Borràs et al. 2007), ultimately aiming at an improvement of the entire society's well-being.

Such goals have been viewed with indifference or distrust by traditional, male-controlled trade unions (Humphries 1981) and today are only incipiently incorporated by those fractions of the labor movement that are sensitive to gender issues. Consequently, only limited changes have affected collective bargaining and the workplace:

> For us, work is a central issue in this debate, as it articulates not only wage work, but also the rest of our time. It is particularly important to take into account its impact on the time for care, for raising children, for looking after the elderly, and also for housework.[5]

In our ethnographic context, renegotiations of the balance between production and reproduction are needed if male steelworkers are to take on a wider range of domestic responsibilities, at least in part in response to their wives' participation in the labor market. This entails changes within the household, in the workplace (through collective bargaining) and in the national–and sometimes international–arena of labor legislation. The patriarchal ideologies that characterize the domestic unit have been denounced by feminist scholars (Hartmann 1979, quoted in Humphries 1981). Similarly, Marxist analysts have criticized State regulations of labor relations as ultimately supporting the interests of the capitalist class, by ensuring the provision of labor, an essential factor of production:

> The matter takes quite another aspect if we contemplate not the single capitalist and the single worker, but the capitalist class and the working class [. . .]. The capitalist [. . .] profits not only by what he receives from the worker, but also by what he gives him. The capital given in return for labor-power is converted into means of subsistence which have to be consumed to reproduce the muscles, nerves, bones and brains of existing workers, and to bring new workers into existence.
> (Marx 1990: 717)

But, as a matter of fact, workplace negotiations take place in relation to each employer, and because the reproduction of the employee's family is not a priority for the individual employer (as opposed to the interests of the capitalist class), the company does not prioritize these issues. Furthermore, as a highly male-dominated sector, the steel industry is quite impervious to the question of family obligations. These circumstances complicate the efforts of households to organize their everyday lives.

Nevertheless, this chapter illustrates workers' growing concerns with, and efforts towards achieving improved working conditions, particularly concerning the use of time and seeking a balance between productive and reproductive activities. Childcare arrangements in particular highlight the constraints and opportunities stemming from fathers' working conditions at the steel plant, and the contradictions between production and reproduction as they are experienced at the level of households and family relations.

Some Theoretical Considerations

The anthropological literature has shown how households "get by", not only in relation to gaining access to income from paid work or other sources, but crucially through a variety of strategies based on reciprocity and on the non-monetary circulation and provision of goods and services (Lomnitz 1983; Stack 1974; Pitrou 1977; Narotzky 2012). Despite the importance of non-monetized relations and exchanges, the organization of reproduction cannot be isolated from the monetary sphere of production, as some dichotomous conceptualizations suggest (Gudeman 2001; Parry and Bloch 1989). On the contrary, the boundaries between both realms are permeable.

This is also the case with industrial work, despite its depiction as a paradigm of the historical separation between production and reproduction (Daly 2001). Although some ethnographies confirm the extent of this separation in industrial workers' imaginaries and experiences (Weber 1986; 1989), research has also shown that the distinction may be fuzzier than suggested by conceptualization of wage work and housework as "cultural opposites" (Ahlander and Bahr 1995: 55). The effects of industrial wage work extend far beyond the specific times and locations where it takes place (Sierra Álvarez 1990) and wage labor is necessarily intertwined with other provisioning logics (Weber 1986; 1989). Conversely, alternative provisioning systems, broadly understood as forms of reciprocity, also contribute to shaping the diverse developments of industrial capitalism in particular contexts and may even be seen as a condition of possibility for capitalist accumulation itself (Narotzky 2010).

The close intertwining of production and reproduction is evident as relations of solidarity and moral obligations regulate care giving and household work (Ahlander and Bahr 1995), but are also at play in relations of production, for instance, in recruitment mechanisms or in the imposition of a work discipline. It follows that power inequalities and exploitation, typical of capitalist production, can also underpin divisions of labor in the sphere of reproduction.

A historical transformation has been underway with the decline of the Fordist male breadwinner-female housewife model in modern capitalist societies (Moss 1991; Hank and Buber 2009).[6] This has not led to a recalibration of the gendered division of labor towards a more egalitarian basis. In fact, despite the reorganization of roles caused by women's return to paid work (Hill and Hill 1990; Leonard 2001; Hook 2006; Craig and Powell 2011), gender differences persevere and may become more acute as children are born and parents reconfigure their household organization in a more traditional manner (Gjerdingen and Center 2005). In these circumstances, many women opt for part-time jobs or limit their career aspirations at least momentarily (Hill and Hill 1990; Maume 2008; Apps and Rees 2002; Candela and Piñón 2013). Some authors anticipate that there will be a gradual convergence of male and female roles as a result of additional sources of income and renegotiations of domestic organization forced by employed women (Hank and Buber 2009; Gershuny, in Hook 2006). Others point to the need for specific policies to induce changes in this respect (Carrasquer and Torns 2008; Borràs et al. 2007; Torns et al. 2007).

Who Takes Care of the Steelworkers' Children?

Despite the company's recalcitrant attitude to workers' claims, significant advances have been made in relation to economic gains, and current wages comply with the minimum levels set by the provincial agreement for the metal sector.[7] On the other hand, working conditions have improved very little, especially concerning shifts and work schedules. A large proportion of workers carry out shift work, working on weekends and holidays, switching from mornings to afternoons and then to nights every seven working days. This requires complicated arrangements within households, particularly if wives are also employed.[8] Work schedules are extremely rigid and workers' needs are rarely accommodated while the employer often makes changes at very short notice, calling a worker at home during his days off and demanding him to join a shift to meet production requirements. Unpaid leave is strictly limited to two days per annum and managers may reject the dates requested if they are deemed to conflict with the priorities of production. Parental leave for fathers has recently been increased in Spain to 15 days (Lapuerta et al. 2008); nevertheless, workers are discouraged by their employer's reticence, to the point that some of those who are entitled will not make use of their right.

Childcare arrangements are a paradigmatic example of a problem households must solve in order to "get by". Steelworkers repeatedly stress this as a major concern for themselves and their families. Rather than talking about how little time they have to care for their children, they observe their failure to fulfill their children's needs and those of the rest of the family. While they may have days off during the week, or free time in the morning, they miss important family and social events that usually take place in the evenings or on weekends. Thus, it is a matter of quality rather than quantity that describes the effects of their "non-standard" work schedules on their social life and domestic routines (Strazdins et al. 2004; Boisard and Fermanian 1999). They tend to see this as an outcome of the lack of workplace support to work-family reconciliation (Glass and Estes 1997).

Given the Spanish State's deficiencies in providing childcare (Meil Landwerlin 1994; Hank and Buber 2009), and given that paid childcare is not an affordable solution for these families, they come to rely on their support networks, especially those based on the extended family and on intergenerational solidarity (Pitrou 1977; Krzyzowsky 2011; Hank and Buber 2009). Steelworkers' families rely heavily on grandparents' help, as Marcos,[9] a worker with a four-year-old son whose wife also worked shifts in the healthcare sector, explained. Shift work, and particularly night shifts would not be possible without this assistance.[10]

In order to deal with these conflicting demands, many women abandon activities other than paid work when they become mothers and adopt more traditional roles (Gjerdingen and Center 2005). Jenny was married to a steelworker in his 40s; she left her voluntary work with an NGO when she returned to employment after having her two daughters. Similarly, Lorena, employed in the Navantia shipyard, had to leave the charity she had founded some years before when she felt overloaded by work and household duties. Fathers, on the other hand, tend to continue with their former engagements, although awareness of the implications of their absence from home lead some members of the younger generations to reduce their involvement in these other activities. However, when fathers prioritize their political commitment, as a necessary sacrifice for reaching collective goals, occasional conflicts with their wives may arise, as the women may not share this order of priorities. This was ironically expressed by Carmen, the wife of a well-known political activist since the days of Franco, who complained that her husband did not take care of their garden, referring to his political activities as *conachadas*, a localism that could be translated as "nonsense".

However, some husbands do sacrifice certain aspirations in order to gain family time. Anxo, a 44-year-old steelworker who would like to study and write nonfiction, assumes that he will have to postpone these aims until his daughters are grown. Similarly, Rubén, an engineer in Navantia who entered the company as an apprentice while studying for his degree in the evenings, believes that now he could not invest as much time and energy in education after his workday, as he has two daughters to care for.

A salient aspect of the parenting experience (Daly 2001) in this group is the sense of "juggling" (Strazdins et al. 2004) to organize everyday activities. This goes beyond unexpected circumstances, such as a sick child demanding "urgent childcare" (Maume 2008). These households face the impossibility of planning their daily routines for more than a week, as men's schedules are always changing. Hence, time management and investment have to be solved almost on a daily basis (Apps and Rees 2002), which adds considerable stress to their everyday lives. Children also experience the consequences of their parents' work schedules. For example, Marcos is convinced that his son's negative attitude towards food is due to the lack of consistency and mealtime routines, as he stays with different relatives depending on his parents' shifts. Some problems appear to be intractable: Jenny's elder daughter refused to sleep away from home, for example, with her grandparents, and thus required her mother's presence when her father was working. These are examples of the limits that children themselves set to the flexibility of household arrangements.

The need to resort to relatives, particularly grandparents, for childcare reinforces the links between households and extended family networks that are also vehicles for other kinds of exchanges (Brandon 2000; Uttal 1999; Hank and Buber 2009). Mutual aid circulates on the basis of moral obligation and solidarity, but does not exclude the possibility of conflicts and negotiations, or the potential unease caused by feeling permanently indebted (Ahlander and Bahr 1995; Reschke *et al.*, 2006; Krzyzowsky 2011). Tensions between self-sufficiency and relatedness may emerge when the widespread ideal of a relatively independent nuclear family cannot be fulfilled and households become more dependent on kin networks than they expected. This is exemplified by Marcos, who was dissatisfied with the childcare arrangements he and his wife had to make, forced to rely on grandparents more than they wished. To avoid increasing the burden on their own parents, they are determined not to have a second child, a decision reached reluctantly and against their original plans. In contrast with what happens during the rest of the year, in his summer holidays Marcos devotes most of his time to his son, avoiding contact with his workmates and minimizing his participation in the workers' committee.

Victoria's case is different. Married to a Navantia worker who has always been very active in the labor movement and virtually absent from home, she proudly describes how she succeeded in bringing up her two children, who are now entering adulthood, without depending heavily on relatives. Although she sometimes accepted help, especially from an unmarried sister-in-law who lives nearby, she managed to combine childcare and housework with paid work and even with advancing her education. She took the two little children with her wherever she went, while her husband attended endless meetings and demonstrations. Victoria appears to be resigned to the fact that her husband will never share domestic responsibilities on an equal basis. She resents that, even if her husband and the children take on some housework, she must take the initiative and keep an eye on domestic organization. For her, the problem is not so much the amount of time allocated to housework by each family member, but the degree of their commitment to and the "quality" of the time devoted to it, a crucial distinction that has also been noted in the literature (Maume 2008).

Sole, the adult daughter of a steelworker in his 50s, whose mother never had a paid job, described the allocation of responsibilities at home: her father brought home a salary and, added to his need to rest between shifts, he devoted much time to participating in the workers' committee. Her mother took on all the housework and childcare, and the little girl had to concentrate on doing her homework and on doing her best at school. Sole now lives away from home and is trying to start a career as a university researcher. Although she does not share her mother's world view and would not like to follow her footsteps, she understands the distribution of roles she grew up with as a pragmatic strategy in terms of domestic survival and reproduction, and even as a condition for her own upward social mobility.

Although childcare was highlighted in workers' accounts, household members frequently confronted other care needs within the family, relating to other dependents such as the sick or the elderly. Jaime, a Navantia worker who took early retirement and had a son and a daughter in his 20s, was looking forward to becoming a young grandfather in the near future. He was enthusiastic about his plans to take his grandchildren with him when he went hiking or camping, two of his favorite activities now that he had plenty of leisure time. Interestingly, his wife Isabel's view was slightly different. Although she was also willing to become a grandmother and she shared her husband's outdoors activities, she was more ambivalent, stressing the workload she would have to take on with the grandchildren because of the moral obligation towards her children. After some years caring for her sick parents, who had died recently, she now preferred to enjoy her freedom before taking on new care obligations. However, she expressed these views gently, and acknowledged she would be available, no matter what her children decided.

Wallace and Young (2007) refer to the impact of childcare on workers' productivity, while other authors point to its implications for parents' career opportunities, especially for women (Carrasquer and Torns 2008; Leonard 2001; Candela and Piñón 2013). These issues did not emerge from our interview data. The absence of comments about workers' careers may reflect the paucity of opportunities for promotion within the steel plant's hierarchical organization.

"Good Fathers" and "Ideal Workers"

How do the inner workings of domestic reproduction affect relations of production and, more precisely, working conditions as they are experienced by workers? Marxist approaches have shown that capitalism draws on mechanisms that are not reducible to capital accumulation, such as reciprocity (Narotzky 2010) or the domestic mode of production (Meillassoux 1977), to ensure continuity through the reproduction of the workforce at local and global scales of interdependence (Harvey 2004). However, at the level of the household, the focus shifts to women as the central actors in the tensions between paid work and domestic reproduction at home, as well as for the reproduction of the working class as a whole (Humphries 1981). To complement this emphasis, the following exploration of the effects of household organization privileges the experience of fathers, at work and at home, a task that has already been taken on by other authors (Lattrich and Blanco 2012). I argue that, while work—along with levels of indebtedness and consumption–determines childcare and other domestic arrangements, the presence of children, and fathers' involvement in their care, also affects working conditions. For example, responsibility for supporting children while paying the bills or making mortgage payments may well hinder workers' involvement in struggles for improvements at work, if they are perceived to entail potential economic losses, such as lower wages during strikes. Manuela, a widow with several steelworker sons, saw this as the main obstacle to mobilization. Likewise, members of the workers' committee stressed the need to choose mobilization strategies carefully, for example by distributing strikes throughout the year, so that salaries were not too severely affected at the end of each month and the workers' families did not suffer the consequences of significantly reduced wage packets. This strategy had been the key to success in putting pressure on the employer over the course of two years, until they obtained an acceptable collective agreement.

In the steel plant, many workers appear to accept exploitative conditions and a dull work experience in exchange for job security. This compromise in the interests of job security, at the cost of enduring drudgery, emerged in conversations with relatively young workers. They joined the plant after having worked for other firms, such as auxiliary companies subcontracted by the shipyards, where work was less monotonous and wages were higher thanks to overtime. However, these jobs were temporary and depended on market fluctuations. Besides, workers had to be geographically mobile. Consequently, when they came to settle down and start a family, they chose to work at the steel plant, trading in their career ambitions for the stability needed to guarantee their family's livelihood.

These arguments suggest that there is a connection between the representation of what a "good father" is, and what employers consider as an "ideal worker" (Sierra Álvarez 1990), in that they submit to the interests of production both through high productivity and a docile attitude. Indeed, it seems that, in the case of men, there is no cultural contradiction between the archetypes of father and worker (Wallace and Young 2007). And yet there is no simple correspondence between them, which becomes evident in the conflicts and negotiations that may disrupt work and production. Labor law and regulations have often been understood as the outcome of the historical achievements of the labor movement in setting limits to individual employers' drive to achieve maximum productivity (Fuma and Cohen 2007; Glass and Estes 1997), while securing the availability of labor through the reproduction of the working class as a whole (Humphries 1981). Ideally, policies pursuing the reconciliation of work and family aim to change attitudes and protect workers devoting more time to their families from being labeled as lazy or unmotivated (Lattrich and Blanco 2012). But, as we have seen, the gender bias underpinning these policies has limited their impact (Borràs et al. 2007).

Anxo exemplifies the possibilities of commitment to struggle, overcoming the material determinisms of capital-labor relations. He has two daughters, and his was the only income in the household while the children were young. But this did not prevent him from playing an outstanding role in mobilizations, and even to represent the steelworkers in the public sphere. This has been noticed by his employer, who has imposed disciplinary measures and threatened legal action against him. Jorge's case is somewhat different for, despite his ideological affinity with the labor movement, his participation in particular conflicts and his awareness of the mechanisms of exploitation that are at play in the steel plant, he is not a member of a trade union and prefers to delegate the collective representation of the workers' interests to others. Like several of his fellow workers, he pragmatically accepts the conditions in the plant as the price for stability. But now he faces a dilemma that is forcing him to reconsider his position. He and his wife are on a waiting list to adopt an African child. As soon as the child is assigned to them, they will have to travel to the country where they applied in order to pick him or her up. They know that the entire procedure will take about a month, while Jorge is only entitled to 15 days of parental leave as stipulated by law. There is no precedent for such a case in the steel plant and he fears his employer will deny permission to leave for a month. Jorge will apply for unpaid parental leave or will try to negotiate an exchange for part of his summer holidays. But he is skeptical, given the extreme rigidity of the human resources managers. If unsuccessful in his negotiations, he would choose to fetch his child and face the consequences, severe as they may be given that his wife is currently unemployed:

> As a final resort, I'd just leave. I'd rather go pick up my child than anything else, of course. I'll try to act in good faith, otherwise I don't know, I'll get a sick leave, or will disappear and let them take disciplinary action... I don't know.

In contrast to what has been discussed, domestic factors can enhance workers' combativeness, particularly in demanding changes in their working conditions. Where conflict erupts, workers rely heavily on material and moral support from their families. This is especially so where the struggle is protracted, as Manuela recalls. During the strike that took place in the late 1970s, she and other women supported their husbands, both privately and in the public sphere by participating in mobilizations, organizing actions (such as demonstrations in front of the employer's home), and by explaining the reasons for the strike in their social environment:

> My father-in-law said why are you letting him get into trouble? You have three children! And I told him, that's exactly why, because I have three children, and because it's his right as a worker. He should stand up for it. Your son is struggling for your grandchildren's bread. I will never tell him to quit the strike. I will always support him.

Francisco, a trade union member with a long history of struggle in the plant, acknowledges his wife's contribution to his militant activity. She offered emotional support, and her work as a nurse reduced their dependence on his wages. She also supported the workers, for example, by lending them her car whenever they needed transportation.

Finally, informal work and domestic production may reduce workers' acceptance of adverse working conditions and increase their bargaining power. Some informants remember that, during the factory's first decades, steelworkers and their families engaged in agricultural activities. This provided a supply of food that helped to complement their low wages. Furthermore, during the two major conflicts of the 1970s, one of which ended with a lockout, workers' families were able to survive in the absence of wages thanks to the distribution of the vegetables grown by steelworkers families. Similarly, Antonio increased his usual fishing activity during the 1971 strike in order to get food and earn some money. Here the "travail-à-côté" (Weber, 1989) shows its two sides, providing resources independently from the factory, but also defusing revolt under unfair economic conditions by enabling households to meet their needs despite low wages.

Final Remarks

The difficulties entailed in organizing family time on a daily basis, and not only in special circumstances or crisis situations, constitute an often-neglected dimension of the precariousness and uncertainty experienced by significant sections of the working class. This adds to other sources of instability, such as the health and safety risks of industrial activities, low wages, dependence on overtime, the uncertainty of temporary contracts or management strategies that undervalue the contributions of workers. Besides these factors, I argue that the inability or the difficulty to match the organization of family time to productive and reproductive needs, rights, duties, expectations and aspirations—what we can call "time precariousness", generates great pressures on individual workers and on their households.[11] The politics of time becomes thus a major factor for the reproduction and aggravation of social inequalities, as patterns of social differentiation emerge not only from income inequalities, but also from the unequal distribution of opportunities to organize productive and reproductive tasks in a balanced and satisfactory manner. The case of industrial workers, particularly those constrained by shift work, shows how time use and availability is both a contributing factor and a consequence of inequalities (Strazdins et al. 2004).

The emic notion of "social" conditions of work, mostly related to time organization, and its growing importance in trade union discourses,[12] can be interpreted as a symptom of an increasing sensitivity towards these issues. Younger workers, aged 45 at the most, are particularly likely to express concerns about family time. But it is unclear whether this recent prioritization of social over economic claims is a symptom of a process of re-signification of gender roles, in the sense that new generations are becoming more egalitarian concerning the sharing of housework duties, as one of our informants suggested and some authors anticipate (Gershuny, in Hook 2006). It does not appear to be so: rather, researchers point out that women's entry into the workforce does not entail major changes in the practice of housework (Hook 2006; Leonard 2001; Hill and Hill 1990; Craig and Powell 2011; Candela and Piñón 2013).

However, even if a radical change in real practices concerning the division of reproductive labor by gender has not occurred, at least a new awareness is revealed on the part of younger men, who are confronted with the need to negotiate their domestic responsibilities as husbands and fathers with their working wives. Regardless of the results of this negotiation and its translation into real practices, this already constitutes a difference from the previous generation of industrial workers in the Ferrol region.

State action does not fulfill steelworkers' need to balance productive and reproductive needs and duties, as, even if labor laws include regulations that aim to improve social well-being, their application is subject to factors that escape formal control, such as the historical peculiarities of employer-employee relationships, the management models implemented, or the bargaining power of workers in each particular factory. Therefore, a deficit in the support afforded by the state to household reproduction is perpetuated despite the existing regulations (Brandon 2000). As a result, households try to counteract the threats to their reproduction by resorting to social networks for support, as in the case of the childcare arrangements discussed above.

This ethnography of a traditionally male industrial sector illustrates how, in a company where jobs are designed as if workers had no care responsibilities beyond their role as breadwinners (Strazdins *et al.* 2004), the contradictions between private and public, production and reproduction, have enduring effects, but also show important changes. For decades, concessions made to employees reflected a paternalistic morality and the employer's particular view of workers and their families. At that time, the company's priorities supported the argument about *the self-destructive character of capitalist society* (Humphries 1981; Polanyi 2001), as, in his pursuit of profits and competitiveness, the individual capitalist did not feel concerned about the reproduction of the working class. This is why regulations were needed—and were partly achieved, with great effort on the part of workers—to govern labor relations. But the social and labor rights that workers derive from these regulations are only potentialities. They are not automatically enforced in the particular spaces and times where work is performed. In this process, the intervention of relationships and ideologies originating from and involving different domains—the family, the firm, the market, public administration—makes the course toward achieving rights particularly tortuous. Only through processes of legitimation and institutionalization (Lapuerta et al. 2008) will legal entitlements become real rights for workers and their households, and will thus have tangible effects at the grassroots level of households' life projects and everyday practices.

Notes

1 The chapter is based on field research carried out by the author together with Susana Narotzky as part of the FP7 Collaborative Project (Grant Agreement No. 225670) MEDEA- Models and their Effects on Development Paths: an Ethnographic and comparative Approach to Knowledge Transmission and Livelihood Strategies and presented at the project's international conference held at the University of Barcelona on 23–24 February 2012.
2 And, since 2010, facing a labor force adjustment plan that was justified by the current crisis in the building sector, which includes steel product buyers.
3 Interview with a long-standing trade union member and worker at the steel plant.
4 The extent to which they really become involved in parenting and reproduction, and they thus contrast significantly with previous generations, would require a deeper insight into their domestic routines and will not be addressed here.
5 Excerpt from a document entitled 'Les dones transformen des del temps i els treballs' ("Women make transformations on the basis of time and [different types of] work"), disseminated by the trade union Comisiones Obreras in Barcelona, June 2009. Translated from Catalan.

6 As Borderías (2001) shows, it is misleading to interpret this model in a dehistoricized way, as it was not applicable, for example, to earlier periods of industrialization.
7 The unions also complain about a productivity bonus that accounts for a considerable proportion of their wages. As it inflates the total amount, it fuels a groundless reputation of work in the steel plant as particularly well paid, regardless of its harshness and other considerations. They also demand extra overtime pay (weekends and holidays) and for economic compensation for health risks resulting from the plant's environment.
8 This situation was not as usual for previous generations of industrial workers in the region, but has now become the norm.
9 All names are fictitious.
10 This arrangement was also made easier by the short distance between both homes, a facilitating factor that is stressed in the literature (Rose 1990; Hank and Buber 2009; Brandon 2000), especially in rural environments (Reschke et al 2006).
11 Since, as we have seen, time is best understood as a family resource (Strazdins et al. 2004).
12 Further investigation would be needed in order to address the gradual incorporation of the new agenda of the "politics of time" into the labor movement, with an analysis of the difficulties encountered when the traditional aims of trade unionism—as well as the foundations of social and labor policies—have to be reconsidered from a gender perspective (Borràs et al. 2007; Torns et al. 2007).

References

Ahlander, N.R., and Bahr, K.S. (1995). 'Beyond drudgery, power, and equity: toward an expanded discourse on the moral dimensions of housework in families'. *Journal of Marriage and Family* 7(1): 4–88.
Apps, P., and Rees, R. (2002). 'Household production, full consumption and the costs of children'. *Labour Economics* 8: 621–648.
Boisard, P., and Fermanian, J.-D. (1999). 'Les rythmes de travail hors norme'. *Économie et statistique* 321–322:111–131.
Borderías, C. (2001). '"Suponiendo que ese trabajo lo hace la mujer". Organización y valoración de los tiempos de trabajo en la Barcelona de mediados del siglo XIX', in C. Carrasco (ed) *Tiempos, trabajos y género*, Barcelona: Publicacions de la UB, pp. 103–128.
Borràs, V., Torns, T., and Moreno, S. (2007). 'Las políticas de conciliación: políticas laborales versus políticas de tiempo'. *Papers* 83: 83–96.
Brandon, P.D. (2000). 'An analysis of kin-provided child care in the context of intra-family exchanges'. *American Journal of Economics and Sociology* 9(2): 191–216.
Candela, P., and Piñón, J. (2013). *Vida, trabajo y relaciones de género en la metrópolis global*. Madrid: La Catarata.
Carrasquer, P., and Torns, T. (2008). 'Les dones i el treball: la transformació de les desigualtats de gènere?' in E. Bodelón and P. Giménez (eds), *Desenvolupant els drets de les dones: àmbits d'intervenció de les polítiques de gènere*, Barcelona: Diputació de Barcelona, Àrea d'Igualtat i Ciutadania, pp. 33–36.
Craig, L., and Powell, A. (2011). 'Non-standard work schedules, work-family balance and the gendered division of childcare'. *Work, Employment and Society* 25(2): 274–291.

Daly, K.J. (2001). 'Deconstructing family time: from ideology to lived experience'. *Journal of Marriage and Family* 63(2): 283–294.
EUROFOUND (2006). 'Reconciliation of work and family life and collective bargaining in the European Union'. Available at http://www.eurofound.europa.eu/pubdocs/2006/06/en/1/ef0606en.pdf
Fuwa, M., and Cohen, P.N. (2007). 'Housework and social policy'. *Social Science Research* 36: 12–30.
Gjerdingen, D.K. and Center, B.A. (2005). 'First-time parents' postpartum changes in employment, childcare, and housework responsibilities'. *Social Science Research* 34: 103–116.
Glass, J.L., and Estes, S.B. (1997). 'The family responsive workplace'. *Annual Review of Sociology* 23: 289–313.
Gudeman, S. (2001). *The Anthropology of Economy*. Oxford: Blackwell.
Hank, K., and Buber, I. (2009). 'Grandparents caring for their grandchildren: Findings from the 2004 Survey of Health, Ageing, and Retirement in Europe'. *Journal of Family Issues* 30(1): 3–73.
Hartmann, H.I. (1979). 'The unhappy marriage of Marxism and Feminism: Towards a more progressive union'. *Capital and Class* 3(2): 1–33.
Harvey, D. (2004). *El nuevo imperialismo*. Madrid: Akal.
Hill, E.M., and Hill, M.A. (1990). 'Gender differences in child care and work: An interdisciplinary perspective'. *The Journal of Behavioral Economics* 19(1): 81–101.
Hook, J.L. (2006). 'Care in context: Men's unpaid work in 20 countries, 1965–2003'. *American Sociological Review* 71(4): 639–660.
Humphries, J. (1981). 'Protective legislation, the capitalist State, and working class men: The case of the 1842 Mines Regulation Act'. *Feminist Review* 7: 1–33.
Krzyzowsky, L. (2011). 'In the trap of intergenerational solidarity: Family care in Poland's ageing society'. *Polish Sociological Review* 173(1): 55–78.
Lapuerta, I., Baizán, P., and González, M.J. (2008). 'Who benefits from parental leave in Spain? A life course analysis'. *DemoSoc Working Paper* 26, available online: http://hdl.handle.net/10230/264
Lattrich, K., and Blanco, R. (2012). 'Conciliación de la vida personal, laboral y familiar en clave masculina'. *Estudios de la Fundación 1° de Mayo* 52, available online: http://www.1mayo.org/nova/files/1018/Estudio51.pdf
Leonard, M. (2001). 'Old wine in new bottles? Women working inside and outside the household'. *Women's Studies International Forum* 24(1): 67–78.
Lomnitz, L. (1983). *Cómo sobreviven los marginados*, México: Siglo XXI.
Marx, K. (1990) [1976]. *Capital. Volume I*, London: Penguin Books.
Maume, D. J. (2008). 'Gender differences in providing urgent childcare among dual-earner parents'. *Social Forces* 87(1): 273–297.
Meil Landwerlin, G. (1994). 'L'évolution de la politique familiale en Espagne. Du salaire familial à la lutte contre la pauvreté'. *Population* 4–5: 99–983.
Meillassoux, C. (1977). *Mujeres, graneros y capitales*, Madrid: Siglo XXI.
Moss, P. (1991). 'School-age child care in the European Community'. *Women's Studies International Forum* 14(6): 39–49.
Narotzky, S. (2010). 'Reciprocidad y capital social: modelos teóricos, políticas de desarrollo, economías alternativas. Una perspectiva antropológica', in V. Bretón (ed) *Saturno devora a sus hijos. Miradas críticas sobre el desarrollo y sus promesas*, Barcelona: Icària, pp. 127–174.

Narotzky, S. (2012). 'Provisioning', in J. G. Carrier (ed) *A Handbook of Economic Anthropology*, Cheltenham: Edward Elgar Publishing, pp. 77–94.

Parry, J., & Bloch, M. (1989). *Money and the Morality of Exchange*. Cambridge: Cambridge University Press.

Pitrou, A. (1977). 'Le soutien familial dans la société urbaine'. *Revue française de Sociologie* 18(1): 47–84.

Polanyi, K. (2001) [1944]. *The Great Transformation. The Political and Economic Origins of Our Time*, Boston: Beacon Press.

Reschke, K.L., Manoogian, M.M., Richards, L.N., Walker, S.K. and Seiling, S.B. (2006). 'Maternal grandmothers as child care providers for rural, low-income mothers'. *Journal of Children and Poverty* 12(2): 19–174.

Rose, D. (1990). '"Collective consumption" revisited: Analysing modes of provision and access to childcare services in Montréal, Quebec'. *Political Geography Quarterly* 9(4): 353–380.

Sierra Álvarez, J. (1990). *El obrero soñado*, Madrid: Siglo XXI.

Stack, C. (1974). *All our Kin. Strategies for Survival in a Black Community*, New York: Harper & Row.

Strazdins, Lyndall, Korda, Rosemary J., Lim, Lynette L-Y., Broom, Dorothy H., and D'Souza, Rennie M. (2004), 'Around-the-clock: parent work schedules and children's well-being in a 24-h economy'. *Social Science and Medicine* 9:1517–1527.

Torns, T., Carrasquer, P., Parella, S., and Recio, C. (2007). 'Les dones i el treball a Catalunya: mites i certeses'. *Estudis* 2, Institut Català de les Dones, available online: http://ideo.sectorweb.es/arxius/Dones%20i%20treball_mites%20i%20certeses_estudis2.pdf

Uttal, L. (1999). 'Using kin for child care: embedment in the socioeconomic networks of extended families'. *Journal of Marriage and Family* 61(4): 845–857.

Wallace, J. E. and Young, M. C. (2007). 'Parenthood and productivity: A study of demands, resources and family-friendly firms'. *Journal of Vocational Behavior* 72: 110–122.

Weber, F. (1986). 'Le travail hors de l'usine. Bricolage et double activité'. *Cahiers d'Économie et Sociologie Rurales* 3: 13–36.

Weber, F. (1989). *Le travail à-côté. Étude d'ethnographie ouvrière*, Paris: Institut National de la Recherche Agronomique et École des Hautes Études en Sciences Sociales.

Afterword

Making Difference
Concluding Comments on Work and Livelihoods

Susana Narotzky

> Men make their own history, but they do not make it as they please; they do not make it under self-selected circumstances, but under circumstances existing already, given and transmitted from the past.
>
> Marx, *The Eighteenth Brumaire of Louis Bonaparte* (1852)

> The angel would like to stay, awaken the dead and make whole what has been smashed. But a storm is blowing from Paradise; it has got caught in his wings with such violence that the angel can no longer close them. This storm irresistibly propels him into the future to which his back is turned, while the pile of debris before him grows skyward. This storm is what we call progress.
>
> Benjamin, *Theses on the Philosophy of History* (1955)

Anthropologists often tend to stress the particularities of the cases they study through intense ethnographic encounter. This provides an extremely nuanced approach to process and practice that has become the trademark of our discipline. It leads us to use complexity as an argument to eschew describing simple laws of movement for social processes. I find this a growing trend that places us in a politically irrelevant position. Often, the ethnographic detail appears as a free floating crystallization of contingent assemblages of items, agents and connections devoid of historical logic. The problem, then, is why and how to explain human projects that seek to change the connections that exist into something different. Designing an image of the future and of the logical process leading to it is, fundamentally, creating the conditions of possibility for its transformation (Bourdieu 2003). The other, often forgotten, leg of anthropological enquiry is comparison which enables similarities to emerge while it renders differences meaningful in the larger picture. Through the pieces in this volume we begin to perceive a thread of commonalities that, paradoxically, serve to underscore the centrality of the differences that are played out as well as produced by the various actors involved in industrial production.

Making Difference, Making History

Walter Benjamin's metaphor of the angel of history looking at the debris of the past piling under its eyes while it is being blown forcefully backwards toward an unimaginable future can be understood as a poetic rendering of Marx's historical materialist approach (Benjamin 2007 [1955]: 257–8). For several decades now, workers in the heavy industry and their families have witnessed the piling of debris of what used to make their livelihood (Hudson and Sadler 1989). This is often remembered as a "stable" period where plans for the future were easier to develop. Often this entailed inherited positions in the local industrial firm(s), a form of training framed by the plant's vocational school and including intra-plant mentorship based on seniority, a certainty about male identity and bread-winner responsibilities, together with clear household divisions of labor and gender-power geometries. These stable albeit unequal structures of mutual obligation, state protection and production organization existed in a Fordist past for the "key" or "strategic" industries (steel, energy, cement, automobile, etc.) but they were often a recent development of nationalizations or import substitution policies that expanded throughout the first half of the 20th century in both capitalist and socialist polities (Dal Forno and Mollona 2015). The "debris" of this industrial past started piling up at an increasing pace in the 1980s unsettling deeply embedded practices and livelihood expectations. It is certain that the form of this debris and the pace of its accumulation varied according to colonial, post-colonial and political histories; uneven regional patterns of capital expansion; the local embedding of "modernization" and "development" economic models; and changing theories of profit maximization.

At the same time these debris resulted from the actual resistance and resilience practices of people in their everyday attempt to make a living and care for proximate others, and from their active engagement in struggles that occurred at different scales, from the very local to the very global. As Beynon, Hudson and Sadler (1994) pointed out 20 years ago, *place* is formed and transformed by the articulated forces of capital, labor and the state (or, rather, various capitalists, workers and representatives of the administration), in the *longue durée*. Place is the domain of actual existing people while space is the domain of abstraction: of capital—as an abstract social relation—although capital can only be realized in places, through places and their differences; of state—as an abstract relation of domination—although its power can only be realized in places through the concrete production and enforcement of difference. Place grows from the meaningful relationships that people build with each other in the long-term and from their engagement and creative production of institutions in particular locations. Place is multidimensional and the primary referent of people's lives (Beynon et al. 1994: 5–6). And it is also multi-scalar, as social, economic and power relationships that produce place occur at various scales (local, regional, national, global) and simultaneously transform the operational scale of political–economic processes (Peck 2002). *Space*, in contrast, is an abstract assessment of the value of localities in political, symbolic and economic terms. It is used by public administrators to lure investment to a locality and by capitalists to generate profits through the mobilization of investment. In the globalized present, it supports a neoliberal scalar narrative where places compete in a global market of locational assets. "Investment and divestment decisions perpetually relate to a spatial dimension, and this can often pose a deep threat to the integrity of places" (Beynon et al. 1994:6).

In the history of heavy industry sometimes capitalist forces have been dominant in the shaping of place and have been able to co-opt the other players in the field, often through a kind of blackmailing that uses jobs, and therefore the very basic ability to make a living, as the ultimate trade off token. As the chapters in this volume show, this has been the case in many places at different moments, e.g., in most of Europe in the early 20th century and then after 1973. At other times the state has been the dominant force as was the case in strong nationalist economies such as that of socialist countries, but also in capitalist countries in particular historical conjunctures. Sometimes unions have become dominant, albeit for a brief period, as the success of some labor struggles might express (Herod 2001) or their conjunctural position as political brokers in some regimes (such as Argentina). But, generally, the tension between these three forces is what creates the "circumstances" that get "transmitted from the past" and set the ground where people "make their own history".

The tension between place and space points to *difference* as it emerges from the human attempt to "make history" in two distinct ways. First, difference results from the everyday *spontaneous* entanglement of peoples' lives as they engage with the spatial expressions of capitalist uneven regional development in place. Second, the *intentional* production of difference appears as a strategy of control by capitalists, the state or workers in space. Therefore, the attempt to "make history" is often an attempt to create "difference" from various positions and at various scales in order to yield power. As Jamie Peck has stated: "hegemonic power (. . .) is reflected in the control of scale and/or the assertion of a particular scalar fix in which certain sectional-political interests are privileged" (2002: 337). Some of the chapters in the volume present this struggle during processes of restructuring (outsourcing, whipsawing, labor flexibility) when difference becomes the argument of a competitive worth that defines a collective in space: a community, a plant, a nation (Kalb, Kasmir, D'Aloisio, Wódz and Gnieciak, Diaz Crovetto, this volume). Other chapters express embedded and individualized processes of differentiation in the workplace, in the household (Kalb, Spyridakis, Perelman and Vargas, Pine, this volume). Ethnography and geography enable us to address the actual relationship between these two processes (spontaneous or intentional) of making history. Comparison of ethnographic cases enables us to understand the various scales that interlock in the concrete places where livelihoods are materially situated. What Doreen Massey (1993) defined as "a global sense of place" helps us understand the kind of structure that connects different locations and is expressed through these differences in their relational value. I have found critical topography (Katz 2001) and power geometries (Peck 2002, Yeung 2005) helpful concepts to think through the tension of place and space in the complex processes of capitalist realization. As a geographer who has worked with dispossessed communities in the Sudan and the US, Katz reflects on how what she observes in these two locations is related and she finds the concept of topography and its associated term of contour lines helpful:

> Topography is associated not just with the description of place but also with measurements of elevation, distance, and other structural attributes that enable the examination of relationships across spaces and between places. (. . .) the effects of capitalism's globalizing imperative are experienced commonly across very different locales, and understanding these connections is crucial if they are to be challenged effectively. Topographies provide the ground—literally and figuratively—for developing a critique of the social relations sedimented into space and for scrutinizing the material social practices at all geographic scales through which place is produced.
>
> (Katz 2001: 1228–9)

She uses the concept of contour lines as a metaphor of the original concept where lines connect different places of precisely the same altitude.

> I want to imagine a politics that maintains the distinctness of a place while recognizing that it is connected analytically to other places along contour lines that represent not elevation but particular relations to a process (e.g., globalizing capitalist relations of production). Such connections are precise analytic relationships, not homogenizations.
>
> (Katz 2001: 1229)

Katz's relational concepts provide anthropology with tools to discover analytical similarities that make sense in structural terms, but they remain mostly descriptive in their aim. In his review of relational economic geography Yeung (2005) attempts to go beyond the descriptive aspect of relationality and proposes a theoretical turn that will enable explanation, what he describes as "theorizing explanations of difference" (2005:42). He proposes to address why and how difference produces power that becomes expressed in concrete outcomes, in place. The geometries of power concept, therefore, attempt to unpack the power tensions between places (2005:44). I will use these methodological and theoretical insights to engage with the cases presented in this volume.

Flexibilities of Work and Life

Restructurings of heavy industry have had similar effects, namely, job losses and the reorganization of production relations around the polysemic concept of "flexibility" (Narotzky 2015). Structural and functional flexibility are imposed by capital in industry allegedly to enhance productivity and become more competitive in a globalized market. The injunction to productivity has become such an entrenched hegemonic discourse that it is rarely argued and is considered as self-evident by all concerned parties. This flexibility results in some common traits, namely the use of subcontract and outsourced labor often composed by workers who have been made redundant from the core staff or by younger generations of workers that cannot get hired into the core staff of the firm. This situation produces difference between types of workers in the plant, even when they work side by side, a difference that is often marked by their distinct overalls. Outsourced, temporary contract workers, are confronted as *another kind* of worker to permanent, core workers in the firm. Stability that had become ingrained in what the "normal" life of a steel, shipyard or autoworker was, suddenly becomes a "privilege" in the face of the growing majority that have precarious jobs, although in turn they represent the living expression of the fragility and instability of this "privilege". These new situations push people to diverse kinds of strategies that operate at different scales. Some of them take advantage of forms of "embeddedness" such as kinship or other local connections (e.g., through the unions) in order to facilitate access to the better jobs (Perelman and Vargas, this volume). Others strive to individually better their competitive position in the local labor market, such as the *sneaks* in Piraeus who accept extremely low wages, or the *rabbits* who become benchmarks for productivity, speeding the work process and consolidating their value for the firm (Spyridakis, this volume). In other cases, the tensions between a union local plant strategy and larger scale, national or even global solidarities, express the ways in which "difference" or its negation through similarity or connection, gets played out on the side of labor (Kasmir, this volume).

This common reality of flexibility, however, presents local variations that relate to history as it has produced place at various scales. In the steel industry case from Argentina, for example, the privatization of the firm strengthened the outsourcing process although articulating it with technical and vocational training systems partially controlled by the unions. In addition to formal credentials, young people now need a further career in the satellite (contract) companies of the firm in order to acquire the proper "work ethic" and "attitude" which might eventually provide employment in the main firm. The expectations of "naturally" following the previous generation into the factory have been shattered and strategies of differentiation are key both for the process of segmented recruitment and for obtaining a stable job. Credentialism appears as a normative evaluation of difference that the firm uses to legitimate its hiring practices that rest on hyper selective incorporation of core employees, which systemically reproduces the pressure on stable employment. Simultaneously, recommendation and union brokerage are the usual practice for anyone who aims at achieving a job at the main firm. These produce another kind of difference by extending responsibility for the worker beyond his or her individual person and expressing the local power they can mobilize through kinship and other personalized links. Unions, here, emerge as crucial actors both in their control of training institutions and in the informal power they are able to yield towards management, probably related to the political power of unions in Argentina's history. This results in particular patron-client networks that young aspiring workers and their families have to cultivate with key union members in order to succeed in the career to stability.

Both these networks and the low salaries and precarious conditions of young people's labor are based on their families' support, and become a form of dispossession of the family of orientation's resources and care work. As in the case of women workers in the Italian Melfi auto plant whose small-scale often informal activities supplement a decreasing income, salaries that are not sufficient to reproduce labor get subsidized by unrecognized forms of work and non-market resources (D'Aloisio, this volume). This is analogous to the support function that subsistence gardens of steelworker's families have in Slovakia (Buzalka and Ferencova, this volume). In a challenge to the labor theory of value, the cost of labor reproduction here is systematically undervalued and labor power exchanged below cost. Colonial and feminist scholars have repeatedly underlined that market exchange is supported by forms of depredation that are embedded in historically produced geometries of power, a process akin to what Harvey has defined as "accumulation by dispossession" (Amin 1970, Elson and Çagatay 2000, Harvey 2005, Kasmir and Carbonella 2008), and this process seems to be expanding in present-day globalized capitalism. In his chapter, Kalb points at an important aspect of this process when he compares two different forms of locally producing labor devaluation or "worthlessness" and their connection through the spatial movements of capital in the white goods sector. This reveals an embedded and changing structure of alienation which is nevertheless connected in a topographic manner to the global movement of capital accumulation and its temporalities. Embeddedness is crucial in this development as it thrives on, reproduces and transforms aspects of inequality deeply entangled with livelihoods, intimate responsibilities and identity belongings. Hence, age, gender, nationality or ethnic factors become structurally entangled in how family relations or community networks contribute to structure present-day forms of exploitation in place and across space. The scalar dimension of social reproduction dialectically embracing the household or family's unequal obligations with larger processes of social reproduction of inequalities and surplus extraction becomes transparent in the chapters of this volume (Narotzky 2004, 2015).

A similar situation seems to emerge in the Galician Spanish case where the mini-mill that has expanded into an international venture has addressed flexibilization mostly in functional terms (Sabaté, this volume). Here, the pressure on reproduction work in the household becomes extreme as wives of younger workers have entered the workforce and the inflexible shift work policies of management are not up for negotiation. Differentiation here hinges on an implicit assertion on the part of management that "traditional" male-breadwinner families are the norm, reassessing an unrealistic gender division of labor that justifies not giving in to work-balance needs for the male workforce. For management, male workers are decidedly another kind of worker (as beholds family responsibilities) which results in a form of dispossession of the kinship network's resources that creates tensions between male and female household members as they try to renegotiate their family responsibilities. Often households extend the care network outwards in search for help, therefore redistributing dispossession. The centrality of the male-breadwinner ideology in producing a kind of identity that sets limits to the kinds of jobs that are acceptable to men is also stressed in Trappmann's chapter on employability. Beyond the issue of employability, however, and similar to the Polish workers in Kalb, Pine, and Wódz and Gnieciak chapters, we can witness a "making of difference" that rests on developing a *feeling of inadequacy* about the capacity to fulfill crucial obligations of social reproduction (whether referred to gender, generations or the nation) that had been produced under different political-economic conditions and contributed to a sense of adequacy, of social worth. It is this attack on personal "worth" that challenges the contours of past "stable" identities that contributes to the present devaluation of labor value. Conversely, the attempt to prevent this situation drives workers and the union local in the GM Saturn plant to a strong cooperation with the firm (making themselves different from the rest of UAW workers, allegedly producing a "new" kind of worker's worth). However, this does not prevent the final self-deprecation of "scab" even as they try to recuperate workers' collective action (Kasmir, this volume). In Piraeus, "sneaks" appear as both inevitable expressions of the place bound and gender inflected individual strategies to earn a livelihood and of the larger structures of global shipbuilding capital (Spyridakis, this volume). The poignant consciousness and embodiment of this devaluation takes different forms that are historically path-dependent along a continuum that spans from more "moral" depictions to more "political" ones.

Geometries of Power and the Production of Moral Economies

Emerging in the comparison of these cases is a topography of capitalist relations of production that defines the precise distinctions that make each place unique as it has engaged historically with diverse social, political and economic forces. But contour lines appear that show how these differences latch into the enactment of a cost cutting, competitive, "supply side" economy. Indeed, in all cases what amounts to the same destruction of workers' value and workers' power is realized through various forms of flexibility. On the one hand, flexibility in the firm, both structural and functional, brings uncertainty to workers. On the other hand, flexible livelihoods of different kinds are forced upon all workers and their families in an environment of skyrocketing relative and absolute surplus population, what neoliberal voices are defining as the structural "acceptable" rate of unemployment (Smith 2011). In practice, however, the changes of labor/capital relations that this restructuring brings forward in each location depend on how each particular place has become an expression of previous capital, labor and state forces and hence sets the ground for working out and working through further transformation.

Moreover, another vision which is not that of contour lines uniting places in a similar relation to industrial capitalist processes emerges configuring a spatial power geometry: that of power differentials between and within places that are played against each other by the different actors. Places in management's vision appear constructed as locations containing assets that can be valorized by capital. These include physical resources (e.g., iron, coal, a maritime port) and institutional frameworks (e.g., labor and environment regulations, trade unions), but also people with their different skills, their kinship networks, their webs of dependencies (both political and economic), their histories of conflict; in sum, people with an experience of making a living and memories of making history. Places in state's vision are territories to govern, firms and citizen's to regulate and tax, but also to provide for and seduce. The state's territory is materially a relational aggregate of places although symbolically it presents itself as an abstract projection of the "imagined community" of the nation (Anderson 1983). Places in workers' vision are where they need to make a living in all the social complexity that this entails, i.e., sustaining life, being a social person, someone with dignity and respect. The attempt to hold back worthlessness is their main purpose and often results in moving from place to place and creating trans-local places (Narotzky & Besnier 2014, Glick Schiller and Çaglar 2008, Pine 2014, and this volume). These various actors' understandings inform practices occurring at multiple scales that take into consideration the values (or value) most dear to each actor and use them to make differences. Some actors will have a great capacity to define, impose and benefit from particular differences between and within places while others will have a limited one. Geometries of power result from the capacity of some actors to define and take advantage of difference both within and between places (and people) in their interest. Making difference between places is also often making difference between the past of these places and an alleged better present or future. Finally, making a difference is always about trying to impose a moral economy (i.e., produce an hegemonic model of the economy that rests on moral imperatives), a set of basic distinctions in terms of what is "bad" and "good" for the larger "common good", not for any particular or parochial interest. These moralities are often presented as universals and tend to get essentialized; but they are always historical and political, the result of struggle. In this struggle of producing differences and juggling them, the scale at which the actors are able to operate is often an expression of the power they can yield. Peck (2002) speaks of hierarchies of scale and asserts that actors' power is generally linked to "the ability to shape extralocal rule regimes that constrain and channel the strategic options and tactical behavior of local actors". Herod (2001) points, however, at the possibility for "local scale models of struggle" to be powerful tools for workers in particular crucial positions in the production process of Transnational Corporations in a global economy. Therefore, local actors can shift the scale hierarchy if they work in a place that "makes a difference" in the production process, enabling them to overturn the power geometry of the firm. Conversely, the GM Saturn plant union local is co-opted into localism through their conviction of becoming part of a new, better, form of labor-capital relations, one based on cooperation rather than confrontation. Their refusal to participate in the national scale UAW mobilizations stands on a misunderstanding of their actual power in the structure of production and points to their co-optation into the firm's moral economy. As workers in the plant increasingly realize this, they attempt to renew struggle at the wider scale of national union solidarity and reassert an older kind of class-based morality (Kasmir, this volume).

We initiated these concluding comments with the methodological distinction that Beynon et al. (1994) propose between what they call *space* as opposed to the more concrete *place*. Do the chapters in this volume support such a clear cut proposition? In my opinion, the tension between abstract and concrete seems appropriate while the placing of particular processes (e.g., the power of capital) in what appears as a fixed higher scale, is not (Peck 2002). The hierarchies of scale that generally favor actors with the extralocal capacity to define difference and act accordingly generally set capital in a position of power, but not always. Indeed, the "space" scale is also concretely dependent on previous historical processes that have configured it as a particular kind of abstraction in relation to "places".

The struggles that the various actors wage through making difference within and between places refer to the value(s) that they seek to produce and reproduce. For capital in the global industrial firm, profits are often tied to the value of shares in the stock market, but this in turn is linked to particular actions that are interpreted as pushing the competitive edge of the firm in production, namely restructuring (e.g., cutting costs and increasing productivity) and playing places against each other (including in symbolic and cultural terms). For workers the main value is a life worth living, which is a complex entanglement of material and social values (e.g., food, health, housing, justice and dignity) and which develops in a different timeframe, one of families, households, generations and memories (Pine; Wódz and

Gnieciak, this volume). The cases presented in this volume show how this makes them struggle in the everyday sometimes through organized contestation, but often pushing them into personalized networks that give access to all sorts of resources (e.g., income, jobs, influence, care). The articulation and permanent tension between the contrasting objectives of capital and labor is coordinated by political brokers (in the different levels of government administration and other institutions) that "take sides" through regulatory norms and their greater or lesser enforcement. In this process policy makers differentiate between values. They define and fix through regulation what is allegedly most valuable for the common good—a commonality produced through hegemony—helping constrict and channel practice for the benefit of enhancing that particular value. Any future of politics of the left is, like any past of politics, the attempt to shift power geometries through making the differences that are useful to make history support the worth of people. And this struggle is always expressed in terms of the common good.

Acknowledgements

I wish to thank all the partners in the European Union funded project "Models and their Effects on Development paths: an Ethnographic and comparative Approach to knowledge transmission and livelihood strategies" (MEDEA), FP7- CT-2009–225670, for their invaluable intellectual engagement and dedication. In particular, my thanks go to the project coordinator, Victoria Goddard, and to the Spanish team Claire Montgomery, Irene Sabaté and Elena González-Polledo. Finally I want to acknowledge the invaluable support of the Generalitat de Catalunya Fellowship Program ICREA-Acadèmia.

References

Amin, S. (1970). *L'accumulation à l'échelle mondiale*. Paris: Anthropos.
Anderson, B. (1983). *Imagined Communities: Reflections on the Origin and Spread of Nationalism*. London: Verso.
Benjamin, W. (2007 [1955]). 'Theses on the Philosophy of History', in *Illuminations. Essays and Reflexions*. New York: Schocken Books, pp. 253–264.
Beynon, H., Hudson, R. and Sadler, D. (1994). *A Place Called Teesside. A Locality in a Global Economy*. Edinburgh: Edinburgh University Press.
Bourdieu, P. (2003). *Méditations pascaliennes. Édition revue et corrigée*. Paris: Seuil
Dal Forno, A. and Mollona, E. (2015). 'Isomorphism and local interests in the diffusion of global policies: an enquiry into privatization policy adoption using computer modelling and simulation', in V. Goddard and S. Narotzky (eds) *Industry and Work in Contemporary Capitalism: Global Models, Local Lives?*, New York: Routledge.
Elson, D. and Çagatay, N. (2000). 'The Social Content of Macroeconomic Policies'. *World Development* 28(7): 1347–1364.
Glick Schiller, N. and Çaglar, A. (2008). 'Migrant incorporation and city scale: towards a theory of locality in migration studies'. Willy Brandt Series of Working

Papers in International Migration and Ethnic Relations 2/07, Malmö: Malmö University.

Harvey, D. (2005). *The New Imperialism*. Oxford: Oxford University Press.

Herod, A. (2001). 'Labor Internationalism and the Contradictions of Globalization: Or, Why the Local is Sometimes Still Important in a Global Economy'. *Antipode* 33(3): 407–426.

Hudson, R. and Sadler, D. (1989). *The international steel industry: restructuring, state policies and localities*. London: Routledge.

Kasmir, S. and Carbonella, A. (2008). 'Dispossession and the Anthropology of Labor'. *Critique of Anthropology* 28(1): 5–25.

Katz, C. (2001). 'On the Grounds of Globalization: A Topography for Feminist Political Engagement'. *Signs* 26(4): 1213–1234.

Massey, D. (1993). 'Power-geometry and a progressive sense of place', in Bird, J. et al. (eds) *Mapping the futures. Local cultures, global change*. London: Routledge, pp. 59–69.

Narotzky, S. and Besnier, N. (2014). 'Crisis, Value, and Hope: Rethinking the Economy'. *Current Anthropology* 55(S9):4–16.

Narotzky, S. (2015). 'The Payoff of Love and the Traffic of Favours: Reciprocity, Social Capital, and the Blurring of Value Realms in Flexible Capitalism', in Jens Kjaerulff (ed) *Flexible Capitalism. Exchange and Ambiguity at Work*. Oxford: Berghahn Books, pp. 268–310.

Narotzky, S. (2004). 'The Political Economy of Affects: Community, Friendship and Family in the Organization of a Spanish Economic Region', in Procoli, A. (ed) *Workers and Narratives of Survival in Europe*. Albany, NY: State University of New York Press, pp. 57–79.

Peck, J. (2002). 'Political Economies of Scale: Fast Policy, Interscalar Relations, and Neoliberal Workfare'. *Economic Geography* 78(3): 331–360.

Pine, F. (2014). 'Migration as Hope: Space, Time, and Imagining the Future'. *Current Anthropology* 55(S9): 95–104.

Smith, G. (2011). 'Selective Hegemony and Beyond-Populations with "No Productive Function": A Framework for Enquiry'. *Identities* 18(1): 2–38.

Yeung, H. W. (2005). 'Rethinking relational economic geography'. *Transactions of the Institute of British Geographers* 30(1): 37–51.

Index

Note: Italicized page numbers indicate a figure on the corresponding page

accumulation strategies 9, 210
Amoskeag Mills, textile workers 34
arigós, defined 63
Asian Tigers 1
automation of production lines 68
automobile industry 4–5; and Taylorism 5; Toyota model 5; Volkswagen 20n8
autoworkers: Fiat 77; Fiat crisis 83–4; growth in 83; internationalism 175–9; introduction 172–4; localism and difference 174–5; Palestinian-American 176; politics and disorganization 181–4; United Automobile Workers 172–3, 179–81; *see also* Chrysler Motors; Detroit, Michigan; gender, gender perspective in FIAT-SATA case; Saturn plant

barter/exchange practices 115; *see also* reciprocity/reciprocal
Bear, Laura 8
Będzin 15, 137–51
Benjamin, Walter 205
Bennett, Mike 174–5, 180–1
Berger's Seventh Man 43
Bhilai steel plant 6
Black Power movement 176
The Border Case (Hunčík) 157
Bourdieu, Pierre 57n6, 57n7, 94, 96, 100, 105, 205n6
Brasilia 13, 62
brasilienses, defined 62
Braudel, Fernand 33
Brazil *see* steel workers, Brazil; Volta Redonda, Brazil
Brazilian National Steel Company (CSN) *see* CSN; *see also* steel workers, Brazil; Volta Redonda, Brazil
Breman, Jan 3
Bromley, Roger 150

Caffentzis, George 2
Calheiros, Waldyr 66
candangos (workers) 63
capitalism: accumulation and transformation 7–8, 128; cognitive capitalism 2; "flexible" post-industrial capitalism 117; global capitalism 36; inequalities in 5–7; liberal/corporatist capitalisms 95; self-destructive character of capitalist society 198; shaping of place and 207; spatial symbolic representation of 148–9, *149*; urbanization projects 4; valorization of capital 130; *see also* necropolitics concept; neoliberal, capitalism
capitalist: accumulation 15; identity 3; power 11
Cassa Integrazione support 84
Catholic: Church 159, 160, 169–70n11; social teaching and theology 124
Central and Eastern Europe (CEE) 124, 157, 166
change competence 93, 101–2
Chrysler Motors 84, 172, 177
Civil Rights movement 176
civil society associations 188
class 2, 6, 32; antagonisms of 127; anthropology of 124; capitalist 189; class-based morality 213; "class interests" 17; consciousness 113, 176; contradictions 130;

218 *Index*

cosmopolitanized state 134; devaluation of the notion of 165–6; "domestic capitalist class" 161; dynamics of 123; identity 173, 179, 181; manual labor 88; middle 70, 83, 95, 123, 133; politics 177; reproduction of 194–5, 198, 57n6, 169n11; solidarity 112–13; subjectivity 176; technical 61; of worker-peasants 166; working 6–9, 12, 13, 15–17, 42, 46–8, 52–3, 55, 79, 81–6, 96, 112, 173–5, 187, 197, 18n7, 21n22, 89n2; working-class estate of Ksawera 137–53; working class family 127–9; working class legacy 159
CLT *(Consolidação das Leis do Trabalho)* reform 61
COMECON market 131
Communism 150, 166
conachadas, defined 192
consumption: centrality of 9; levels of 14; mass 128, 130; middle class 123; needs linked to 87
contract 2, 4, 16, 19n11, 20n7, 47–52, 57n4, 77, 82, 84, 102, 110, 114, 115, 116, 118n3, 162, 164, 172–84, 184n3, 179, 197; between citizen and state 8; social 138; worker 51; *see also* employment
corporate housing policy 128–9; *see also* policy
corporatist capitalisms 95
credentialism 4, 50–3, 209; *see also* steelworkers
critical junction 127, 128, 130, 134, 135, 167
CSN 13, 60–71; *see also* Brazilian National Steel Company (CSN); Volta Redonda, Brazil
Czechoslovak Velvet Revolution (1989) 160

Dal Forno, Arianna and Mollona, Edoardo 67, 206
Day, Sophie 33
debt/indebtedness 1, 14, 53, 84, 116, 132, 157, 192, 194
deindustrialization: auto industry 175; impact of 7, 14; shipbuilding industry 109–10; steel industry 164
deregulation 6, 16–17, 116, 137
Detroit, Michigan 1–4, 128, 179
domestic reproduction 194–6; heavy industry workers and family 187–98; *see also* flexible, familism; household, Spain and childcare considerations; male breadwinner model; socialism, children of factory workers family

Edensor, Tim 144
egoismos notion 111–12
Eindhoven 15, 123, 124, 127–35
embedded/embeddedness 10, 102, 115, 118n1, 123, 188, 206, 207, 209, 210
emotional geographies 8–9, 138
employability 4, 14, 93–104, 211; institutional support systems 102–4; masculine identity and 93–7
employment 3, 8, 14, 20n14, 34, 36, 38, 46–50, 55, 61, 62, 65, 68, 69, 80, 85, 86, 93–7, 101–4, 105n7, 109, 113–17, 118n1, 137, 141, 159, 161, 169n8, 178, 184n2, 187, 191, 209; access to 69, 71; employer-employee relationships 197; employment history 102; formal/informal employment conditions 114–17, 109–11, 114, 162–4; male 98, 99; overemployment 44n2; policies 52; of women 96, 104n4, 105n8; *see also* contract; redundancy; skills, transfer of; underemployment; unemployment
Escola Técnica Pandiá Calógeras (ETPC) 61, 66, 67, 70
ethnography/ethnographic 5, 6, 15, 31, 35, 47, 52, 60, 62, 70, 71, 80, 83, 88, 109, 110, 118, 119, 174, 183, 187, 188, 198, 205, 207, 214
European: financial crisis 14, 110; global rhythm of capitalism 124
European Capital of Culture (2013) 163
European Commission 14, 93, 94
European Economic Recovery Plan 94
European Employment Strategy (EES) 94
European Union (EU) 32, 93
Europe 2020 strategy 93, 94

family 6–12, 16, 17, 31, 33, 35–44, 46, 47, 48–55, 60, 62, 66, 70, 79, 79, 81–3, 87, 100–1, 115, 116, 126–9, 137, 141, 157, 158, 160, 163, 166, 169n5, 170n11, 188, 189–98, 199n11; breakdown of family ties 43; care 31, 40–1, 95–6, 99, 129, 188–93, 198, 210, 211; expectations 50; family ties and job access 47, 66,

70, 163; relations 55; support 52–3; transitions 38; wage 188
female: exploitation 124; part-time-carer model 95; pragmatism 85; *see also* employment; family; labor; labor market; unemployment
feminism: feminist perspectives on the economy 10; *see also* female
Ferber, Marianne and Nelson, Julie 10
FIAT: crisis 83–4; Fiat Melfi workers (*fiatists*) 14; FIAT-SATA (*see* gender, gender perspective in FIAT-SATA; Melfi, Italy)
FIOM trade union (National Metalworkers' Federation) 84, 86; *see also* Metalworkers' Day; trade unions
flexible: familism 10–11, 127–30; flexibility 103; flexibilization 4, 46; flexible work 20n17; post-industrial capitalism 117
Fordism/Fordist 1, 37, 128, 82, 87, 137, 173, 18n8; corporate programs 179; decline 3; Fordist localism (USA) 175; and Keynsianism 8; male breadwinner 190; Post-Fordism 2, 87, 137, 18n8, 89n2; Post-Fordist model 79; past 206; production 77; working class 181
French Italian Association 140
Friedman, Jonathan 134–5

Galicia, Spain 17, 187, 210
Gellner, Ernest 56
gender: female pragmatism 85; gender and employability 95; gender-blind concept 95; gendered habitus 96; gender ideologies 6; gender interests and class interests 17; gender perspective in FIAT-SATA case 77–89; gender-power geometries 206; "traditional" patriarchy 130; urban-industrial patriarchy 124; *see also* masculine
General Electric 1–2
General Motors (GM) 2, 16, 172–3, 177, 179, 211, 213
generational: discourse 7; disrupted 12; and households 213; inter-generational solidarity 191; of jobs 13, 46–8, 50, 52, 55; of memory 11; transmission of skills 7
generations 5, 7, 13; in Brabant 129–30; and gender roles 197; lost 31–44; and memory 141; of steelworkers in Brazil 60–71; in times of crisis 29; of workers 187, 188
geometries of power 211–14
Germany (West) 11, 14, 94–105; *see also* steelworkers
Gibson-Graham, J.K. 2–3, 10
globalization 11–12, 111
Goodbye Lenin (film) 31–2
Greek shipping industry 14, 109–18; *see also* shipbuilding industry
Grieco, Margaret 34
grilheiros, defined 64
Gudeman, Stephen 10, 158, 189

habitus 94; as gendered 96
Hareven, Tamara 33, 34, 38, 43
Harvey, David 2, 37, 52, 137, 138, 173, 174, 181–3
Hayter, Teresa 181
heavy industry 6, 79, 96, 161, 187, 205, 207, 208; Herderian nationalism 158
homo economicus concept 10
household 4, 6, 10, 14, 17, 189–90; and gendered divisions of labor Europe 95; Greece 110, 115–6; household division of labor 194–7, 206, 207; Melfi 80; and redundancy South Wales 100; Slovakia 160; and social reproduction 33, 210; Spain 188, 189, 192; Spain and child care 192, 193–8; working class Eindhoven 128, 129
Hunčík, Péter 157

Import Substitution Industrialization 3, 131, 206, 56n3
individualization 11–12
Industrial Revolution 4
industry: Cowley 183; industrial, landscapes, old and new 3–5; industrialization 4, 61, 78–80, 159 (*see also* Import Substitution Industrialization); privatization 131–2, 161–5, 169n8; privatization/restructuring 123–4; *see also* automobile industry; class; Paryż coal mine; shipbuilding industry
IndustryALL 21n26; *see also* trade unions
inequality/inequalities 5–9, 11, 47, 56, 172, 186, 190, 197, 210, 18n2
informal: economy 35, 85, 110, 117, 161; employment conditions

Index

114–17; labor force 37; work under socialism 34; *see also* labor
internationalism 175–9
internationalization 4–5, 161
International Labor Organization (ILO) 3, 6
Iron and Steel Trades Confederation (ISTC) 103
Italian automobile manufacturing *see* FIAT

Japanese: automakers 173; competition 16, 79, 173; production model 77, 81, 87; *Toyotism* 68
job insecurity 100, 102, 113, 164

Katz, Cindi 208
Keynesianism 8, 137
kinship 6, 7, 10, 11, 16, 17; and generational transmission 32; importance of 158–60; kinship hierarchies 127; and labor 32; patriarchal 11, 209–12; ties 43, 123, 126
knowledge 15, 129, 19n12, 57n6; acquisition 70; based 2, 4, 38, 93, 137; and capabilities 93, 101; new 101; regimes in Poland 31–44; technical 69
Košice 159, 163–5
Ksawira estate 138–49; *see also* class; Paryż coal mine; place; space

labor 9–12, 16; agricultural 80; alternative sources of 118n1; in Brazil 68; casual labor (Greece) 110–14, 117; challenges 68; class and 18n7; Communitas (training) 103; concept 11; concrete 134; conditions 69; conflict 173; costs 173, 177, 210, 118n1; day laborers 110; demand for 50, 117; devaluation of 134, 211; division of 4, 16, 96, 115, 190, 197, 206, 211; domestic 37, 41, 100, 104n5; elite 173; flexibility 207; geography 177; in Greece 110–18; household 17; informal 37, 80, 110; insertion 57n6, 57n7, 63; kinship and 32, 34–5, 42; labor agreements (USA) 175–9; labor-capital relations 212, 213; labor-exchange 103; labor-management cooperation/conflict 173–5, 178–9; *Labor Notes* journal 178, 180; learning to/training 55, 70, 169n8; living 125; local 163; manual 88; migrant 37, 63; mobility 105n10; models of 65; movement (Spain) 187, 188, 199n12; movement (USA) 175; National Labor Relations Act USA 177; niche 48; outsourced 209; in Poland 32–44; power 95, 111, 112, 118, 125–6, 189, 212–13; precarious 85; process 65, 109, 112; reform 61; regulations of 189, 195, 197–8, 212; reproduction of 16, 60, 63, 210; struggles 173–84, 123, 207; studies 96; sweatshop 37; unionized 172; unions 79, 84, 132, 175, 176, 72n7, 90n6; union Solidarność 130, 131; value of Polish 133–4; women's labor 80, 81, 127, 89n4; work and identity 82, 101, 102; worth and 36; young people's 210; *see also* "contract" worker; skills; trade unions; unskilled
labor market 42, 50 (Argentina), 85 (Southern Italy), 95 (UK and Germany); adverse 110, 113; European 104n2; female participation 94, 96, 97, 189; and gender 97; hierarchical character 111; institutions 94; local 37, 111, 209; policy 94–5, 103, 104, 105n10; segmented 5, 11; struggling in the 117
labor theory of value 125, 210; value regimes of labor 126; value theory of labor 125; *see also* labor
Lancashire mills 34
Latvia 33
League of Revolutionary Black Workers 176
localism 174–5, 178–81, 192, 213
Łódź, Poland 35–44
longue durée 33, 206
Lublin, Poland 13, 31–44

male breadwinner model 95–6; *see also* family; gender; household; labor
Marchionne era (Italy) 83, 90n6; *see also* FIAT
Marx, Karl 126, 134, 135, 189, 205; *see also* Marxist/Marxian
Marxist/Marxian 114, 124–6, 128, 183, 194, 205; analysts 189; anthropology 134; autonomist Marxists 18n6; Leninist groups 176

masculine: defined 98–100; in Germany and UK 93–105; identity 100, 189; jobs 103; masculinity, ideals of 6, 7, 14; masculinity and protest (USA) 176; redundancy concerns 99–100, 102; roles 98; *see also* gender
Massey, Doreen 9, 207
Mečiar, Vladimír 161
Melfi, Italy 14, 77; *see also* autoworkers; FIAT
Members for a Democratic Union (MDU) 181
memory 7, 11, 32–3, 36, 38, 48, 81, 89; experiences 138–48, 151n1; social 139–40
Menem, Carlos 50–1
Metalworkers' Day (Argentina) 48–50
modernization process: auto industry 77–9; capital expansion and 206; steel industry 63; under socialism 157–8, 166, 168; World War II economic boom 87
Mollona, Massimiliano 3, 35, 88
moral/morality 7, 9, 10, 11, 16, 32, 33, 35, 125, 130, 132, 135, 147, 158, 160, 190, 192, 193, 196, 198, 170n12; economies 211–13
Morris, Lydia 8, 21n23, 34

National Collective Working Agreement 110
National Labor Relations Act (USA) 177
necropolitics concept 8, 17
neoliberal: agency 11; capitalism 7, 46
New Directions Caucus 183
New Directions Movement 178
Niemeyer, Oscar 64

Ohno, Taichi 77
Ost, David 150, 157, 166

Papa, Cristina 80
Parry, Jonathan 6, 12, 18n4, 21n21, 189
Paryż coal mine, Poland 15, 138–51; *see also* place, in Ksawera estate
Perama, Greece 109–18
Pfau-Effinger, Birgit 95, 96
Philips 124–30
Piketty, Thomas 5, 18n4, 20n19
Piraeus, Greece 14; *see also* Greek shipping industry
Pittsfield General Electric 1–2

place 206; and difference 206–7, 211, 212–13; disposable places 8; experienced 138; importance of 6; in Ksawera estate 137; and/of memory 138–40, 147; naming of 141; obligations to 16; power of 139; production of 5, 209; and scale 206, 209, 210; silenced 44; and sociality 53; and space 206–7, 210, 213; and spaces of the economy 3; state-place 62; time and 11, 15, 123–4, 130; topography and 208; trans-local 212; for Yi-Fu Tuan 138; *see also* workplace
Podbrezová, Slovakia 159–65
Poland 9, 13, 15; EU accession 38, 123–34, 138–51, 157, 159, 166, 169; knowledge regimes 31–44; post-socialist Poland 130–4; textile industry 32; working class struggles 15
policy 52, 84, 109, 150, 177, 20n15, 89n5; hiring 47; housing 128; incompetent 146; labor market 94–5, 104; makers 5, 6, 188, 204; social policy 127, 129, 188; *see also* CLT (*Consolidação das Leis do Trabalho*); European Economic Recovery Plan; European Employment Strategy; Europe 2020 strategy; National Labor Relations Act (USA); Import Substitution Industrialization
Polish People's Republic 140, 142
populism: mobilization and 164–7; *see also* Russian populism; workers, and populism
Post-Fordism 2, 87, 137, 18n8, 89n2; Post-Fordist model 79; *see also* Fordism
post-peasant: identities 16; political culture 15, 158; populism (*see* worker, and populism); proletariat 167–8
post-socialist transformations 15–6, 43, 123, 132, 134, 158–62, 167; capitalism 170n11
precarity/precarious 4, 10, 13, 14, 17, 39, 47, 51, 69, 85, 87, 109, 114, 115, 197, 209, 210, 20n17; precariat 18n6; *see also* labor
privatization 4, 7, 9, 11, 13, 209; in Argentina 46, 51–3, 209; in Brazil 61, 63, 65, 67, 68, 70; Eindhoven 130–1; EU membership

and 161; industrial privatization/ restructuring 123–4; in Poland 123, 132; in Slovakia 161–2, 165, 169n8
productivity 68, 79, 85, 87, 111, 112, 128, 132, 194, 195, 209, 213; bonus 198n7; of labor 125

Reagan, Ronald 8
reciprocity/reciprocal 33–8, 54, 55, 189, 190, 42, 53, 57n7, 83, 125; *see also* barter/exchange practices
redundancy 14, 84, 85, 94, 97, 99–103, 105n8, 105n10; redundancy payments 85; *see also Cassa Integrazione* support
reproduction 113, 119; and division of labor 190; gendered division of labor and 107, 190, 210; of labor 210; of the labor-force (Volta Redonda) 60; *see also* domestic reproduction; household
Revolutionary Union Movement 176
Russian populism 158

San Nicolás, Argentina 13, 46–56
Saturn plant 12, 16–17, 10 (footnote 17), 173–9, 211, 213; *see also* autoworkers
Second Generation (Raymond Williams) 182
Sélim, Monique 80
shipbuilding industry: formal/informal employment 114–17; as global industry 211; in Greece 14, 109–18; Navantia shipyards (Spain) 187, 194; worker competitiveness 111–14
Siderar company 46–57; *see also* SOMISA
Skeggs, Beverley 9, 10
skills 4, 6, 7, 13, 85, 87, 94, 101; Communitas 103; intensive 127; language 42; management 78; physical 69; previously acquired 66; skilled labor 123, 163; soft 94; Steel Partnership Training 103; of survival 36; technical 52; transfer of 35, 37, 42; *see also Escola Técnica Pandiá Calógeras (ETPC)*
socialism: children of factory workers 35, 36–7; collapse of 7, 13, 15, 16, 31–6, 157, 161–2; ethical socialisms 125; lives under 32–4; material world of 31; memory of 36, 38; modernization process under 157–8, 166, 168; prestigious position of workers under 164; "really existing socialism" 123, 131, 159; revolt against 150; scarcity economy under 158; transition from 15; and unionism (Western world) 129; Western socialism 158; and workers 164–6; worst of 132; *see also* post-peasant
SOMISA 47, 49, 55, 56 (footnote 3); *see also* Siderar company
space 206; coal mine examples 140–2; differentiation of 5; division of labor across 4; empty spaces 32; labor unions and 175, 184; leisure spaces 130, 141; new spaces 62, 148; and place 206–7, 210, 213; place and spaces of the economy 3; and place in Ksawera estate 137; production of 9; public and private 34, 62; representation of capitalism 148–9, *149*; ruins of mine infrastructure 142–4, 142–8; socio-political 37; and time 7, 38; urban 60, 144; *see also* Harvey, David; Massey, Doreen
Stalinism 33, 36
steel: Bhilai steel plant India 6; British steel industry 19n19; Chinese steel 19; as commodity 3; footnote 10; Lancashire steel mills 34; steel and masculinity 98–100, 189; steel as strategic industry 206; Steel Partnership Training 103; steel Sheffield 35; steelworks Argentina 46
steelworkers/steel industry 35, 47, 98–100, 162–4, 189; Argentina 13, 209; Brazil 13, 60–71; and credentialism 50–6; India 21n21; Poland 137, 146, 148, 149, 150; Redcar plant (UK) 19n10; Slovakia 159–65, 210; Spain 17; Spain family steel plant 187; steelworkers and generational transmission 46–50, 66–9; Taranto plant (Italy) 19n11; West Germany and United Kingdom 14, 93–104; *see also* domestic reproduction; heavy industry; masculine
Stewart, Michael 167–8

Taylorist/Taylorism 5, 20n17
temporality 7, 17, 33, 197, 210; politics of time 188; re-mapping process 33
textile industry 32, 33–5
Toyota Motor Company of Japan 77

Toyotism 68
trade unions 47, 54, 57n5, 84, 86, 188, 207, 210; Community 103; *see also* FIOM trade union; labor; IndustryALL; United Automobile Workers (UAW)
transnational 64, 65, 124, 131, 132, 133, 134, 213

underemployment 11–12
unemployment 2, 6, 11, 14, 16, 19n10, 20–1n20, 34, 39, 40, 43, 78, 86, 95, 101–3, 109, 113–17, 161–3, 169n8, 212; acceptable rates of 212; benefits 103; female 80, 89n4; plant liquidations 137; shipbuilders in Greece 109, 113
United Automobile Workers (UAW) 172–3, 179–81, 211
unskilled: laborer 97; labor/work 37, 127, 128; *see also* labor; skills
Upper Silesian Industrial Area 149
US Rust Belt 1–2; comparisons with 18n3
US steel belt 1–3
US Steel Corporation 162, 19n13, 169n7, 169n10
UTE (Technological Elementary Unit) 82–3

Vargas, Getúlio 61, 64
vocational training 47, 50, 52, 209
Volta Redonda, Brazil 13, 60–71

Weston, Kath 17, 18n8
Whirlpool 124
Williams, Raymond 173, 182; *see also Second Generation*
Willis, Paul 52, 57n6, 119n8
Wolf, Eric 55, 57n7, 58n12, 126, 128
women's work *see* gender
workplace 5, 11, 13, 14, 16, 48, 54, 82, 110, 112, 115, 188; competition 164; differentiation in the 207; knowledge of the 36; learning at the 52; and living-place 62; masculinity and workplace 101; negotiations 189; in post-socialist capitalism 170n11; promotion in the 47; socialist 34; as state-place 62; and work-family reconciliation 191; workplace and class identity 173
work: conditions 65–70, 69; work and masculinities 6–7, 101; *see also* labor
worker: competitiveness 111–14; cooperatives 132; identity 47, 18n6; and populism 157–68; self-management 131; worker-controlled privatization 9; *see also* gender; labor
World War I 5
World War II 87, 140

Yi-Fu Tuan 138

Zarycki, Tomasz 166
Zawadzki, Aleksander 140, 147–8